IN *the*

GARDEN *of*

DESIRE

ALSO BY WENDY MALTZ

Incest and Sexuality

The Sexual Healing Journey

Passionate Hearts

IN *the*

GARDEN *of*

DESIRE

The Intimate World of Women's Sexual Fantasies

Wendy Maltz
& Suzie Boss

BROADWAY BOOKS   NEW YORK

BROADWAY

A hardcover edition of this book was published in 1997 by Broadway Books.

IN THE GARDEN OF DESIRE. Copyright © 1997 by Wendy Maltz and Suzie Boss. All rights reserved. Printed in the United States of America. No part of this book may be reproduced or transmitted in any form or by any means, electronic or mechanical, including photocopying, recording, or by any information storage and retrieval system, without written permission from the publisher. For information, address Broadway Books, a division of Bantam Doubleday Dell Publishing Group, Inc., 1540 Broadway, New York, NY 10036.

Broadway Books titles may be purchased for business or promotional use or for special sales. For information please write to: Special Markets Department, Bantam Doubleday Dell Publishing Group, Inc., 1540 Broadway, New York, NY 10036.

BROADWAY BOOKS and its logo, a letter B bisected on the diagonal, are trademarks of Broadway Books, a division of Bantam Doubleday Dell Publishing Group, Inc.

The names and identities of the women whose stories appear in this book have been changed to protect their privacy. In some instances, stories have been dramatized.

First trade paperback edition published 1998.

Designed by Nancy Singer

The Library of Congress has catalogued the hardcover edition as:

Maltz, Wendy.
   In the garden of desire : the intimate world of women's sexual fantasies : a new path for enhancing passion, pleasure, and self-discovery / by Wendy Maltz and Suzie Boss. — 1st ed.
      p.   cm.
   Includes index.
   ISBN 0-553-06770-2
   1. Women—Sexual behavior.   2. Sexual fantasies.   I. Boss, Suzie.
II. Title.
HQ29.M36   1997
306.7'082—dc21   96-40217
                                                                      CIP

ISBN 0-7679-0161-4

98 99 00 01 02 10 9 8 7 6 5 4 3 2 1

To the women who shared their stories

Acknowledgments

This book began as a fantasy. We are indebted to the many people who have helped to make it a reality. Although we can't begin to name them all, we wish to single out a few for special thanks.

Literary agent Felicia Eth recognized the importance of this book when it was an early idea. She was instrumental in helping us find our focus and wisely encouraged us to tackle the intimate issues that affect women's lives. Editor Janet Goldstein has been a steady source of enthusiasm and expertise, helping us shape research findings into concepts all women can take to heart.

Many clinicians, therapists, and educators generously shared their time, knowledge, and personal curiosity to help us ask the right questions and broaden our understanding of fantasy. We owe thanks to Lonnie Barbach, B. H. Barkley Jr., Karla Baur, Stephanie Covington, Gayle Delaney, Diane DeSylvia, Clyde Ford, Lori Galperin, Steven Gold, Toni Cavanagh Johnson, Carol Koenig, JoAnn Loulan, Sharon McIntosh, Eva Norvind, Julie Rosenzweig, B. J. Seymour, Bee Sholes, and Mary Widoff.

Many friends and colleagues in the writing community contributed enthusiasm and ideas to this project. In particular, we are grateful to Jo Robinson, Lauren Kessler, Laura Davis, Cathy Van Horn, and Elizabeth Claman, whose critiques helped us improve the manuscript. Sincere thanks, also, to Diana Russell, Geraldine Kudaka, Stella Cameron, Marilyn Sewell, and Hank Estrada, who helped us explore cultural and social influences on women's sexuality.

Members of several organizations were helpful in our research, including AASECT (American Association of Sex Educators, Counselors, and Therapists), VOICES (Victims of Incest Can Emerge Survivors), and SIECUS (Sexuality Information and Education Council of the United States). Thanks, also, to the staff of *The Healing Woman* newsletter.

Our families buoyed our spirits and kept us going with their encouragement and support. From Wendy, a special thanks to my husband, Larry, who nurtured this project with a continuing supply of personal and professional wisdom. Your love is the wind beneath my wings. Thanks, also, to family members Sara Allman, Bill Becker, and Suzanne Jennings for your time, expertise, and creativity. I am also especially grateful to my children, Jules and Cara, who respected my busy work schedule and kept me grounded in the reality of everyday living.

From Suzie, special thanks to my husband, Bruce Rubin, who has been a smart reader and a great listener. To my mother, Trudy Boss, thanks for your unwavering encouragement. To my sons, Danny and Jay, thanks for your patience while I monopolized the phone and stayed up too late.

Finally, our deep gratitude to the many women and men who shared their most personal stories with us in workshops, questionnaires, discussion groups, and interviews (and who will go unnamed to protect their privacy). Your contributions not only made this book possible, but expanded the scope of knowledge about a subject that touches all of our lives.

Contents

IN *the* GARDEN *of* DESIRE

Preface

"Your sexual fantasies are normal and harmless. Don't worry about them. Just relax and enjoy."

This was the standard line I was taught more than twenty years ago in postgraduate training. It was considered the best advice sex therapists could give women who asked questions about their sexual fantasies. Back then, when sex therapy was still a relatively new field, it felt permissive and positive to encourage women to fantasize in order to improve their sexual response. The common wisdom was "If it leads to orgasm, it's got to be good."

This permissive, sex-positive view challenged entrenched and more judgmental attitudes about sexual thought. It was Sigmund Freud, the founder of psychoanalysis, who laid the groundwork for being ashamed or afraid of fantasies with his earlier assertion "A happy person never phantasizes, only an unsatisfied one." It didn't matter that he had long since been proven wrong. Numerous studies during the 1970s and 1980s showed that nearly everyone fantasizes about sex. Nonetheless, some researchers in the mental health field continued to investigate sexual fantasies as potentially serious business, even a predictor of criminal behavior or symptom of pathology. Many early studies labeled and sorted sexual fantasies according to the so-called perversion of the fantasizer.

These conflicting views of sexual fantasy left a lot of room for confusion. Was sexual fantasy fluff or was it heavy and dangerous? And how does it affect us?

When Nancy Friday published *My Secret Garden* in 1973, she broke new ground by recording women's entertaining and boldly sexual fantasies.[1] This popular anthology proved that women *do* think about sex, in all sorts of interesting ways. I added her book to my library of erotica which I used to loan out to clients who wanted some new ideas to fuel their own fantasies. But in my personal life, and in the stories I was hearing from many women clients, it was becoming evident that sexual fantasies were more complex than either Freud or the early sex therapists had imagined. They could be a source of pain as well as pleasure.

During the 1980s, I began to specialize in working with survivors of sexual abuse and other sexual trauma. I wrote *The Sexual Healing Journey* (1992) to describe my approach for healing the sexual problems caused by abuse. In my book, I briefly addressed the concerns that some survivors had experienced with *unwanted* sexual fantasies. I was amazed by the reaction. I began receiving immediate feedback from survivors, from other therapists, and from women I'd never met before who drew me aside at workshops or lectures to ask questions about their own sexual fantasies. I didn't have all the answers, but I began to suspect that there was a significant connection between our fantasies and our life experiences.

Intrigued, I pored through books and articles on the general topic of women's sexual fantasies. Although I had heard men express similar concerns and questions about fantasies, I focused specifically on women because the issues they were raising were more reflective of my clinical experience and expertise. I was disappointed to find that most of the existing research failed to address the specific questions women wanted answered. There was little information about where fantasies come from and only a cursory exploration of how and why women's and men's fantasies differ. None of the studies that I found paid attention to the individual history of the fantasizer herself or how she felt about the contents of her erotic imagination. That struck me as ironic. How could we begin to understand a woman's fantasy if we leave the woman herself out of the picture?

I started to suspect that the full, complex range of female erotic thought had been overlooked or overly simplified in social science, popular culture, and even pornography. Women's fantasies seemed far more multidimensional and interesting than anyone previously imagined.

For the next five years, I explored the subject of women's sexual fantasies from many different angles. I discussed fantasies with dream experts, religious educators, and other therapists in the sexuality field. I conducted clinical research to find the answers I couldn't find elsewhere. I listened closely and paid more attention to the sexual fantasy problems my clients brought up in therapy.

As my knowledge grew, I started offering workshops for women who wanted to heal unwanted sexual fantasies and learn new tools for exploring the contents and erotic power of their sexual thoughts. The more I learned about sexual fantasies, the more I became impressed with how much we all can learn by looking more closely into our fantasy life.

Sexual fantasy is an intimate world where mind, body, and emotion come together. Like dreams, our fantasies can tap into the unconscious and express deep-seated desires or conflicts. They often speak to us in a symbolic language. They don't have to obey laws of physics or stay within the bounds of common sense. And also like dreams, fantasies can range from delightful and uplifting to troublesome and nightmarish.

By daring to explore the meaning of our erotic thoughts, we can gain incredible insights about ourselves. Understanding our fantasies can help us enjoy better sex lives, better relationships, and improved self-esteem. Knowing more about how fantasies work can leave us feeling more free and less inhibited in our own imagination. Not only do we have the power to create fantasies of infinite variety, but we can be empowered by them.

In recent years, I've been eager to share the exciting information I have been learning. In fact, I've become passionate about opening up this area so we all can feel more permission to talk about sexual fantasies and learn from each other's experiences.

My friend and coauthor, Suzie Boss, a journalist, has helped me extend my research to include a wide cross section of women. In a large new study we conducted specifically for this book, we gathered detailed information from more than one hundred women about their sexual fantasies. We deliberately took an informal, anecdotal approach rather than using a more traditional or scientific research model. Some of our subjects submitted lengthy questionnaires. Others talked with us in personal interviews. All of them were given an open-ended invitation to share their stories, woman to woman.

Knowing that women's fantasies can reflect different life experiences, Suzie and I actively sought a diverse population. Thus, the stories in this book come from women of varied ages, races, occupations, ethnic backgrounds, religions, sexual orientations, relationship statuses, and sexual histories. Some women have been faithful to one partner for a lifetime while others have enjoyed casual sex with more lovers than they can count. A few work in the world of sexual fantasy for a living, including a phone sex operator, a stripper, and a professional dominatrix. The group includes women who have lost breasts to cancer, were raised in a foreign country, have physical disabilities or a history of sexual abuse.

Once women were given an opportunity for sharing and a chance to learn more about themselves, they often opened up to this personal topic quickly, candidly, and with humor. Many women got a kick out of telling us about their unusual and unconventional objects of desire—including such surprises as the curly-haired comedian Gene Wilder, former Disney Mouseketeer Annette Funicelo, cave-dwelling gargoyles, and chocolate-covered éclairs. A few women became emotional during interviews when they recognized the significance of what their fantasies were really saying to them. Many women made insights that would have remained hidden if they hadn't learned to look at their fantasies more consciously.

This book is based primarily on the stories Suzie and I collected, but it also includes information gathered from my early research, clinical work, and fantasy workshops. Although we've written the book for women, we know that men will also find valuable information about themselves and their intimate partners.

We've designed this book to be both entertaining and informative. We know that people will read it for a variety of reasons. You may be reading out of curiosity about a subject that's been in the dark for too long. You may seek a vicarious thrill from listening to women's juiciest sexual secrets. Perhaps you want to actively use this material to answer questions or concerns you have about your fantasy life or that of a partner.

Our goal has been to offer you an opportunity to develop a rich and dynamic understanding of women's sexual fantasies. In the following chapters you'll learn a new way of exploring fantasies that emphasizes a woman's personal experience. You'll find out how you can benefit from using an exciting new language for describing fantasies, investigating the early sources of your sexual thoughts, recognizing your own sexual style, and evaluating the pros and cons of how particular sexual fantasies operate in your life. You'll learn how other women have been able to gain personal wisdom from tracing the evolution of their fantasies and analyzing them closely to unlock their hidden meaning.

Later in the book you'll hear more in-depth stories, coupled with strategies and techniques to address the specific fantasy issues many women share. You'll hear how women can successfully transform and eliminate troublesome and unwanted sexual fantasies. You'll learn how sexual fantasies can affect your intimate relationship and whether it's wise to share your fantasies with a lover. With all this information, you'll have what you need to create new fantasies that you love.

As you read women's stories and come upon the questions and lists in this book, you may want to pay close attention to your own responses. By noticing your reactions, you can gain important clues and information about your sexuality and your own fantasy life.

The women who explore their fantasies with us in the following pages are our pathfinders in this fascinating garden of desire. They help illuminate the universal truths about women's sexual fantasies and teach us not to be afraid or ashamed of this subject. Listening to their stories, we discover the answers to our own questions. Along with understanding where fantasies originate, what they mean, and how they can lead to better sex, we are assured that the realm of sexual fantasy is safe, open, and valuable for all of us to explore.

Wendy Maltz
Eugene, Oregon

❦

CHAPTER 1

Our Most
Private Thoughts

Faye was nervous. A mother and computer programmer in her midthirties, with a robust laugh and an ample build, she had never told anyone about her sexual fantasies before. In fact, she wasn't sure that she had anything valuable to tell us now. "I don't know that I've ever had a sexual fantasy anyone else would find significant or even interesting," she said. After considering for a moment, she added, "Let me tell you about one experience, though, that I often think about when I want to feel sexy."

With that, Faye adjusted her eyeglasses and took a deep breath. "I didn't deliberately plan this out as a fantasy. It began unexpectedly when my husband and I were attending a classical guitar performance in a large concert hall." As she began to share this story, the nervousness in her voice gave way to excitement and the unmistakable ring of pride. Clearly, this was a sexual fantasy she loved:

In my fantasy, my husband and I have seats so close to the stage that we can hear the musician's fingers slide across the strings. The guitarist performs solo, with a single beam shining a pool of light around him. His eyes are closed, his head turned down and at an angle. From where I sit, I can see his exquisite profile. I notice his lips trembling when he plays one passage with great emotion. His straight, black hair falls across his forehead and moves in rhythm with the music. The performance is so flawless, the notes so clear, that when my husband slides his arm around my shoulder (which he did in real life), I can feel goosebumps rising on my bare arms. As I'm listening and watching, I begin to imagine that it is my body cradled in the musician's arms in place of the guitar. When he wraps his left hand around the slender neck of the instrument, I feel his tender grip on my own neck. The curve of wood that fits across his thigh becomes the curve of my hip. And the strings, when he plucks and strums them with his strong fingers, echo with a throbbing rhythm between my legs. I can barely sit still as the music soars to a climax.

As she came to the end of her story Faye paused for a moment, then added, "The night of that performance, when my husband began to touch me in bed, I let those images from the concert hall wash over me. I deliberately lay across his lap and guided his hands to the places I wanted played. Only that time, there was no holding back at the crescendo." Smiling shyly, she asked, "Tell me, does this qualify as a sexual fantasy?"

Does it ever.

From the outside, no one can imagine what thoughts or images might be thrilling a woman's senses, igniting her passion, and leading her to heights of sexual pleasure. Nothing about Faye's outward appearance hinted at her lyrical approach to lovemaking or her enjoyment of sensuous sexual fantasies. That's why it takes some detective work to discover what really goes on inside a woman's erotic imagination, and why.

When women like Faye accept their sexual fantasies as natural, normal, and worth exploring, they're taking the first step on a fascinating adventure. By using a new approach for unlocking the mystery of our fantasies, we have a chance to make important discoveries about ourselves, our sexuality, and our intimate relationships. This new approach isn't any more complicated than paying attention to what our dreams have to tell us. But because we're dealing with an explicitly sexual subject, it does require a fundamental change in how most women think about sexual fantasies. In order to learn all that fantasies have to teach us, we need to consider them as treasures—not taboos.

If we're willing to look at our fantasies more closely and from many new angles, we can discover why certain thoughts excite us and others leave us cold. Our fantasies can not only teach us more about our sex lives but also offer insights into *our whole lives*.[1] Rather than brushing off our fantasies as embarrassing secrets or idle thoughts, we can start using them as the wonderful resources they truly are.

COURAGE AND CURIOSITY

It takes courage for women to talk about their sexual fantasies as candidly as they do in the upcoming pages. We have encouraged women not to hold back in describing their fantasies, and we haven't censored their language or omitted the sexual heat from their stories. Rather than telling women what we mean by fantasies, we have invited them to describe this world in their own words. "What do you think about," we might ask to get the conversation rolling, "when you're making love, daydreaming about sex, or masturbating?"

Many women are motivated to answer this personal question because they want to make sense of fantasies that have left them puzzled or mystified. They may be eager to figure out where certain images have come from, and why they are such reliable turn-ons.

Gale, a thirty-year-old woman, wondered why, when she makes love with her husband, she often imagines herself surrounded by women bathing topless at the beach. The images feel so vivid to her, she can imagine the smell of suntan lotion and feel the sun warming her skin, just like when she was a girl growing up near the ocean. Yet, she has no idea why thinking about the curves, contours, and nipples of other women's breasts is guaranteed to make her climax.

Sybil, forty-three, wondered why she needs to imagine herself getting punished in order to get in the mood for sex. In real life, she said, her lover is tender, caring, and romantic, "everything a woman dreams about finding." Yet, to get turned on enough to enjoy sex with him, she has to imagine his hand slapping her bare bottom and squeezing her breasts hard. To keep her sex life interesting, she regularly browses porn magazines and reads erotica to find new ideas that she can file away in memory and hook onto during sex to turn up her own response. "Pictures of people fucking don't turn me on, though," she said with a shrug. For reasons she can't explain, she hungers for stories about naughty girls, spankings, and light bondage.

Brooke, twenty-eight, wondered if she was secretly being unfaithful to her new lover when she thought about her old boyfriend during sex. She explained, "These memories from my first real love affair pop into my head so unexpectedly. I imagine my old boyfriend touching me, kissing me, and stripping off my clothes. Then I get turned on. After sex, though, when I open my eyes and see my new boyfriend lying next to me in bed, I start feeling guilty."

Women's natural curiosity about sexual fantasy is far-ranging but typically comes down to these five basic questions:

- "Am I normal?"
- "Where do my sexual fantasies come from?"

✿ "What do my sexual fantasies mean?"

✿ "If they are upsetting, what can I do about them?"

✿ "Can fantasies enhance or improve my sex life?"

These five questions are compelling, and we'll answer them in more detail in the chapters ahead.

As soon as we start hearing more about other women's fantasies, though, many of us will have a nagging thought. Suddenly we want to know "How do I measure up?"

If we're prone to judge or compare ourselves against other women, we may start wondering if our own fantasies are too raunchy or too politically correct, too sexy or too prudish. We may worry that we fantasize about sex too often or not enough. And that's a big mistake. Exploring our fantasies isn't a competitive exercise. There's no right or wrong way to think sexy thoughts. Although almost all women and men fantasize about sex at some time in life, there's no magic formula that equates certain sexual fantasies with a great sex life.[2]

Instead of measuring ourselves against other women's fantasies, we can use these stories as an opportunity to find out about the range of women's experiences. We've included a wide variety of stories because they illustrate variations and similarities from one woman to the next. As we'll hear, some women love their fantasies and call them up at will to enhance sexual pleasure. Others despise the erotic images that invade their minds during sex. Still others appreciate how reliably their fantasies work, but feel stuck or bored with them. Women nearly always express delight when describing fantasies that have carried them into peak sexual experiences.

By paying close attention to our own reactions as we hear these stories, we gain an immediate sense about whether certain fantasies arouse us or turn us off. And that quick insight can be a helpful clue as we become more conscious about our own fantasy life. Long after their erotic buzz subsides, many of these stories will continue to resonate because of the lasting truths they also tell us about our own sexual style.

DETAILS AND CLUES

Daphne is a twenty-two-year-old woman whose graphic fantasy aroused her for many different reasons:

> *In this fantasy, I imagine that my boyfriend and I are at a seedy bar with another couple, Pamela and George. When I make my way to the ladies' room, Pamela follows me. As soon as I lock the bathroom door, Pamela pulls down my pants and begins licking my clit. I can hear our boyfriends talking just outside the door, and I quietly slide up on the white porcelain sink and push her face further into my cunt. After we have been in there quite a while, our boyfriends start pounding on the door, calling our names. Pamela sucks all the harder. Just then, I notice that the bathroom walls are tiled with shards of broken mirror. As I watch myself come, my image is reflected in a hundred pieces of mirrored glass. It is like watching an art film.*

If we had asked Daphne to describe her fantasy in just a couple words, she might have said it was an oral sex fantasy. We never would have heard about the "art film" quality of the images that excited her or understood how the chance of being caught was part of the sexual thrill of her fantasy. Without taking time to hear more about her life, we never would have known that she considers her boyfriend a wonderful lover—but that fantasy allows her to indulge her desire for what's not possible to experience sexually with him.

Really listening to women's sexual fantasies is an active process. We need to ask lots of questions in order to bring out all the facets of a fantasy. The right questions can help a woman figure out whether a particular fantasy holds a significant psychological message or whether it's just plain fun. As we'll see, fantasies get even more interesting when we look at them in such detail.

When women explore what's so special about their fantasies, we also find out how varied and complex this world of fantasy really is. One woman explained how, as a young mother, she often eroticized the sensation of babies nursing at her breast. "I loved the softness of skin, the way their little heads smelled, and I would weave those sensations into my fantasies during sex." Clearly, she said, she wasn't having fantasies about incest. "I would never want to have sex with my children." But for her, those skin-on-skin sensations proved powerfully erotic.

Many women highlight the relationship dynamics as key ingredients in their fantasies. In fact, the actual sex in women's fantasies is often only one moment in a much longer erotic story. As one woman said, "When the sex is over in my fantasy, I imagine my partner holding me and talking to me, not just rolling over and falling asleep." When a woman in her twenties explained why she often fantasized about Denzel Washington as her imaginary lover, she said his intelligence reminded her of her real boyfriend. But unlike her young and rather inexperienced boyfriend, who tended to rush through sex, she imagined the older and wiser actor appreciating her sensuality and spending more time on foreplay.

From listening closely to the details of fantasies, we find out that women think about sex in all sorts of interesting ways. Some of us entertain only fleeting thoughts, as quick as an unexpected smile. Others create fantasy scripts that are as intricate and carefully plotted as a full-length suspense film. Some women describe lusty images of erect nipples and hard penises, soft breasts and tight butts, as explicit as any porn film. Others speak in ways that evoke the soft, moody light of perfume ads.

While women most often have fantasies during sex or self-stimulation, boosting arousal at a specific place in their sexual response cycle, many also experience fantasies in nonsexual settings. We'll be hearing from women who make up sexual fantasies while swimming laps, cooking dinner, driving through rush-hour traffic, or speaking in public. Some have sexual daydreams that help them relax, but stir no sexual response. A few women describe fantasies so erotic to them that they climax on the strength of their thoughts alone, with no accompanying stimulation.

Whenever a woman says she's not sure that her own fantasy "qualifies" or "fits in," we've learned to listen closely. Those are often the moments when a woman's creativity has challenged old stereotypes and myths about sexual fantasy and expanded the boundaries of what we know. Some women find erotic thrills in roller coasters, saxophones, ocean waves, and mangoes, for instance. Sexual fantasies can include sensory experiences that don't follow a narrative script (like Faye's guitar story) or even involve images we would not normally define as being sexual.

These variations have led us to a new definition of sexual fantasy that is broad enough to take in the widest range of women's experiences. *Sexual fantasy includes all sexual thoughts and images that alter our emotions, sensations, or physiological state.* We label these thoughts as sexual either because they have an erotic effect or because they include images we commonly associate with sex.

POWERFUL INFLUENCES

Given this expansive definition, only a handful of women said they never fantasize about sex at all. When they explored why not, they often realized that their innate ability to fantasize was inhibited by past experiences, repressive beliefs, or common misunderstandings about fantasies.

One woman, for instance, said she had assumed that having a sexual fantasy would mean picturing herself as a *Playboy* bunny, Marilyn Monroe, or some other cultural stereotype of how a sexy woman should look. She said, "I don't want to think of myself as a silly woman or a slut in order to be sexual." Realizing that she has the power to see herself however she chooses has helped her to become much more free and playful within her erotic imagination.

Women shut down their ability to think about sex for many different reasons. Among the strongest influences that can limit a woman's fantasy life is a history of sexual trauma. Similarly, a sexually repressive childhood or religious messages against fantasizing can also affect a woman's fantasy life in profound ways. The lasting impact of such experiences makes it important to trace a woman's personal sexual history when we begin to explore her fantasies.

For example, a woman whose father forced her to pose for kiddie porn when she was a girl wound up feeling afraid of the whole subject of fantasy. "It's a place my mind cannot go now, however much I might want it to as an adult," she said. Another woman also censored her own sexual thoughts after adolescence, but for a very different reason. She planned to become a nun. At age fifty, after she left her religious order and began dating men, she was delighted to experience her first erotic fantasy about a male friend kissing and sucking on her fingers. The pleasure generated by that sweet fantasy made her eager to invite bolder and more graphic sexual thoughts into her imagination.

Women's fantasies evolve and change over the course of a lifetime for all sorts of reasons. One young woman said she fantasizes less frequently now that she is comfortable enough with her lesbian orientation to begin a long-term relationship with a woman partner. "Who needs fantasy now, when the real thing is right here beside me?" she said, patting her lover's thigh. In contrast, another woman said that she started fantasizing more often after falling in love in her forties. "I got back in touch with being sexual after a long dry spell and my fantasies have started up again," she said with a satisfied smile. Women have also noticed that their ability to fantasize has been affected by such biological factors as aging, stress, and hormone levels.

A PERSONAL APPROACH

The way women talk about their own fantasies has helped shape our approach for further exploring this complex aspect of our sexuality. We take what we call a *personal experiences approach*. This way, we look at fantasies within the context of an individual woman's life. One woman understood immediately how much sense it makes to explore our own fantasies in this new way. She said, "A fantasy is like a beautiful piece of cloth made up of all the threads of who you are. It takes you your whole life to weave it together." As we apply this personal approach to fantasies, we also assume that each one of us is our own, most reliable sleuth for identifying where our fantasies have come from and figuring out how well they work for us in our everyday lives.

Just how does this personal experiences approach work? Let's use it to take a look at one fantasy theme that we've heard many women describe in different variations. This fantasy is typically about a teacher seducing a student. Yet, no two women tell this erotic story in exactly the same way. When one woman described her teacher-student fantasy, the story unfolded like this:

I imagine a young girl, just starting to develop breasts. She lives on a farm way out in the country, and is often lonely. One day, a traveling salesman stops by. Her dad offers to let him stay in the hayloft. Late at night, the man and the girl start talking. She's excited to have a new friend. As they talk about more personal matters, she mentions that men seem attracted to big-breasted women. She worries that hers will stay small. In his travels, he says, he has gotten to be friends with many women. Once, one of them told him the secret for growing big breasts, and now he'll share it with her.

First, he tells her she needs to massage her breasts and nipples before she goes to bed. He suggests that she do so in front of her bedroom window. That way, he can watch to make sure she's doing it right. Then, he offers to teach her some new strokes to "wake up the growth hormones." Next, he mentions that having someone suck on her nipples will make her breasts grow. Hasn't she noticed, he asks, that nursing mothers have big breasts?

Each time the salesman comes back to stay in the hayloft, he brings her another new secret tip to make her breasts grow. She feels lucky to have her own tutor, even though she doesn't notice much change in her breast size. He assures her it's working, though. In fact, he tells her the same exercises can make a man's penis grow. He asks her to massage his penis, and she's amazed to see it grow before her eyes. He has one more lesson to teach her, but says he'll need her help. He has her undress, then shows her how well his hard penis fits into her body. After he shows her how their bodies fit and move together, he tells her she's finally all grown up.

If we only hear the story without learning any details about the woman who told it, we don't have a clue about why it excites her or how she feels about it. How might a woman feel about this fantasy if she were young and sexually inexperienced, inventing erotic thoughts during masturbation? How differently would the fantasy seem if, instead, she were much older and eager to recapture the thrill of her sexual awakening?

In fact, this farm girl fantasy was shared by a forty-six-year-old woman named Janette who described having mixed feelings about it. She said she liked the friendship and sexual playfulness between the man and the farm girl. She found the breast stimulation to be especially arousing. If she entertained this fantasy when she was actually having sex, she would get excited enough by the explicit graphics of the fantasy to reach orgasm. Yet, even though the fantasy helped her enjoy sex, she also felt a nagging dislike for it.

As we heard more about Janette's history, we learned that she had been introduced to sex by an older brother. When she was still a child, her brother had fondled her while pretending to be her "teacher." The farm girl fantasy reminded her how she had been robbed of her own innocence. That's why it bothered her. Yet, for a woman who hadn't been abused, the same kind of story might have seemed like a purely playful, fun fantasy to entertain.

Like dreams, the contents of our fantasies can't be evaluated on the surface or by an outsider as "good" or "bad." Each woman herself is best qualified to interpret her own sexual fantasies according to how she feels about them. As we gain new information from exploring fantasies, we need to trust our own intuition about how best to use these insights.

Once we understand our fantasies better, we may decide to use certain ones more deliberately to bring specific benefits to our sex lives. Or, we may be eager to create new fantasies as a playful route to personal expression. Exploring our fantasies gives us fresh information and new options for how we choose to think about sex.

With an open mind about fantasies, we're ready to learn more. The first new tool to help us is a fantasy vocabulary that respects women's own personal experiences.

CHAPTER 2

Describing Our Fantasy Style

"Private Party: Two Girls Together"
"Luscious Nurse Becomes Doc's Willing Sex Slave"
"Slut Wife Stories"
"Ladies! Get Spanked!"

Every day, titles such as these are posted on adult-oriented computer bulletin boards, luring viewers with descriptions of very specific sexual situations. From a quick glance, it might appear that the Internet has thrown open the topic of sexual fantasy for full and complete discussion.

A closer look, however, shows that this high-tech medium describes and categorizes sexual fantasies in the same narrow way that X-rated videos and skin magazines are shelved in adult bookstores catering to men. Classifying fantasies according to sex act, sex object, or fetish is nothing new or original. A woman who works as a phone sex operator told us that the most popular male-oriented fantasies she hears are so stereotypical and predictable that she can usually tell, within the *first minute* of getting a call, what kind of fantasy a man wants to enact. Once she figures out his category, she knows exactly what kind of script will take him to climax.

When women describe their own sexual fantasies, in their own words, it usually takes longer than a minute. It's seldom so predictable or so focused on achieving orgasm. In fact, very few of the women we interviewed said that a particular sex act, body part, or partner was enough to make a fantasy enticing. Instead, they took time to explain how they saw themselves, what sort of role they imagined playing, and what kind of sexual energy was portrayed in their fantasies.

Many women told us their fantasies are too complicated for a one-line description to capture. "My sexual fantasies are about much more than just suck-suck-suck, lick-lick-lick, pump-pump-pump," one woman said. Indeed, what makes women's fantasies erotic and memorable to them is often emotional content, relationship dynamics, and many different varieties of sensory stimulation.

The importance of these specific details to women is consistent with more general findings about gender differences. Past studies have shown, for instance, that men's fantasies tend to be more visual and graphic than women's, and that women's include more tactile stimulation. Men's fantasies tend to get to the sex act more quickly, while women's often involve a longer buildup and more foreplay.

One woman explained how these differences in the biology of desire play out in her life. Describing how she and her husband make different uses of pornographic magazines, she said, "He looks at the pictures and gets hot. To him, visuals are the whole point of fantasy, an instant turn-on. I need more of a setup to enjoy sex. I take more time to read the stories, and imagine myself engaging with certain characters who appeal to me for emotional reasons. Then I find myself getting excited, too."

Much of the past research about sexual fantasy has focused on sex acts but has overlooked the context for the imagined sexual experiences. Yet, context plays a big part in determining how women feel about their fantasies. Two women, for example, both fantasized about having group sex. One imagined a violent abduction and brutal rape by a motorcycle gang, while the other fantasized about being aboard a luxury cruise ship and receiving the delightful and welcome sexual attention of each member of the crew. Because these imagined sex acts took place under such disparate circumstances, the two women were left with very different feelings about their group sex fantasies.

Past studies have also categorized men's and women's fantasies according to sexual fetish, location, or imagined partner in addition to a particular sex act. We've learned, as a result, that men's most common fantasies are about having sex with attractive, eager, willing partners, while women are more likely to fantasize about being the object of another's desire. One researcher during the 1980s summarized the five most popular fantasies for men: different sexual positions during intercourse, woman as aggressor, oral sex, sex with a new female partner, sex on the beach. And for women: sexual activity with current partner, reliving a past sexual experience, different sexual positions during intercourse, sex in rooms other than the bedroom, and sex on a carpeted floor.[1]

Yet, when women describe their own fantasies, they report images that don't neatly fit into these kinds of categories. They tell complex stories that lose their erotic value if condensed or cataloged according to sexual activity. Maggie, for example, is one of many women we met whose fantasies eroticize the sensuousness of being female. Her private thoughts are about the curves and shadows and softness of the female body. Yet in real life, she enjoys having sex with men. Trying to explain her fantasies is difficult, she said, "because I don't have the right words for it. It's not a lesbian fantasy, even though it's all about women. It's more of a celebration of being female." Similarly, some lesbians shared fantasies that involve penises, dildos, and the turn-on of eagerly masculine energy.

Women's descriptions of their own fantasies also differ in

striking ways from the boldly sexual world of pornography. The typical pornographic formula of instant sexual pleasure, graphically portrayed, didn't excite many of the women we interviewed. Unlike the fantasies that women often describe, male-oriented pornography fails to offer much context for sex. There's not usually much in the way of story lines or intimate relationships, and porn seldom offers imagery that's sensual as well as sexual. The more physical aspects of sex, though often graphic, are usually only part of what makes a particular woman's fantasy memorable or worth repeating.

A classification system that is more woman-friendly includes the full range of women's experiences with sexual fantasy. It gives names to the different roles women see themselves playing in their own fantasies, and it pays attention to the specific sensory elements of fantasy that women find most erotic. Using this new classification system for describing our own fantasies, we gain a better sense of why some fantasies turn us on while others turn us off.

In general, women describe two main styles of fantasies. One style is the *scripted fantasy*. These fantasies follow a narrative story line with a plot, identifiable characters, and perhaps some dialogue. The second style is the *unscripted fantasy*. These fantasies focus on sensory images that echo or enhance whatever a woman is experiencing sexually. Unscripted fantasies amplify the sights, sounds, or other physical sensations a woman associates with sex. Unscripted fantasies don't unfold like a traditional story, with a clear beginning, middle, and end and defined characters. Rather, they focus on sensory impressions of sexual energy building and releasing.

Most women find that their fantasies fall somewhere along a spectrum from highly scripted to completely unscripted. The key elements that women seem most interested in describing in the more scripted fantasies relate to plot, character roles, and relationship dynamics. The key elements in more unscripted fantasies relate to whatever images most excite a particular woman's senses.

There's no telling why some women invent scripted fantasies and some create unscripted ones. One woman who writes fiction for a living said she spends her workdays thinking about characters, plot, and dialogue. In her active sex life, though, she's never had a scripted sexual fantasy. Both scripted and unscripted fantasy styles can work well to stimulate the senses and enhance sexual enjoyment. In fact, we found no correlation between either type of fantasy and a better sex life.

SCRIPTED FANTASIES

Fantasies with scripted plots and identifiable characters are by far the most common type of fantasies women describe. These tend to be the most well-defined fantasies and also the ones that are most often seen in the larger culture.

To better define and understand our scripted sexual fantasies, we can categorize them according to six different roles. These character roles correspond to how a woman sees herself within the context of her own fantasy. The six most popular roles women play in their sexual fantasies are

- Pretty Maiden
- Victim
- Wild Woman
- Dominatrix
- Beloved
- Voyeur

In essence, these six roles create a new set of fantasy stereotypes that are general enough to allow each of us to fill in the details of who we are and what we do within a particular fantasy role. With this shorthand way to describe our own experiences and learn about other women's fantasies, we can talk more readily about the special opportunities and limitations of each role.

To determine which of these six roles we play in our own fantasies, we can ask ourselves a few simple questions:

- ❧ Am I more active or more passive in this imagined sex scene?
- ❧ Am I more of an initiator or more of a recipient?
- ❧ Is the interaction a mutual sharing, or is one person controlling the other?
- ❧ Do I resent the sexual interaction or welcome it?
- ❧ Is the sexual energy an expression of caring or hostility?
- ❧ Am I part of the sexual action, or do I watch from the sidelines?

While these fantasy roles can help us identify what sort of sex we are attracted to in imagination, they don't necessarily reflect who we really are or what we really want. Fantasy can be a place to try on roles that elude us in real life or explore sexual situations we would never want to enact. As one woman explained, "In my life, I run the show. I talk the most. I'm the loudest. In fantasy, I can shut up, lie back, and be submissive. Fantasy gives wings to my shadow self." In examining these roles, we also can see which ones we may have identified with in the past and which ones we might want to experiment with in the future.

THE PRETTY MAIDEN

I am in a candlelit bedroom wearing a dark green negligee with spaghetti straps. The door opens, and I gasp to see the gorgeous Hawaiian man whose flashing black eyes met mine earlier that day in the hotel lobby. On this warm evening, with an ocean breeze billowing the curtains, he has stripped down to his tight jeans. I yearn to touch his smooth brown skin, but hesitate to make the first move. I wait, my downcast eyes catching a glimpse of his snakeskin boots as he steps behind me. He begins kissing and stroking my neck and shoulders, applying a gentle pressure that sends ripples of pleasure down my body. Murmuring, "Trust me," he blindfolds me with a silk scarf and pulls me onto the bed. Not being able to see or control what happens next only heightens my arousal. I grab hold of the bedposts and release screams of delight as he works his way down my body and begins to lick and bite between my thighs.

Judith's favorite fantasy is about playing the role of the Pretty Maiden. In this role, women enhance their own desirability and often eroticize the loss of inhibition. Picturing herself as the passive object of desire, a woman in the Pretty Maiden role eroticizes the message many women have grown up hearing: that it's feminine and pleasurable to be sexually submissive. Because this is such a prevalent, socially acceptable message, the Pretty Maiden role is one of the most common fantasies that women describe.

Although she's clearly passive in her fantasy, Judith said her imagined encounter feels romantic. Her fantasy lover would never want to harm her; on the contrary, his actions take her to new heights of sexual pleasure. She said, "The love I feel is part of the turn-on, along with feeling out of control, not knowing what's going to happen, and letting him take over." Although she described herself in real life as an assertive feminist, Judith said she prefers a passive role in bed and in her fantasies. "I like to be made love *to*. That's how I define a sexual, desirous woman."

In this role, women interpret "pretty" in a variety of ways. Some envision themselves much as they are in real life, while others change their appearance to match cultural ideals of beauty. Some women say it's an inner beauty, humor, or intelligence that drives their imagined partner wild, like that of Shakespeare's sharp-tongued Kate, who attracts her mate with her rapier wit in *The Taming of the Shrew*.

Women who eroticize being a Pretty Maiden are giving themselves a role in which they can freely enjoy sexual pleasure without feeling guilty or inhibited. That's why it's a fantasy role that appeals to some women who hesitate to more openly enjoy sex. Because they are "done to," they don't have to feel any shame about the pleasure they imagine experiencing. They can picture being wantonly sexually responsive and leave out any thoughts of negative consequences or condemnation from others. In this role, a woman can consider herself virtuous, even mysterious, by having hidden passions. Being swept away by her partner's desire also sweeps away any need for her to be an initiator to let her passions out.

While some women describe the Pretty Maiden role in romantic terms, others highlight the thrill of sexual power. They may imagine scenes of bondage or group sex where they are the object of everyone's desire. Yet, even if a woman describes her fantasy partner as sexually forceful, she never sees him as cruel, demeaning, or hurtful. "I like to imagine being overwhelmed sexually, but never actually hurt," one woman said. Another noticed that her fantasy relationship remained the same whether she imagined her partner as a stranger, a favorite television actor, or a real-life boyfriend. "He's always forceful. I'm always swept away. But it's not like being raped. I choose to let him have all the control. I don't have to tell him what to do to please me. He already knows."

Although this kind of fantasy might seem to perpetuate a sexual role of being helpless, women sometimes describe an erotic power that comes with being the Pretty Maiden. One woman felt powerful as a forbidden object of desire in her fantasy of being kept after class by a favorite teacher. She said, "This gorgeous, bearded man finds me so attractive, he just can't help himself. The fact that it is so wrong for him to seduce me is a big part of the thrill. I love imagining myself as so irresistible that something sexual *has* to happen." Far from feeling powerless or taken advantage of in this role, she explained, "I have the power to drive a man wild. By acting innocent, I'm letting him think it's all his idea for us to have sex. But I'm setting up the whole scene to please myself."

Looking back, some women could see how they had eroticized the Pretty Maiden role since childhood when they first imagined being the focus of another's passion. They also pointed out the many cultural images that reflect the role of woman as object of desire. In the classic musical *The Music Man,* for instance, Marian the Librarian appears mousy and asexual until Professor Harold Hill removes her eyeglasses, revealing her beauty and igniting her passion. The Professor happens to be a scoundrel, but he's tamed into goodness by his love for Marian.

Although Pretty Maidens are plentiful in literature, film, and fairy tales, the enduring popularity of romance novels may be the best evidence of how many women find pleasure in this fantasy formula. Indeed, regular readers of romance novels have more frequent sex, and report greater sexual satisfaction, than nonreaders. Clearly, the Pretty Maiden role has some loyal followers. Whether romances are set in historical periods or the contemporary era, whether the heroine lives on a lonely moor or works as an international spy, she always gets to enjoy a happy, and often erotic, ending by attracting, winning over, and transforming the man of her dreams. "From the moment they meet," writes romance author Susan Elizabeth Phillips in an essay collected in *Dangerous Men and Adventurous Women,* "he is a goner. All his muscle, wealth, and authority are useless against her courage, intelligence, generosity, loyalty and kindness."[2]

In their own fantasies, women describe a wide range of settings in which they imagine playing out the Pretty Maiden role. Fantasy settings are often distant in time or place from the present. One woman described herself riding home at night in a carriage, circa 1800, with a man who couldn't resist making love to her on the spot, fighting his way through the layers of her frilly garments while the horse clopped down cobblestone streets. Another woman imagined being in a cottage in Bali "where a dark-eyed man undresses me with his passionate glance." Many women say this historical or physical distance is significant. Their fantasy is a way of taking them away from the present time and place, where they may be feeling more insecure, tentative, or ambivalent about expressing sexual desires.

While some women say this fantasy role has helped them overcome inhibitions, others worry that it reinforces a passive role in real life. As a Pretty Maiden, a woman has to wait for her fantasy partner to initiate sexual contact. She doesn't get to mentally rehearse being the initiator. One woman who enjoyed her frequent Pretty Maiden fantasies also saw the limitations of this role. "This culture has taught me to see my body as a source of pleasure for men. It's ingrained," she said.

Women who like this role, though, often stress that the Pretty Maiden fantasy gives them a feeling of control they don't always enjoy in real life. In her own Pretty Maiden fantasy, a woman decides how quickly or how leisurely sexual events will unfold. She selects the fantasy partner who seduces her and decides how body parts will be stimulated. She orchestrates the scene within her imagination to suit her own comfort and pleasure.

THE VICTIM

I am alone in a fortresslike setting, with heavy drapes blocking out all sunlight. As I smooth oil on my body and dress in a flimsy costume that shows off my breasts, the phone rings. It's my boyfriend, telling me in a gruff voice to be ready. He's on his way home, and he's bringing a friend. When the two men arrive, I serve them drinks on a silver tray. The guest pulls me across his lap and begins slapping and squeezing my breasts and reaching under my skirt to fondle me. I can feel his penis getting hard. "She's hot, huh?" my boyfriend says to his guest. "The bitch lets me do anything to her." When I hear this, I know I have done my job well. Both men

*will want to have rough sex with me, one after the
other, and bring me to orgasm by delivering a potent
combination of humiliation and pleasure.*

In Nita's fantasy, her imagined sexual passivity goes beyond
a loss of sexual inhibition. She sees herself as a Victim. Instead of
being desired by a kind captor or swept away by a sweet hero,
women who adopt a Victim role imagine being forced into sexual
situations against their will. They link sexual excitement with images of being controlled, dominated, or even hurt.

While both the Pretty Maiden and Victim roles focus on a
woman's sexual passivity, the two roles represent different views
of sex and different conditions for sexual relating. The Pretty
Maiden role creates pleasure from spontaneity, love, physical attraction, and often playfulness, while the sexual energy in the
Victim role springs from fear, hatred, danger, or sometimes violence.

Women who see themselves in this role sometimes describe
being held captive, tied up, or even tortured. They often say they
feel intense sexual pleasure as a result of the fantasy and the
adrenaline rush that comes with it. Temporarily and without any
real danger, they can indulge their curiosity about dangerous sex.

In the Victim role, women describe themselves as powerless.
The perpetrator has all the power and holds all the cards. To
highlight this power imbalance, women sometimes describe the
Victim as a child, young woman, or at least smaller and weaker
than the dominator.

The Victim role often grows out of early associations women
have made between sex and power, pain, terror, or shame.[3] Lori
Galperin, a sex therapist and clinical codirector of the Masters and
Johnson Sexual Trauma and Compulsivity Program, said she has
frequently seen the Victim fantasy play out with clients whose
histories have included sexual violence. She explained, "If a
woman's arousal patterns unfolded in the context of incest, bru-
tality, or violation, that sets a machinery in motion. It brings

together elements that, under normal circumstances, wouldn't have been paired."

Nita, for example, was a young teenager when her strict Muslim father caught her kissing a boyfriend. Although they were living in a middle-class suburb in the Midwest, her father expected her to behave like the girls in his Middle Eastern homeland. He called her a whore and beat her so badly that she needed medical care. "I still feel guilt over being a sexual person," she said. "The only way I can enjoy sex is to imagine being punished for my sexuality and for being female."

Victim fantasies, even when women describe them as erotically powerful, often leave women feeling demeaned or humiliated. These fantasies can be so powerful that some women feel they must either surrender to them or shut down sexually to avoid them. One woman who had a recurring rape fantasy explained, "I don't understand why I would replay such a horrible event over and over. I do enjoy the climax, but afterward I cry, probably because I feel so guilty achieving orgasm this way." (As we'll see in chapter 8, women can learn to erase or replace troublesome fantasies and experience sexual desires in a new way.)

The erotic pleasure women derive from a Victim fantasy can be an attempt to resolve the unpleasant or horrible experiences they endured in the past. If a woman erroneously blames herself for previous abuse, the fantasy can represent self-punishment. If she fears the intensity of her anger, the fantasy can inhibit the expression of her rage. If she feels scared, fantasy offers proof that she can survive the worst scenario imaginable. In a Victim fantasy, a woman can essentially play out abuse scenarios for psychological purposes while avoiding the horrible realities and negative consequences of actual violence. Thus, a woman who pictures herself being beaten in a fantasy emerges without the bruises she would suffer in real life.

Alice, for example, was badly hurt during an attempted rape when she was a girl, then date-raped as a young woman. Although her real-life lover is kind and caring, she said she finds the greatest sexual pleasure by fantasizing about "faceless males who hold my ankles and rape me violently. Eventually, I add all the perpetrators so that they are penetrating my mouth, my anus, my vagina. When they start to swear and slap me, I finally come."

There are plenty of cultural models for the Victim role. It's a part that Hollywood never tires of casting. In the 1950s, Vivien Leigh portrayed the fragile Blanche Dubois, savaged by Marlon Brando in *A Streetcar Named Desire*. In the 1990s, it was Elisabeth Shue playing a prostitute gang-raped by college students in *Leaving Las Vegas*. When Hollywood films depict rape scenes, the victim is almost always female.[4] When a man is sexually assaulted on film, as in *Deliverance* or *Pulp Fiction*, the scene is so unfamiliar that it shocks audiences otherwise accustomed to screen violence and the resulting adrenaline rush.

In real life, when a woman's Victim fantasy fades, she may feel upset by the distance it has created from her real partner. One woman set out to change her Victim fantasies when she realized how this role kept her from feeling closer to her boyfriend. "He was thinking about me when we made love, but my thoughts had nothing to do with him." Similarly, another woman said she felt guilty whenever she had Victim fantasies during lovemaking with her lesbian partner. "I felt dishonest. I wasn't enjoying the tender kind of sex she thought we were having."

Of even greater concern is the potential for Victim fantasies to set women up to be revictimized in real life. When a woman repeatedly engages in Victim fantasies, she is reinforcing a link between pain or danger and sexual pleasure. Mentally, she is rehearsing risky or dangerous scenarios without any of the negative consequences of real life. This could fog her judgment and blind her to the risks of being in a situation where she might be hurt or humiliated in real life.

As Ellen Bass, coauthor of *The Courage to Heal,* wisely notes, "The Victim role is not about a woman's essence, her true self. Women mistakenly think this fantasy says something about who they really are, rather than recognizing it as a response to an outside force. It helps to remember that a fantasy is only a role we have learned, not a destiny."

THE WILD WOMAN

I'm in a cottage with a group of beautiful women. The women fuss over me, painting me with makeup and dressing me in high-heeled shoes and the tiny bottom half of a bikini. When I am ready, the women leave and twenty handsome men, wearing only boxer shorts, enter the room. They are drinking, laughing, and watching me as I dance seductively to the music that has suddenly started playing loudly. When I'm in the right mood, I take a chair in the center of the room and instruct the men to come to me, one by one. They are looking for pleasure, and so am I. I tell each one to make love to me in a different way. And they do, all night long.

Bernadette, who has been sexually affectionate only with her husband throughout their fifteen-year marriage, enjoys being a Wild Woman in her favorite fantasy. Casual, anonymous, sometimes raw sex is the norm for women who take on the Wild Woman role in their fantasies. This role gives women a chance to enjoy sex without rules, limits, or commitments. As the Wild Woman, they describe a feeling of breaking free from traditionally submissive female roles and actively seeking out pleasure on their own terms. They enjoy initiating sex without relying on a partner's lust to ignite sexual fireworks.

Although the typical Wild Woman is actively satisfying her own desires, she does so without hurting or humiliating her fantasy partners. Pleasure, rather than power, is the driving force in this fantasy role. Like the Pretty Maiden, the Wild Woman also requires conditions of safety and consent for sex to occur in the fantasy. Similarly, the Wild Woman might heighten her excitement by weaving in elements of adventure, spontaneity, suspense, or playfulness. As one woman explained, "My fantasy tells me I am worthy of receiving as much love and attention as I can possibly get. I enjoy a total lack of guilt. I don't have to give anyone a blow job in my fantasy to get all the oral sex I want for myself."

In the Wild Woman persona, some women exaggerate their sexual prowess and energy. Greta, for instance, fantasizes about being a wealthy, independent businesswoman, full of energy and creativity. In her Wild Woman fantasy, she imagines approaching men at a party and boldly unzipping their pants to initiate sex. She imagines herself having multiple sexual experiences daily, often as an exhibitionist who disrobes in public. Her fantasy creation, she said, "is much more sexually expressive than I am in real life. In fantasy, I'm not concerned with social pressures or conventions. I'm wanton, wildly sexual, with no consequences. A free spirit."

Often, women imagine playing out this role in public places, with multiple partners, or in other ways that boldly flaunt sexual conventions and restrictions. Erika, for example, said she fantasizes about being in a noisy pool hall with laughter echoing over loud rock and roll music. "One of the men I've been shooting pool with dares me to dance on top of the table. I eagerly climb up to perform. I love for the men to look at me with overt, erotic desire, even though in real life I am uncomfortable with that kind of attention," she confided. "Then, as the fantasy continues, I invite one of the men—a gorgeous hunk—to get up on the table and dance with me. I tell him to strip. When he does, I notice that his cock is even bigger than I had imagined. We start kissing, fall to the table, and go at it. The other men watch and cheer me on. In this fantasy, I'm very bold in getting what I want. I tell the hunk exactly how to please me. After I've climaxed with him, I take on all the other men, one after another."

Some women imagine being a temptress, vamp, or prostitute in this kind of fantasy, playing out a role as old as the biblical Jezebel. But unlike real-life prostitution, where sexual violence and humiliation are routine, being a fantasy whore poses no such risks. One woman described her fantasy as a romantic comedy. Imagining herself as her boyfriend's "special whore," she pictured herself dressed in sexy Frederick's of Hollywood garter belts and performing like a sexual acrobat, laughing her way through one sex act after another. Like the hooker Julia Roberts played in *Pretty Woman,* this woman fantasized about rich clients who fall in love with her.

The Wild Woman is the Cosmo girl, knowing her erogenous zones. It's Madonna, strutting her sexuality. It's characters like Elaine on the popular television sitcom *Seinfeld,* luring sexual partners with her wry humor. These cultural images show women who are bold about seeking sexual satisfaction in their real relationships.

While many women enjoy the freedom and heightened pleasure of the Wild Woman role, some feel uncomfortable with how differently they behave in real life. Others notice a dissonance between how their fantasy partners respond to their imagined sexual aggression and how their real-life partners would react if they were more direct about getting their sexual desires met. Because the Wild Woman role typically focuses on achieving physical pleasure, sometimes in a selfish way, some women miss feeling a deeper intimacy or equality within the fantasy or with their real partners.

Women sometimes try on the Wild Woman role in fantasy to explore sexual relationships they feel curious about, but have not yet experienced in real life. A forty-year-old woman, for example, said she sometimes fantasizes about having sex with another woman, although she's never had a lesbian encounter. She imagines a scene of mutual sexual discovery with a woman who looks much like herself. "I'm aroused by my sense of exploration and curiosity. I undress my fantasy partner and kiss and caress her body in a way that's exploring, passionate, but most of all gentle. Then she does the same to me."

For some women, the Wild Woman role gives them the freedom to carry real-life desires and sensations to new extremes. Maureen, for example, is a thirty-four-year-old who fantasizes about being with partners who set no limits on what they will allow in sex. "I fantasize about a partner who makes all of herself available for touching. I enjoy complete permission and trust to frolic with her body in any way I wish. This is a wild turn-on for me, but there's no hint of humiliation or degradation. We're both totally into sensations, but it's not out on the edge of danger. It feels free, extravagant, with abundant pleasure."

THE DOMINATRIX

I like to fantasize about hunting men. I'll imagine that I pick out an attractive man in a crowd and go after him. It's easy to imagine controlling men with sex. I think about giving him a little taste of power, just enough to let him think he's in charge. Then, when he can't live without me, when he's completely addicted to me, I switch it on him. I'm in control then. I'm calling all the shots. He's there just to please me. And when I've had enough pleasure, I'm through with him. He doesn't know what hit him. That's my game.

Monica was describing a Dominatrix fantasy. In this role, a woman is aroused by her own power and her erotic control over others. Her fantasies focus on getting a partner to do what she wants.

As she described her fantasy, Monica explained how she had adopted this fantasy role in reaction to her past experiences with sex. "I'm only twenty-one," she said, "but I do feel a lot older. I've been through a lot. I've seen enough of sex already in my life to conclude that every relationship has a dominant and a submissive partner. I've had fantasies where I've been the Victim, and I've decided that I will not be dominated, ever again. That only leaves me one option: to fantasize about being on top." Similarly, other women say they are attracted to the Dominatrix role out of a desire to claim sexual power, master past sexual hurts, or avoid feeling victimized in sex.

Like the Wild Woman, the Dominatrix actively initiates the sexual encounters that she wants for her own pleasure. But while the Wild Woman initiates sex against a backdrop of safety and consent, the Dominatrix may not be as concerned with a fantasy partner's sense of safety or long-term emotional well-being. She gets an erotic thrill from power.

Women have reported a wide range of experiences with Dominatrix fantasies, from playful to horrendous. One woman said she toys with this role only in fleeting thoughts when she fantasizes about being more demanding in bed. In real life, she has never acted out this fantasy or shared with her partner her specific sexual desires for more control.

An elementary school teacher said she and her boyfriend take turns being dominant and submissive to lend occasional spice and the thrill of power to their sexual encounters. They use sex toys such as handcuffs or scarves in a playful way, not intending to inflict pain. For her, she said, "This isn't about who I really am. It's just for fun, something different to do together if we're tired of vanilla sex. We play with all kinds of roles in bed, and this is just one of them."

Rather than approaching the Dominatrix role for fun or variety, a few women we met said they were attracted to sadomasochistic sex, or "S/M," as an attempt to master past sexual hurts. They had been victimized by sex in real life and wanted to experience mastery, at least in fantasy, over what had hurt them in the past.

The female Dominatrix stereotype is also one of the popular male fantasies found in pornography, film, and other cultural arenas. The sex industry caters to people who enjoy this role by selling bondage toys and metal-studded leather outfits.

A woman who works in the commercial sex industry said she receives frequent and increasing numbers of requests from men who ask to be sexually dominated.

One woman who has acted out the Dominatrix role as a paid performer explained the appeal of this highly scripted fantasy. She said, "Sex can be both soft and rough, tender and harsh. Some people need that contrast. It creates a state of arousal in the whole body, not oriented only in the genitals." The Dominatrix role, she said, "is not just something you act out to inflict pain. If your partner wants to be spanked, you spank 'with love.' You start slowly and gradually, so that the skin yearns for more. What's interesting for me, as a Dominatrix, is for the submissive to share his vulnerability with me."

While the Dominatrix role is culturally visible, it's also often treated with scorn or contempt. This is the role of the evil seductress who uses sex to get what she wants, such as Demi Moore in *Disclosure* or Glenn Close in *Fatal Attraction*. In this film formula, a beautiful woman's sex appeal diminishes if she starts acting too superior, strident, or sexually demanding. Unlike the Wild Woman, who is driven by her quest for sexual pleasure, the Dominatrix is more often portrayed as sexually threatening and emasculating.

Because the Dominatrix role is about control, a woman who acts it out can risk damaging a relationship built on love and trust. One woman said she split up with her lover because of S/M sex play. She said, "My partner liked me to call her names like 'dirty slut' or 'piece of shit.' But I'm basically a gentle person. When I make love, I want it to be soft, caring, loving. This was the exact opposite. I didn't like the person either of us became in our fantasy roles."

The women who seem most fond of this fantasy say that they don't let the Dominatrix role define or color their intimate relationships. Rather, as one women explained, "It's something I can use when I want to push the edges and bring more intensity to sex, but I always know that it's just a fantasy."

THE BELOVED

> *I have known my imagined partner for some time, but we have held off becoming intimate until this moment. He has spent the day showering me with attention, listening to me over lunch, looking at me with a burning desire as we have walked together, hand in hand, along crowded city sidewalks. Now, back at my apartment, he holds me close and whispers his feelings for me. He lets me know that I'm the center of his life, the only one who has ever made him feel this way. This excites me and makes me want him all the more. Our kisses at first are tender, then we both become more passionate. We collapse on the floor, pulling at each other's clothes, then pause in our frenzy and take time to look at each other. When our bodies finally come together, it's not just sex but the merging of two people, hearts and souls.*

Jayne, twenty-nine, described the soul-mate attraction of the Beloved fantasy. This role plays out in the realm of emotional intimacy where lovers experience lust that starts in the heart. Typically in this role, the woman and her partner feel lucky to have found each other. They are star-crossed lovers like Romeo and Juliet, with a connection that feels rare, special, even spiritual. As one woman explained, "My fantasy partner believes in me. He's not threatened by my intellect or my ambition. He's strong and self-reliant. But he can't get enough of me, nor I of him. We're the only ones who can quench each other's desire."

In the role of the Beloved, the woman enjoys a feeling of equality and strong mutual attraction. A young woman named Kim, for example, said her most exciting fantasy "is not about a serial killer or a rapist. We're just two normal people in love." What adds drama to her fantasy, she explained, is imagining that she and her fantasy lover (who is a dead ringer for an old boyfriend) are frequently kept apart by their careers. She sees herself as a correspondent for *Time* magazine's Asian bureau and her lover as a successful, globe-trotting television producer from Australia. In one fantasy, she imagines their far-flung paths crossing in Los Angeles. "When I step off the plane, my lover is waiting for me in a studio limousine. We begin kissing passionately and want to tear each other's clothes off right there. But we take our time. We go back to his hotel room where he has a Chinese dinner waiting. I pick up my chopsticks and begin to lick and suck them with every bite. He knows I want to do this to him, and smiles wickedly. Under the table, our feet are touching and our legs intertwine. We talk about what's been going on in our lives, in our careers, in the world. We talk about everything, in fact, but sex. Our bodies are having that conversation." Eventually, when they begin to make love, he whispers in her ear how he has missed her. Finally, their groans of pleasure drown out his declarations of love.

Women like the Beloved role because it allows them to blend intimacy and caring with sex. Some women fantasize about the first time they had sex with a real partner, celebrating the newness of their love. Others imagine themselves and their partner being younger and more energetic in bed. Some women weave into their fantasy a desire to conceive a child, creating new life from their love.

Maxine, for example, pictures a Beloved-type fantasy in the outdoors to reflect the love she feels for her husband, Jeff. "I imagine that we are camping in the mountains near a clear lake. Summer wildflowers dot the ground, and the air is sweet with the scent of pine. We're in a secluded spot, very private, and decide to go skinny-dipping. Once we're in the water, we instinctively move closer to each other. At first, we hold one another to keep warm, then we look at each other with desire. When we kiss, I feel our throats, hearts, and bellies touching. Our breathing quickens, and soon we move into our tent that's been warmed by the late-afternoon sun. As we begin to touch each other, we whisper our affections. I feel Jeff's devotion for me through his fingertips, and I return my appreciation for him as we begin kissing and licking each other's genitals. He enters me as I sit in his lap, and we rock back, forth, and around. Smiling, even laughing at times, we feel our passion build until we both explode in rhythmical pulsations, taking in deeply the other's essence. Still inside me, his head on my chest, Jeff lies down with me and we fall asleep, feeling all sense of separateness dissolve. I am at one with everything."

Maxine said her camping fantasy celebrates the love she and Jeff share. But other women, when their Beloved fantasy fades, sometimes say they feel saddened by the contrast with their real-life relationships. "The men in my life come and go, but my fantasy man never dumps me," said one woman who also described a history of heartbreak in real life. Another complained that she has never met a real partner who could fulfill the Beloved fantasy partner role. "In real life, when the man is not the center of attention or the focus of the woman, he gets insecure and threatened. I'd like to meet a man who finds equality as sexy as I do." Sometimes women said they had created Beloved fantasies to resolve the pain of a relationship that went sour. In real life, one woman's boyfriend betrayed her and ran off to marry another woman. But in her fantasy, she pictured him returning to her for a scene of tender, mutual lovemaking.

For women who have tasted the pleasure of a Beloved-type relationship in real life, this kind of fantasy may feel too poignant to indulge in when death has taken their partner away. Rosie, for example, is a sixty-two-year-old widow who enjoyed a happy marriage for nearly forty years. She and her husband had shared an active, exciting sex life. But since her husband's death, she has been unable to sexually fantasize about him, even though that used to be an erotic turn-on for her. "It would be too sad now. Fantasizing would remind me of how much I have lost," she said.

When women see themselves in a Beloved fantasy, or in any of the four previously described popular fantasy roles, the erotic attraction of the fantasy comes from a sense of being part of the action. Sometimes, however, women find the most heat when they imagine watching others carry on a sexual relationship.

THE VOYEUR

> *I imagine that I'm back in college, and another woman is in my dorm room. We're listening to music, dancing around, dressing up in shawls, hats, and outlandish outfits. She lies down on her bed and begins to masturbate. I pretend not to notice, but it's obvious what she's doing. Then she starts talking to me, saying she has to touch me. I sit there like a statue while she rubs up against me and climaxes. I don't engage in sex in the fantasy. It's like I'm offstage from my own fantasy. I'm watching her, and watching her want me. It's like I'm seeing myself in a home movie. The images run through my mind like flickering old film clips.*

For Eileen, imagining herself in the Voyeur role is an erotic fantasy experience. This role can allow a woman to step back and have some emotional distance from her own fantasy. She can vicariously enjoy watching a scene without having to feel as if she's participating in the story. Her voyeuristic fantasy gives her a buffer zone from the erotic action, almost like a fantasy within a fantasy.

Women who fantasize about being a Voyeur often incorporate other fantasy roles into the story that they imagine watching. Eileen's roommate fantasy, for example, incorporated the Pretty Maiden role along with the Voyeur. She was fantasizing about watching herself be the object of another woman's desire. Similarly, other women might create a Voyeur fantasy that contains the relationship dynamics of the Wild Woman, Victim, Dominatrix, or Beloved.

As Voyeur, a woman can enjoy the heat of a sexual scene without having to take on a particular role herself. One woman, for example, had fantasies of watching a girl get sexually tortured but cringed at the thought of viewing herself as a Victim. Because so many different roles get played out in Voyeur fantasies, the interpersonal dynamics of the imagined sex scenes can vary widely. One woman fantasizes about watching two newlyweds arouse each other to a mutual sexual frenzy, while another imagines watching a woman dominate another woman in a prison cell.

In the Voyeur role, a woman can remain passive in terms of the primary sexual action. Her power and excitement come from choosing to watch. The erotic tension she feels can be heightened if there's a chance she will be discovered. One woman, for instance, imagines herself hiding in a closet, watching a prostitute perform oral sex on a male client. She also imagines masturbating and moaning with pleasure while watching, further increasing her own sexual excitement and risk of getting caught. Some women said they enjoy this thrill of the taboo that the Voyeur role offers. By infringing on others' privacy, in imagination, they can break social conventions—and even the law—without negative consequences. One woman explained, "I don't think about how anything feels to the characters I fantasize about. I don't identify with them. What turns me on is watching them, listening to the grunts and groans and other sounds they make during sex."

By remaining removed from the sexual action, a woman can feel less responsible for what occurs during the fantasy. She can enjoy watching a scene that she might not feel ready, able, or interested in experiencing herself. As the Voyeur, she can create a safe emotional distance from the dynamics of a fantasy that is bothering her for some reason. It can also be a safety zone when a woman wants to test out a new fantasy or when she's working to change a troublesome one.

Although the Voyeur is always about being a spectator, women's experiences with this role differ depending on their imagined perspective and how much of themselves they bring into the fantasy. Several women, for instance, might describe Voyeur fantasies about an orgy. The first woman might picture herself reclining on a couch in the middle of the orgy, with people engaging in wild sex all around her. Another might remove herself further from the action and fantasize about watching the sex scene through a window. A third woman might let the orgy scene play out in her mind with no consciousness of herself being present. A fourth might picture herself participating in the orgy, but feel as if she's watching herself from a distance.

In Voyeur fantasies, women sometimes invent props to distance or dissociate themselves from the sexual action that they imagine observing. They might imagine, for instance, that they watch through a one-way mirror, or underneath a bed, in a theater, or from behind a screen. Some women imagine eavesdropping on lovers through a bedroom wall or listening to the sounds of sex over a telephone.

For some women, the attraction to the Voyeur role may have been rooted in an early exposure to pornography. By watching others have sex, and becoming aroused, they created an erotic pattern that has stayed with them in fantasy. A few became so conditioned by this pattern that they could not become aroused in real sex unless they imagined watching their lover having sex with someone else.

Although some women enjoy the distance created by imagining themselves a Voyeur, this distance can also pose a drawback. By keeping herself on the outskirts of her own fantasy, a woman can deny herself the full benefits another fantasy role has to offer. She may feel she's not worthy of the attention, intimacy, or power that the fantasy characters enjoy. "My Voyeur fantasy reflects other parts of my life where I'm an observer, not actively engaged," one woman explained. "Sometimes I feel like I'm watching my life pass me by, including my fantasy life." Another woman said she's always felt distanced from the people around her in real life. "I'm always on the outskirts, watching what's going on with everybody else. I'm not in the mix. And in my fantasies, I'm also on the outside, looking in."

※

Most women who experience scripted fantasies find that one of the roles fits them well. Indeed, many women say they *prefer* a certain role over the others. Often, women can connect a particular fantasy role with a particular time in their lives. "I used to be a Pretty Maiden," one woman said, "but now that I've had more sexual adventures in real life, I've become a Wild Woman in my fantasies." Occasionally, women feel stuck in a particular fantasy role. Instead of feeling like a preference or passing fancy, the fantasy role may be the only route that leads to sexual satisfaction.

Some women find that they readily shift and change roles from one fantasy to the next or even within the same fantasy. One woman, for instance, shared an intricate fantasy that started with her being a schoolgirl who is kidnapped and taken to an underground cave. After she described the rest of this fantasy, we could go back and label all the different roles she had included. She said: "I am tied up with a group of other captives [Victim]. A Dominatrix wielding a whip orders a male captive to his knees and tells him to perform oral sex on her. I watch [Voyeur]. Somehow, the man and I escape from the cave and make our way to a hidden room with a couch in it. I either fall asleep and wake up with the man causing me to scream with joy [Pretty Maiden], or else I become the initiator and tell him just what I want to enjoy [Wild Woman]."

Some women not only change roles during a fantasy but also imagine changing genders or orientations. One black heterosexual woman, for instance, imagines herself as a gay white male. Another woman imagines that her gender is magically changed so that she becomes a well-endowed man, eager and able to please a parade of women.

Once we understand these definitions of women's most common fantasy roles, we can talk about our sexual desires more clearly. One couple came to Wendy for counseling because they were having problems with their sex life. By talking with them about fantasy roles, she helped them see that they were both desiring a passive role in sex. The woman was envisioning herself as a Pretty Maiden and wanting to be swept away by an aggressive partner. The man was imagining himself with a Wild Woman who would initiate sex. Their sex life was stagnant because both of them were waiting for the other to initiate lovemaking—in their fantasies and in real life.

UNSCRIPTED FANTASIES

When women describe the ingredients of their favorite fantasies, they often get very specific about little details: the scent of a particular perfume; the taste of chocolate melting on the tongue; the wail of a saxophone; the texture of leather or silk; the crash of ocean surf; the afternoon heat of a summer's day. While this is true with many women who describe scripted fantasies, it is even more pronounced among women whose primary fantasies are unscripted and focus on sensations rather than character roles.

A woman named Rani said she can feel many different physical sensations soaring to an intense peak when she experiences what she calls a "fire breath orgasm":

> I lie on my back with my knees bent and my feet flat against the floor. I visualize energy moving up from the earth, into my feet, up through my legs and toward my genitals. As I feel this energy building in me, I start rocking and pumping from the pelvis. Instead of letting go, I build the energy up more. I imagine looping the energy around and around through my body so that it builds up a reservoir. I breathe with it. I work with this energy, squeezing my pelvic muscles as I let my breath

out. When the energy starts to feel locked in my geni-
tals, I touch myself there to let the energy out and help it
move through me. As the energy builds, my breathing
intensifies. I open my throat and let sounds emerge. My
voice changes as I get deeper into orgasmic sounds. I
keep the energy looping around and around through my
body until I feel the orgasm moving up from my pelvis
and my G-spot, into my heart. When the orgasm
reaches my throat, my body arches and the energy fi-
nally explodes from me. The sounds I make echo what
I'm feeling throughout my body. My voice wavers and
soars like the call of a wild jungle bird.

When Rani describes her fire breath orgasm in words, she highlights the key sensations that take her to such peak sexual experiences. She focuses on thoughts that intensify her breath, feelings of physical energy, and the sounds of sex. "I'm not a very visual person," she said, explaining why these other senses are more important to her.

By looking more closely at which senses are being excited in a fantasy, we often learn new information about our natural sensory preferences and sexual styles. Women who are more visual, for example, may become easily aroused by fantasizing about images or pictures. Women who are more auditory may get excited by hearing sexy words, moans, music, or other sounds they associate with sex. One woman likes to mentally replay songs by her favorite rock group, Duran Duran, when she makes love.

Similarly, women sometimes identify their sexual style as more focused on body movement. Women who share this "kinesthetic" approach to sex like to feel the physical dance of desire. They focus on how their whole bodies feel in motion as they undulate and touch during sex. For them, fantasy often starts with a strong physical sensation. Then, they search for words to capture the memory of their kinesthetic experience. Sarah, a woman in her sixties, said she used to think of herself as someone without sexual fantasies. But with one favorite partner, she said, "I kind of disappear during sex into some altered state. It's a feeling of merging with him, almost like spinning off together out into space. Our bodies are part of the whole universe. I can't create this feeling on purpose. But when it happens, it's very special."

Lonnie Barbach, Ph.D., a well-known sex therapist and author on sexuality, said she can't explain why certain sensory modes are more important than others to individual women. "But it's crucial to understand that different women have different modes for getting aroused sexually. If a woman is very visual, then the images of her fantasies can be just as important to her sexual arousal as clitoral stimulation is to another woman. If a woman is auditory, then she needs to hear things during sex. If her partner's not talking to her, she can lose an important part of the arousal process." In her fantasies, a woman can incorporate or enhance stimulation for whatever senses drive her desire.

When we think more closely about which sensations are most involved during sex, we may identify one or more of these as being significant:

- visual, relating to sights
- auditory, relating to sounds
- tactile, relating to touch
- olfactory, relating to smells
- kinesthetic, relating to body movement
- flavor, relating to taste

In unscripted fantasies, women sometimes increase erotic pleasure by using imagery that highlights one of these specific sensory modes. They may describe fantasies that someone else might consider to be nonsexual. Such images offer new metaphors for sexual energy. One woman with kinesthetic fantasies, for instance, imagines a train going uphill while she is having sex. When she reaches the top of a steep incline, she climaxes. Her sexual response cycle matches the rhythm of the train. Another woman pictures her sexual desire as a river inside of her body. When she feels the first stirrings of arousal, she imagines a trickle of water from a mountain stream. As she approaches orgasm, the stream swells to a rushing river. At orgasm, she pictures a waterfall. Other women describe images of storm clouds gathering then spilling their water, or flowers opening from bud to bloom, releasing perfume.

A woman named Jenny explained how images from nature best capture how she feels during peak sexual experiences. "Once, when I was making love with this person I really adored, I remember having a vision of a tree. I imagined that this was the tree of life, with roots going down into the center of the earth, and leaves and branches reaching out to the sun. I felt like I was this tree, and my lover was the sun. I could feel his life energy coursing through my body." Thinking back on that powerful sensory experience, she said, still gives her goosebumps.

Yet when another woman considered the erotic appeal of bringing nature images into her bedroom, she said, "I guess I'm not a nature person. I'd be worrying about bugs instead of sexual pleasure." Clearly, the images or sensations we choose to weave into our fantasies need to ring true for our own personal definition of the erotic.

Because of their unscripted nature, these fantasies don't involve relationship issues or stereotyped sexual roles. As a result, they may be less likely to leave women feeling upset about power dynamics or troubled by their fantasy self-image. Only rarely do women describe sensory fantasies that they find intrusive or unwanted. Typically, these relate to physical pain, bad smells, or other images that may feel like flashbacks and often relate to past abuse experiences.

Most of the unscripted fantasies that women have described are unique and very inventive. One woman, recognizing that she equates the color red with passion, said she decorated her bedroom with art and fabric in scarlet hues to remind her to "think red" during sex. Another, who said she is turned on by her sense of smell, sprinkles her bathwater with rose petals so that she can inhale the sweet floral fragrance from her own warm skin while making love.

Food is a popular element in many women's fantasies, adding a flavor and erotic satisfaction that sometimes overshadows the pleasure of sex. In an anthology called *Ladies' Own Erotica,* several women contributed stories that highlight the erotic qualities of oysters, asparagus, and peaches. In a story called "Just Desserts," writer Rose Solomon explores the sensory appeal of chocolate:

> She took the biggest strawberry and dipped it into the fondue. The chocolate was still very warm, and some of it slipped off the cool berry and dribbled down her arm. Lilah watched the rest congeal and adhere to the strawberry before she popped it into her mouth. . . . By now Lilah's dress was splattered with chocolate. She licked the larger spills, careful not to waste a precious drop. Then, very slowly, she lowered both hands into the remaining fondue, raised them up, and watched the chocolate glaze ooze. She sucked each finger, dipped them in again . . .[5]

Marge Piercy describes the pleasure of weaving all the senses into thoughts of sex in her poem "Wet":

> . . . Deeper and deeper into
> the thick warm translucence
> where mind and body melt,
> where we see with our tongues
> and taste with our fingers;
> there the horizon of excess

folds as we approach
into plains of not enough . . .[6]

Many women who enjoy these kinds of sexual images say that it takes time, sexual experience, maturity, and a willingness to get creative for them to entertain unscripted fantasies. Models for these kinds of sexual images aren't obvious or common. In fact, unscripted fantasies have been largely overlooked in past research about sexual fantasy. Pornography does focus on the visual and auditory aspects of sex, but it typically portrays a very narrow and graphic view that doesn't meet all women's sensory needs. Women who enjoy unscripted fantasies often say their sensory-based images help them feel more free and spontaneous during sex.

᎒

Although we've looked at scripted and unscripted fantasies separately, women have the ability to blend and overlap these styles so that they can enjoy the benefits of both types of fantasies. Thus, scripted fantasies with a story line can more fully engage the senses, and unscripted fantasies can take on the excitement of a more dramatic plot.

By getting comfortable with this new language for describing women's fantasies, we're on our way to understanding our own sexual thoughts better. But figuring out whether we entertain Beloved or Voyeur fantasies, or perhaps a more sensory, unscripted variation, is only a start. Next, we can use this new language to explore where our fantasies come from and how they change over time.

❦

CHAPTER 3

Where Sexual Fantasies Come From

Outside her car window, the wide open spaces of Montana rolled on endlessly. Twelve-year-old Annie glowered at the scenery from the backseat of the family station wagon. If only she were home, she could be meeting her friends today at the neighborhood pool, or maybe going to the mall. Instead, she was trapped here, next to her little brother, with a stack of *Seventeen* magazines she'd already read, wasting her summer on a family road trip. Before her mom or dad could turn around again to tell her how beautiful the West was, she closed her eyes and pretended to sleep.

Out of nowhere, she started thinking about the black-and-white Western they had watched last night on a motel television. She especially loved one scene where the cowboy rescued a young woman from a runaway stagecoach by scooping her onto the back of his horse. She could imagine her own arms wrapped tightly around his waist, her hair and skirts flying in the breeze, and the horse galloping off with them into the sunset. With her head pressed against the cowboy's shoulder, she could smell his cologne (never mind that cowboys probably didn't use aftershave). As she imagined how the supple leather of his jacket would feel against her cheek, she suddenly noticed the tingle of a sensation that she had never felt before, right where her thighs would grip the saddle.

"Hey, Annie!" her little brother shouted, poking her in the ribs with his toy pistol and destroying her fantasy. "Want to help me look for license plates?"

⁂

Sexual fantasies often begin in childhood with romantic or sensual ideas that become more sexual as girls mature. After looking back to remember her earliest sexual thoughts, Annie told us about this Pretty Maiden fantasy that came to her spontaneously, at a time when many different sources in her life converged to make her feel aroused, passionate, and wanting to be more in touch with her sexuality. She could see that, in early adolescence, she was aroused not only by a certain kind of fantasy relationship, but also by a combination of visual and kinesthetic sensations. She appreciated how young she was when she started to concoct her own signature blend of elements that, as an adult, she defines as being pleasing and erotic.[1]

Looking back at our earliest thoughts about sex, most of us can see, in hindsight, that we invented our first sexual fantasies with no one having to teach us how.

Women's earliest fantasies are often a natural extension of daydreaming, make-believe, or other childhood play. Role-playing and imaginative play are the tools children intuitively use to make sense of the world and tackle developmental challenges. Through their active imaginations, children can use inanimate objects such as dolls, toy trucks, playhouses, stuffed animals, and model trains and create lively new worlds full of drama, adventure, and characters of their own choosing. Through fantasy, children also create a very private, inner playground. It's a perfect place for girls to develop and explore all sorts of new ideas, including their private sexual thoughts.

The sexual fantasies females create as children often relate to early yearnings for love and the sexual questions they are most curious about at that time in life. In sexual fantasy, girls can ponder their natural curiosity about female bodies, boys' bodies, and those warm, pleasant sensations they may have discovered between their own legs.

Fantasy development seems intimately tied in with sexual development. The circumstances under which our sexuality unfolds in childhood can have a lot to do with the types of fantasies we are drawn to or create.

Our early sexual fantasies are inspired by many different sources. A fantasy might start with a real-life experience or chance discovery of a new, pleasant physical sensation. It might replay a favorite scene from a movie or continue an erotic thought that first surfaced during a dream.

Clearly, sexual fantasies don't begin in a vacuum. As girls, we took in all sorts of messages about sex and about being a sexual woman that we heard from parents, friends, siblings, teachers, and church leaders. We soaked up more messages from magazines, books, movies, and television. When we consider the personal impact of these early influences, we often can tell which messages we ignored and which ones have remained important in our adult sex lives.

Although a number of different factors may have shaped our earliest sexual fantasies, we're going to examine six different sources and influences separately. As we're listening to other women's experiences with these fantasy sources, we can ask ourselves questions to see how our own personal sense of the erotic first took hold:

- ❀ Was I excited about becoming a woman?
- ❀ What were my earliest sexual thoughts?

    What were my early hopes, confusions, or fears about sex?

    Did my sexuality bubble up naturally in a way that felt comfortable and welcome?

    Did I feel rushed or forced into sex before I was ready?

"HOW LOVELY TO BE A WOMAN"

In *Bye Bye Birdie,* the classic musical salute to female hormones, the character named Kim has a memorable scene where she has just been pinned to go steady. She dances around her bedroom singing "How Lovely to Be a Woman." Although she's still a teenager, she's imagining herself fully grown into the role of woman. And clearly, she's in love with the whole idea.

This movie scene speaks to many women who fondly remember their rite of passage from girlhood to being a woman, and the feelings that often come with that romantic stage of life. Hollywood celebrates this important coming-of-age story over and over again. In such films as *West Side Story, Romeo and Juliet, Gigi,* and *Flower Drum Song,* the nubile female lead gets a scene to express her excited yearning to become a woman. And as girls watch from their theater seats, they rehearse their own dreams of becoming a sexually mature female and may experience the same physical sensations that the actresses are enjoying on screen.

As part of their quest to understand who they are, girls from a young age try on different fantasy images of what it means to be female. Gender is one of the first certainties of identity. Girls' early role-playing about outward appearances often exaggerates qualities they identify as being feminine. Many women probably remember teetering on their mother's high heels, stuffing an older sister's bra to fit, or smearing their faces with borrowed makeup. During these moments, they were experimenting with how their young bodies would feel as grown-up women.

Even today (and often to the chagrin of parents who want to

raise their children free of rigid gender roles), many little girls still love to dress up in their mother's clothes and jewelry, dress their Barbies in exotic costumes, and preen in front of the mirror like runway models. As girls embrace the role of the female, however superficially, they are trying on the hopes and dreams of the woman they might become. Developmentally, they are also latching onto a positive sense of adult sexuality.

A woman named Eve, now in her sixties, has enjoyed a long, successful career as a university professor. She has been through a number of life passages, including marriage, motherhood, being single and dating again later in life. She loves sex and has had passionate encounters with both male and female lovers. It's been a long time since she was a girl, unschooled in the ways of love. But, gazing out her high-rise apartment window, Eve had no trouble remembering her first sexual fantasy.

As a little girl, Eve used to lie awake for hours in her canopy bed. She never complained to her parents about this persistent childhood insomnia. Rather, it was one of her favorite times of day. She would tuck the sheets around her body just so, transforming herself in her imagination from a five-year-old in candy-striped flannel pajamas into a beautiful young woman in a strapless satin evening gown. Then, letting her fantasy and its accompanying sensations unfold, she would picture herself dancing with her favorite suitors to jazzy Glenn Miller tunes.

The details of those first fantasies were so vivid that Eve can recall them even now. "I had two imaginary boyfriends, Dick and Bob. They were both handsome, and both madly in love with me. They competed for me because, you see, I was so popular." Eve nurtured her romantic, Beloved-type fantasies for at least a decade. Like the radio soap operas her mother followed religiously, her fantasies took dramatic plot turns. She would see herself marrying Bob, have him die in a tragic accident, get back together with Dick, and then make Bob magically reappear.

Gradually, as she matured physically, started dating, and learned more about sex, her fantasies became more explicit, more arousing, and more likely to involve masturbation. But from an early age, she had defined being a woman as being desired by others. As an adult, she said, her fantasies continue to focus on romance and being desirable.

Looking back at her childhood, Eve saw that her parents gave her positive messages and useful guidance about sex, but also time to develop at her own pace. She wasn't pushed into sexual acts or exposed to sexual images before she was old enough to understand them. "And I always knew I could ask my parents about anything, including sex, and get a straight answer," she said. "For their generation, they were very unusual. They gave me the idea that sex was a good thing."

A woman named Diane also grew up hearing sex-positive messages. Her grandfather used to tell her often, and with pride, "Lebanese blood is always boiling." From a young age, she understood, "We were supposed to be passionate, sexual people. That's the sort of line that sticks with you your whole life." She remembered how her first fantasy evolved from her natural curiosity about being female.

Diane's earliest fantasy focused on the physical attributes of being a woman. She was about eight years old when her curiosity led her to a key erotic discovery. In the back of her uncle's grocery store, she chanced upon a stack of *National Geographic* magazines. She was fascinated and excited by the pictures of bare-breasted women from a distant continent. The next time she opened an *Archie* comic book, she noticed that Betty and Veronica wore tight clothing that showed off their prominent bustlines. Diane's earliest sexual fantasies, as a flat-chested little girl, were all about women with full breasts. That was the image which first jolted her into thinking, "So *this* is a real woman." That was exactly how she wanted to look some day.

As an adult, Diane said, this visual aspect of "being female" remains a turn-on. While making love with her husband, she often flashes on images of women's breasts to enhance her own arousal.

Although our own personal sense of what's erotic will shift

and evolve over a lifetime, these early impressions often stay with us throughout life. One woman, now in her late forties, remembers being intrigued as a child by the Vargas girl calendars hanging in her dad's dusty basement workshop. In her earliest sexual fantasies, at about age nine, she imagined herself as a showgirl sitting in a crescent moon–shaped stage prop, wearing a see-through gown and singing a love song. Ever since, her erotic fantasies have involved women dressed in sexy Vargas girl costumes, although her fantasies have become more boldly sexual as she has matured. She described her earliest fantasies as the Pretty Maiden variety, in which she was an innocent object of desire. As an adult, she fantasizes about being a Wild Woman who designs sexy women's wear, then puts on her own revealing creations to seek out exciting erotic experiences.

In contrast to Eve, Diane, and the young Vargas girl who all explored sexuality at their own pace, many women created early sexual fantasies in the midst of feeling confused about sex. Fantasy offered a healthy escape where they could privately celebrate being female and sensual and not have to feel ashamed about their bodies or their natural desires. They maintained a place where it felt okay to be a sexual female, even when other messages were confusing or inhibiting.

Angelina, for instance, was raised by her strict Spanish-American grandparents. "I didn't have a clue about sex. The word never came up in my household," she said. In fact, it was only through traditional Spanish dance lessons that Angelina was permitted an outlet for her sensuality. "I loved being on stage with a ruffled dress and a flower in my hair. I could express the beauty within myself that way. When I saw the older girls performing, I wanted to emulate them, become them. They were madonnas, so beautiful and passionate."

Angelina's grandmother sewed her dancing costumes with full, swirling red skirts and low necklines, even though she criticized any girl who dressed or walked in a provocative way offstage. Angelina was well aware of the irony. "My grandmother tried to erase sex from my mind. The day my period started, she screamed and cried in Spanish like she blamed me for turning into a woman. But she also thought dance was creative, artistic, part of our heritage. So she didn't stop me from dancing."

The fantasy that has stayed with Angelina since girlhood is about dancing to Spanish flamenco music. She said she can still imagine the strumming of guitars, the pounding of drums, and her body comes alive with the thrum of desire. "If I like somebody, I picture dancing with him in a way that draws him into my sexual energy."

Many women can see how they were affected by limited cultural models for what it means to be a sexy woman. An African-American woman in her twenties said she spent her childhood imagining she was one of her white Barbies. A lesbian woman, now in her forties, remembers feeling invisible when she was an teenager. "I wasn't giggling about the boys, and I didn't have anyone to giggle with about the girls. Nowhere did I see a love story where two girls got to hold hands and walk on the beach at sunset," she said.

"I'VE GOT A CRUSH ON YOU!"

First fantasies often begin as crushes. From elementary school until well into their teens, girls often shower their romantic hopes and dreams on a love object who typically doesn't know they exist. Since the days when Frank Sinatra sent bobby-socksers swooning, girls have been plastering their walls with posters of stars like Elvis, James Dean, Jim Morrison, or their favorite Beatle. The tradition carries on today, of course, with heartthrobs like Brad Pitt, Antonio Banderas, Keanu Reeves, Coolio, an assortment of rap stars, and even k.d. lang and Jodie Foster shouldering the weight of young female lust.

Crushes often involve a massive outpouring of energy. Some women remember joining fan clubs, writing love letters, or spending all their allowance on memorabilia of whomever it was they once found fabulous. For a young girl, coming to terms with her changing body and her budding sexual feelings, crushes are a safe, acceptable outlet. This is culturally sanctioned sexual fantasy. Crushes are fine to gossip about at slumber parties or to talk over for hours on the phone.

Typically, most women remember fantasizing about someone who was not only drop-dead attractive, by their personal definition, but also completely unavailable. As a result, they were free to imagine falling in love with none of the risks of a real entanglement. Not everyone confined their crushes to Hollywood. Many women remember having a crush on a favorite teacher, an older brother's friend, or a classmate. But usually, they kept these close-range crushes a secret.

In a positive way, a girl's crush reinforces her view of herself as being worthy of love and attention. The fantasy tells her she's lovable, a match for someone attractive. As part of the starry-eyed logic of crushes, girls imagine that their dreamboats would truly "Love Me Tender," if only they had a chance to meet in real life.

Even better, some girls fantasize that their love can heal. They imagine that, through the power of their own affection, they would somehow transform or save their imagined beloved from unhappiness. When James Dean scowled, thousands of girls fantasized that they could make him smile. And when Ricky Nelson sang "Travelin' Man," about his worldwide web of girlfriends, plenty of girls imagined themselves as the one who could make him stop globe-trotting and happily settle down. However corny these early fantasies might seem to us as adults, they served an important purpose earlier in life, by acknowledging our capacity to bring joy and love to another.

Developmentally, crushes offer girls a chance to define for themselves what they will eventually find attractive in a real partner. It may be as general as skin color or as specific as the fullness of an imaginary lover's lips. Or, the magnetism might have to do with personality even more than looks.

A woman who grew up attending Catholic schools, for instance, remembers her crush on the parish priest, an object of desire who couldn't have been more inaccessible. "He was about twenty-eight, dark-haired, Italian, and gorgeous. He was so kind to all the kids, but especially to the girls. If we were upset about something, he would put his arm around us and comfort us. It was almost worth falling down on the playground, just so he could pick you up," she said. Those real touches, although nonsexual, fed her fantasies. She learned early that she was attracted by a tender kind of sexiness.

In the context of a crush, girls can not only explore what they want in a partner, but also make sure potential partners exist. Corrina, for example, used fantasies to help her decide on the type of man she'd like someday for a partner, even though she was years away from being ready for a relationship. From childhood, she was an avid reader who loved classic children's books. At about age nine, she fell in love with Robin Hood. She started daydreaming that she would find someone like him in real life. "He seemed like a true man to me. So when I stepped out of my books, I would think about different men in my life—teachers, or an uncle, or a family friend—and I'd pick out one to fixate on. I'd think of someone who was dapper, with good manners, someone who could talk to kids without being condescending, and I'd think, 'Now, there's a man. A true man.' "

Corrina wasn't sure exactly how her life would change once she found a man worth loving, but she sensed there was something good waiting for her out in the world of relationships. Her crushes on decent, caring, attentive men helped her plan for the day when she felt ready to have a partner. "I was aware that there was a secret men had. They had some secret, greater knowledge that I really desired." And in her fantasies she could safely explore what that secret might be, and imagine herself a match for it.

The personal characteristics of our early crush objects can point to what we longed for in a relationship, and why. Lois, for example, remembered having a series of intense crushes on movie

Add a little sunshine to your life!

- Jackie
-
- Call   Shelly
  Susan   O. Jackie
- Goldia House sitter 2-6147
  Home
-

©Colorbök

stars, starting in her early teens. By the time she was a college coed, she had developed a powerful attraction to the blue-eyed comic actor Gene Wilder. She watched reruns of his old films. She read everything she could find about him. She kept current on the details of his romance with actress Gilda Radner and was moved to learn how Wilder tenderly cared for her when she fell ill with terminal cancer. Even though, intellectually, Lois knew her life would never intersect with Gene Wilder's, she didn't hesitate to fantasize about the sexual escapades they could share.

When we asked what had first attracted her to Gene Wilder, Lois blurted out, "It's the eyes!" Then, pondering why eyes would be such an erotic magnet, she made a connection she had never before considered. As a little girl, growing up with an often angry and critical father, she had learned to watch her dad's eyes to read his moods. "It didn't happen very often, but once in a while he would be happy with me. He wasn't angry or yelling then, and everything was okay. The twinkle in his eye was just incredible. It melted me. In that twinkle, that's the only place I ever saw his love." Fantasy helped her keep that actual experience of love alive. And in the eyes of Gene Wilder, she spotted the sweet, tender love that she yearned to discover again in real life.

During childhood and adolescence, crushes can offer a way to develop and maintain a positive view of sex. These early fantasies can keep a woman's sexual development on track, even when real life throws up obstacles. Luanne, for instance, was molested by an older brother when she was seven. But for this dreamy, imaginative farm girl, fantasy became an outlet for healthy sexual development. It helped that her parents offered her a role model of a loving couple. She would giggle with delight to watch her dad pull her mom onto his lap. By the time she reached junior high, Luanne started developing a series of crushes on boys at school. She would write their initials in the sand at the riverbank near her home, and daydream about holding hands or kissing. She didn't mind when her parents teased her about being boy crazy.

In fantasy, unlike the experience with her brother, Luanne

got to control the pace of how fast sexual activity unfolded. "In a very healthy way, I can see that fantasy let me envision how sex would be fun and safe, not yucky or frightening like it was with my brother," she said. Fantasy helped Luanne develop a dream of romance and love with someone worthy and respectful. As a forty-three-year-old adult, she continues to invent fantasies that focus on the fun, playful aspects of sex with her real partner.

Another woman suffered serious injuries in a car accident in her late teens, just when she was becoming comfortable with her lesbian orientation. By having a series of secret crushes on different hospital nurses and wholesome actress Annette Funicello, she was able to keep her sexuality alive throughout a long and tedious recovery. Fantasy kept her from feeling asexual. It also substituted for the dating she couldn't enjoy because of her temporary disability.

In a crush, girls also find a place to sort out sexual feelings they might be too young to experience safely in real life. For example, they can visualize the male genitals they may not be ready to see up close, or mentally undress a fantasy partner they aren't eager to really meet yet in the flesh. Because they adore the crush object, they can fantasize about his body parts, his hip movements, or the curl of his lips without feeling they're objectifying him. In the magic land of fantasies, they get to sexualize and adore their ideal partner at the same time. From the safe distance of the crush, a girl can imagine going the full length of her desire.

To work well, crush fantasies usually need to keep this distance. That seems to be part of the magic that makes them work. One woman said she still remembers how, at home, she fantasized about a certain boy kissing and fondling her. Later, when she would see him at school, she would feel so embarrassed around him that she couldn't even talk to him. Another woman remembered feeling ostracized in the third grade when a female classmate discovered she was the object of her affection. "The fantasy had been so great, until she found out about it from one of our class-mates. Then she was really mad at me, and all of our classmates teased me."

When crushes get too close for comfort, they are no longer such fun. A young girl's sexual energy needs to travel a one-way street in a crush. While she lavishes her affection onto an imagined partner, she may not be developmentally ready to feel any sexual energy coming back at her. One woman remembered having a terrible crush on her junior high math teacher. But it only felt safe when he stayed up at the chalkboard. She said, "At the end of seventh grade, we were having a pool party. This teacher was a chaperone. Someone started a water fight, and so of course I aimed my water balloon at him. He joined the fray, picked me up, and was going to throw me into the pool. I was terrified, even though I'd imagined for months what it would feel like to be wrapped in his arms. He must have seen the petrified look in my eyes, because he gently set me down and walked away."

For another woman, it was a different story. At about age nine, she would often sit in her driveway and watch a teenage neighbor boy practice shooting baskets. She craved his attention. One day he invited her inside his bedroom to play cards, and she didn't hesitate to follow. But when he began fondling her, she was overwhelmed. He abused not only her body, but also the young love she had been testing in the safety zone of her imagination. Because of her crush, she was left feeling guilty about what had occurred, even though she had done nothing shameful or wrong.

As we navigate this tricky path from childhood toward sex-ual maturity, we eventually outgrow our early crushes. The post-ers come down from bedroom walls. We stop sending secret Val-entines. Developmentally, crushes allow us time to rehearse for real relationships and to imagine a target for the new sexual en-ergy we discover in our own bodies. In this melding of idealized romance and new sensations, we begin to shape our personal sex-ual style.

"WHAT A FEELING!"

Sexual awakening sometimes happens suddenly when real life delivers an experience that stimulates the senses in a new, unexpected way. These spontaneous circumstances might deliver a quick jolt of unexpected pleasure, a tingling sensation in the genitals, a rush of radiant heat. In a flash, we understand what our girlfriends and older sisters have been giggling about. We finally "get it."

Women's memories of this first rush of sensation are varied, but often very specific. Maybe it was feeling a jet of bath water on their vulva. Or a lovely throb of sensation while seated on a bike or mounted on horseback. Some women remember a roller-coaster or elevator ride that sent their stomachs tumbling and spread a warm sensation down their thighs. Others felt a thrill when they slid down a banister, rode a seesaw, or smoothed body lotion on their nipples. And because it felt so good and exciting, they often went looking for that feeling again, in their fantasies.

One woman remembers her first genital pleasure catching her by surprise when she jumped, spread-eagle, into a cool swimming pool. Now, forty years later, she can still climax just by recalling that splash of unexpected sensation as she took the plunge. Another woman vividly remembers an early fantasy of sitting naked with her legs around the branch of a cherry tree. She developed this unscripted fantasy when she was only ten and growing up in rural Japan. But the memory of that fleeting image and the sensations it generated have stayed with her for twenty years. In that momentary flash, she first felt her sexuality stir.

Women describe these early sexual feelings as sometimes starting with a trickle, and sometimes flooding them with erotic sensation. Madeline, for instance, was blindsided by her first sexual sensations. A tall, pale, smart girl in a small, cliquish Southern town, she didn't attract boys like the girls who seemed to know how to flirt by instinct. It didn't help her social life that she attended a conservative Baptist church where being sexual and being virtuous were considered mutually exclusive. In fact, because of her modest demeanor, her Sunday school class had voted Madeline "Best Christian."

One day in ninth grade, Madeline was sitting in band class when she felt the boy in the next chair pressing his leg against hers. "We were both playing, of all things, the trumpet. Well, I felt his leg, and I saw his face getting red, and I had all these warm feelings come over me. It was more than warm—it was a flame. And my fantasy was that he was turning red because of his desire for me. That's when I knew what sex was all about. I wasn't scared at all. I was very excited."

Halfway around the world, in Malaysia, another girl was feeling similarly strong sexual feelings after attending her first dance at age twelve. A tall boy invited her to dance a fast number, then a slow one. She put her arms around his waist and felt the sweat on his shirt as they swayed in time to the music. Her genitals swelled as she felt herself awaken to the thrill of another's touch. All the way home in her parents' car, she replayed the dance in her mind. She wondered what it would have been like if he had bent down for a kiss. That night in bed, she swayed back and forth, kissing her pillow, dreaming of what had just happened and hoping to re-create those marvelous sensations again.

Some women remember experiencing their first boldly sexual feelings or thoughts in a dream. Like other sources of pleasure, sexual dreams can leave us surprised or amazed, and often eager to re-create this new sensation. One woman, for instance, recalled a dream she had after her mother tried to explain to her what sex was all about. She said, "I was in about fourth grade. My initial reaction was disgust. Also, my mom used pretty foggy language, and I couldn't quite imagine how the bodies would fit together. Not long after our little chat, I had a dream where a young man and I were in bed, touching one another. He snuggled behind me, spoonlike. I felt aroused. But before we had intercourse, I told him that was enough. He smiled, rolled over, and went away. Then the dream ended. I woke up feeling excited that sexual feelings applied to me, too."

For Juanita, a nineteen-year-old woman, dreaming has been a safe way to allow her sexual feelings to bubble up on their own. "My parents are old-fashioned Mexican-Americans with conservative values," she said. "They tell me that sex is something special and encourage me not to rush into it." Although Juanita represses her sexual feelings in waking life, when she is in a semiconscious state, drifting off to sleep or just waking up, her thoughts turn to erotic sensations that feel good and loosen her inhibitions:

> *I'm in a field of wheat with a dark-haired lover. Everything's a mellow yellow color—the field, the sky, the afternoon light. There's this golden glow all around us. We're completely alone. We spread out a blanket, open our picnic basket, and start kissing and touching each other. I begin to fantasize about what it would be like to let myself get more passionate and actually make love to him. I can see myself thinking about it, even though I'm still sort of dreaming, and I don't feel guilty at all. I wake up with my heart pounding, wet between my legs.*

Many women remember experiencing their first feelings of sexual pleasure during innocent childhood sexual play that involved kissing, touching, or hugging. A woman named Ellen said she vividly remembers the kindergarten classmate who showed her how to masturbate. "She called it 'beeping.' She would lean on the windowsill and rub up and down against the ledge. I knew right away that it felt good, and also that I didn't want anyone else to know that I was doing this. I could wave to people outside my window, and they would have no idea what I was doing."

As an adult, Ellen still finds it arousing to think about another woman masturbating right in front of her. As she has matured, she has created more scripted fantasies that still involve self-stimulation. Like many women, she has discovered that thinking sexy thoughts *and* touching herself creates even more erotic excitement by pleasing both mind and body.

Although Ellen enjoyed her earliest sexual play, interactions with peers can also create confusion, sometimes leaving women with mixed feelings about their first sexual sensations or fantasies. Nicole, now in her forties, remembered her sexual feelings being awakened under less than ideal circumstances when she was a young teenager. In a friend's basement, she was dancing with a boy her age to Motown music. Everything about the mood, the movement, the moment matched how she had fantasized falling in love would feel. Suddenly, the boy pulled away, leaving her all alone in the middle of the makeshift dance floor.

"I thought I had done something wrong, and that he didn't like me. I was hurt," she said. Not until years later did she learn from a friend that the boy had ejaculated while they were dancing close and fled out of embarrassment. Her sexual awakening combined arousal with feelings of shame and confusion. Yet as an adult, she said her most passionate fantasy still starts with the sensation of slow dancing. As she matured, Nicole was able to overcome her earlier shame and hold on to the original erotic heat generated on the dance floor.

Just as Nicole was confused about what happened to her under those dim basement lights, other women remember some discomfort concerning their earliest sexual feelings. One woman, for instance, worried she had somehow "broken" her clitoris by masturbating as a child. "I was told there was something 'down there' and if I broke it, no man would marry me. I believed for years that I was ruined. Not until I was in my twenties did I realize I had my clitoris confused with my hymen." Another woman remembers her grandmother's strong reaction when she noticed her touching her genitals. "Don't touch there!" her grandmother screamed. "That's where God is. If you touch there, you'll let Him out!" She felt both horror and fascination, amazed that her own body was the seat of such power.

Sometimes, these negative messages about our natural sexual feelings or shaming messages about sexual thought were so strong and relentless that women reacted by inhibiting the development of positive, comfortable sexual fantasies. On top of repressive messages, some women had to face even more overwhelming hurdles to the development of enjoyable sexual fantasies.

BEAUTY AND THE BEASTS

Sometimes our sexual awakening fills us with feelings of anxiety or fear. Rather than representing girlish dreams and desires, the fantasies that grow out of these intense early experiences often seem more psychologically driven and serious.

Jodi, for example, was about eight years old when she became spellbound by a scene in the movie *King Kong*. Breathless, she watched as the ape reached out a giant, hairy paw to capture a pretty young woman who squirmed with fear. Jodi's body squirmed, too, as she reacted with a strange, erotic excitement she had no words to describe. It took years for Jodi to figure out that she was sexually aroused by the idea of being frightened and overwhelmed by a powerful male.

Like many other girls, Jodi had soaked up the message that being female means being sexually vulnerable. Girls get this message in all kinds of ways—from having boys chase them on the playground, overhearing news stories about rapists, watching movies where women are stalked, being cautioned by well-meaning parents to stay away from strangers. Jodi took in warnings about the real danger of sexual exploitation and wound up feeling both afraid and excited by the idea that a man was going to swallow her up with his sexual energy.

For months after seeing *King Kong*, Jodi turned her bedroom into an imaginary jungle, complete with a make-believe waterfall made out of flowing fabric. She would always choose her prettiest doll to play the part of the jungle girl. With her erotic fantasy and make-believe play, she was bringing forth a cultural scenario about female beauty and male power. "The more beautiful the girl was, the more I assumed King Kong would love and cherish her, and not want to hurt her."

The fantasy formula that Jodi came up with is a classic: Female beauty tames raw, dangerous male power. This is the myth we find at the heart of so many romance novels and fairy tales. Growing up, most women see repeated models of a beautiful female being objectified, controlled, and overwhelmed by a man who then falls in love with her. Her beauty and charm bring a strong man to his knees. Many women took this cultural message in during childhood and are drawn to Pretty Maiden fantasies as adults.

In fantasies that follow a "Beauty and the Beast" pattern, we eroticize fears or other emotional distresses. It's easy to confuse, or even fuse, fear and sexual excitement, when we consider how similarly the body responds to these situations. In both, the physiological response is to speed up the heartbeat and breathing, and pump up the adrenaline. Thus, we can quickly turn something scary into a turn-on, capable of generating pleasure instead of pain.

By looking at childhood fantasies that sexualize distress or conflict, we get a glimpse of how creative women can be in wrestling the forces that threatened their sexual development. We also see how these early fantasies can set up a lifetime arousal pattern. A woman who really longs for love and caring as an adult may find herself aroused by thoughts of sexual aggressiveness, danger, and betrayal, because those are the ideas she first wired up as being erotic.

Marta is a young woman who developed her early fantasies to help her cope with a powerful infusion of sexual shame. She grew up on an island in the South Pacific and spent much of her early childhood running through the waves naked or barely clothed. She and her friends explored each other's bodies, playing doctor games, satisfying their curiosity about human anatomy. Because these explorations were mutually desired, Marta never felt afraid or humiliated about her early sexual feelings.

Then, when she was old enough to start elementary school, Marta left her island home and returned with her family to the U.S. mainland. Her new American playmates told her that sex was dirty. She was introduced to the uncomfortable feeling of shame. Around the same time, she saw her first scary film. In her fantasies, she wove these new impressions together. "My sexual fantasies suddenly took on a horror movie edge, like there was a dark green overlay over all my feelings of pleasure. I would imagine a Dracula figure leering over a sleeping woman. That scene was so erotic to me. I turned my shame into a source of sexual thrills."

Women described seemingly endless variations on this theme of being overwhelmed or seduced by male sexual power. One woman remembers inventing a sexual fantasy of this sort with a teenage girlfriend. "One of us would pretend to be a woman sleeping, with her nightgown riding high on her thigh. The other would be a burglar who sneaks into the house at night, carrying a flashlight. His light would shine on the woman's body. He would pull the sheets back and turn the flashlight on every inch of her body. Of course, he'd forget all about robbing the house. We became aroused by the combination of imagined danger and real erotic excitement." Through their mutual fantasy, they discovered that passion can feed on tension, and that sexual pleasure can bring relief.

Sexual fantasies that women invent to address more general emotional distress, such as fears of abandonment and loss, are no less powerful. Shirlee, for example, learned at a young age to eroticize her deepest needs. When she was about five, she lost contact with her father. He moved back to his native China, leaving Shirlee with her American mother in New York. By the time she was in her teens, Shirlee was an active, creative fantasizer. In one of her favorite scripts, two boyfriends would compete for her affection, often with dramatic results. In one fantasy, she would run away from sexually aggressive Peter and flee to the safer arms of Eddie, who lived on the eighth floor of an apartment facing Central Park West. But Eddie, too, tried to embrace her, and she retreated in fear. "I'd slip and be hanging from the window ledge, terrified, eight stories above Central Park. He would pull me back inside the apartment, then we would fall on the floor and make passionate love. Of course, I was still a virgin. But I could fantasize what sex would be like."

By fantasizing the range of emotions from fear, to arousal, to sexual satisfaction, Shirlee created a fantasy that actually soothed her anxiety. Climax brought her relief from tension, even though the real conflict in her life was not about sex. Her deepest need, to be loved by her father, wasn't a sexual need. But she eroticized this longing, then satisfied it with her fantasy lovers. It was no accident that she always had two fantasy boyfriends. She said, "That way, I'd always have at least one of them around. I'd never be abandoned again."

By looking at these early, fear-based fantasies, women often discover what worried or frightened them as children and how they may have soothed those fears with sexual energy. Such fantasies can result from real experiences, such as childhood sexual abuse, in which fear and sex were linked up. Or, like Shirlee's fantasy, they can be sexual solutions to more general childhood anxieties. But the result is similar: Through her fantasy, the woman transforms something fearful into something pleasurable. Her fantasy gives her the sense of control, power, and safety she lacks in real life. She not only survives whatever threatens her, but masters the danger. She turns her fear object into a love object. In her fantasy, she gets to tame the beast.

"SO THIS MUST BE SEX"

When we reminisce about childhood, most of us remember feeling curious about sex. If we didn't get satisfactory answers to our early questions, we may have set out to discover the "truth" about sex on our own. This curiosity led some women underground into a whole world of ready-made, readily available sex fantasies. Prepackaged, pornographic images and scenarios sometimes seduced, tantalized, and molded their earliest erotic thoughts.

As a six-year-old, one woman found her older brother's *Playboy* magazines under his bed, then stood in front of her own mirror in the seductive way the topless models posed. She imagined presenting herself to a man and saying, "Here I am—do with me as you please." She was especially excited by a photo of a nude woman with her wrists tied above her head. From the start of her sexual awakening, she eroticized a "take-me" energy that carried over into her Pretty Maiden fantasies as an adult.

Another woman snuck a look at the erotic novels on her mother's top closet shelf and was amazed to discover stories of Victorian-era sexual seduction. Although she lived in a middle-class, suburban home, she started imagining herself as a chambermaid in an English mansion, seduced by the lord of the manor.

Yet another woman discovered her dad's stash of *Penthouse Pictorials* when she was about seven. In her fantasies, she put those images of women's bodies together with her favorite science fiction television shows. "I imagined myself a grown woman with big breasts, kidnapped by a man and taken to a sexual laboratory where he injected me with drugs to make me submissive. I was kept in a honeycomb-like cell with hundreds of other women, all of us wearing string bikinis. It was a cross between *Penthouse* and *Buck Rogers*."

Although pornography answers some basic questions about sex, it tends to present a limited, narrow view of how people behave sexually, with women typically portrayed as objects for men's sexual pleasure. The models in porn have unrealistic bodies, setting women up for feeling self-conscious or inadequate in comparison. Porn teaches "sex for sex's sake" and fails to equate sexual arousal with emotional intimacy, caring, or respect. To varying degrees, an early exposure to porn can affect our adult fantasy life. Some women's Victim fantasies mimic pornographic images of women being abused and degraded.

Robyn, now 21, was in the sixth grade when she caught her first glimpse of pornography. A girlfriend showed her the Playboy Channel on her dad's television set. Robyn was captivated. "I saw these women touching themselves and moaning and I thought, this has got to feel good. I wanted to understand what was so exciting." Back at her own house, she flipped on the same channel. No luck. Since they weren't subscribers, all she got was a scrambled picture. The sound came through a little bit, though, and that was enough to spark Robyn's imagination. Listening to the moans of pleasure, she explored her own genitals and fantasized about what might be happening on screen. To this day, she credits fuzzy television reception with teaching her to create crisp fantasies on her own.

As an adult, Robyn said she likes hot, heavy sexual escapades. She fantasizes about having sex with strangers—male and female—while her boyfriend watches. She asks her boyfriend to call her names while they're making love and gets even more turned on if he says the degrading things (such as "Fuck me harder, bitch") that she first heard in porn. She dresses up for him in the sleazy outfits that she thinks a prostitute would wear. Although her boyfriend sometimes wants to take his sweet time in bed, she prefers sex that's hard, fast, and raw.

Latoya also saw porn videos on cable television when she was young. But her view of sex wasn't imprinted as strongly. She said, "I just saw it as something silly and pleasurable. What I like in sex as an adult is romance, intimacy, and touch." When she saw videos that showed oversize body parts, or exaggerated sexual prowess, she reacted by giggling. One video featured a Pinocchio-like male character. Only when he told a lie, it wasn't his nose that grew longer. "This gigantic penis seemed funny to me," she said.

In addition to being influenced by pornography, some women's fantasies were affected by seeing or overhearing actual sex at a young age. Marilyn, for example, grew up in a series of hippie communes on the East Coast. She saw a lot of naked bodies and a lot of sex during childhood. "We lived for a while in a cabin, and my mom and her boyfriend would have sex right above us. It was like an earthquake. The whole cabin shook. It felt yucky, like I was intruded upon, but it was very stimulating." Her earliest fantasies felt secretive but erotic. "It was about being with someone in the dark, whispering and touching each other, but making sure no one could hear us," she said. As as adult, she said, her fantasies have included this element of secrecy. "I'll imagine that I'm in a convertible, driving down the highway, and I spot someone in another car. Without exchanging a word, we recognize each other. It's like we're the same species. We drive somewhere secluded, rip off our clothes and have sex, without ever saying a word."

For some women, childhood curiosity about sex led them to more information than they were developmentally ready to handle and shaped their fantasy lives in powerful, sometimes lasting ways. But for a few other women we talked with, their sexual development was not shaped by their own curiosity. Instead, they were pulled into someone else's fantasy life, with no choice or power of their own. As adults, they can see how these early experiences had an impact on their ability to create and enjoy sexual fantasies of their own.

HOSTILE TAKEOVERS

Instead of getting to explore sexuality at their own pace during childhood, women who were sexually abused as children were introduced to sex prematurely and often traumatically. When they look back, they often describe childhood as a time of sexual manipulation and control instead of being a stage of safe sexual discovery. Often, the developmental tasks that should have been tackled during childhood—such as learning to trust, to feel good about one's body, to feel strong as a separate individual, and to take initiative—had to wait until much later in life. In some cases, their fantasy life was similarly sidetracked or taken over by someone else.

In extreme cases, where abuse involved elaborate fantasy scripts and role-playing, some women lost track of their own identity. They began to define themselves by the part they were first assigned in someone else's fantasy. As adults, they can see how the abuse interfered with their ability to develop fantasies that were really their own.

Emily, for example, said she will never forget the slick, slippery feel of the black negligee her father started dressing her up in when she was about eight years old. The gown was way too big. But if she sat still as a statue, with one strap slipping down her shoulder the way her dad liked, the negligee would stay in place. Then he could finish taking his pictures faster, and she could go back to bed.

Emily realizes now, as an adult, that she never got a chance to toy with thoughts of romance or sexual pleasure in a playful, healthy way by herself. Her father's fantasy world of kiddie porn became her reality. From age eight to twelve, she was routinely awakened at midnight to sit through his photo shoots in a cold basement. "I lost my whole childhood. I never daydreamed about boys or had crushes on movie stars. I never dated. I feel like I lost out on my whole adolescence."

Emily also remembers how, as a girl, she had trouble identifying with the sexy feelings her father wanted her to evoke for the photographs. She hadn't had a chance yet to figure out what it meant to be a sexual woman. "I tried my best to look the way he wanted, to get it over with faster. But I could never understand it.

My mom wasn't overtly sexual, so I couldn't mimic her. He would show me magazine pictures of nude women and tell me to copy them, but I just couldn't pull off that look. He thought I was being stubborn. But to this day, I don't know what it means to look sexy or seductive." As an adult, Emily's fantasy life remained shut down until after she worked to recover from childhood abuse. Not until thirty years after those experiences with her father did she start entertaining sexual thoughts that she found pleasing.

June, now in her late twenties, was just entering her early teens when her stepfather drew her into his fantasy world. At the time when her body was starting to change with adolescence, her stepfather began calling her "Lolita." She didn't recognize the nickname until he gave her a copy of Nabokov's novel about a pedophile named Humbert Humbert and his love object: a young "nymphette" named Lolita.

Over the next few years, as her stepfather courted her with gifts, took her out on dates, and began to molest her, June identified more and more with Lolita. Gradually, she said, she took on the fantasy. "I studied that book. It became my framework for understanding who I was, and what was going to happen to me. I realized that Lolita was sexy and questioning and curious, and so was I. She was developing her power. And I wanted the goodies of what she had. The fantasy for me was getting to dress up and go barhopping with my stepfather when I was only fourteen. I got to be the princess. I felt sexy. I looked grown up. And I wanted that attention. I realized I had to take this other stuff from him to get what I wanted."

When her stepfather became more sexually aggressive, June wished for her body to stop becoming so mature. "I thought that becoming a woman was what was making this all happen to me. I wanted not to have breasts, not to have hips. Then maybe I wouldn't become Lolita." It took a decade for June to realize how deeply her stepfather's fantasy affected her self-image. When she finally began to heal and reclaim her own identity, she took her copy of *Lolita* and wrote "NO!" in big letters across each page.

In more subtle ways, other women also remember how they were drawn into another person's fantasy life. One woman remembered her mother dressing her up in sexy costumes when she was just a girl and parading her around as a lure to attract men. Another related how her father's fixation with big breasts twisted her own self-image. Their home was filled with stacks of topless magazines, and their backyard swimming pool always seemed to be overflowing with chesty women in skimpy bathing suits. "I wear a 36D bra, but I've always felt like I'm not quite voluptuous enough to please a man," she said.

҉

To varying degrees, all of the women we interviewed could see how their early life experiences had imprinted them, for better or worse, with an idea of what sex is all about. The sexual fantasies women experience as adults often contain some truth or insight about their past. Some women can see how their fantasy lives developed to reflect what they enjoyed as girls, while others have created adult fantasies as a way to overcome the past.

Women's fantasies don't stop evolving when they mature from adolescence into the more sexually active period of adulthood. Instead, a woman's fantasy life is often a reflection of her search for sexual power, pleasure, and identity that started in childhood. By the time we leave adolescence, most of us have collected a unique set of erotic impressions that help us to define our adult sense of sexual pleasure. Now that we know more about where fantasies come from, we can see how we put them to use in our adult lives.

CHAPTER 4

ᎧᏇ

How Fantasies
Help Us

Sexual fantasies help us in all sorts of ways. Sometimes the benefits are immediate and easy to detect. We might entertain a certain fantasy, for instance, and enjoy a thrilling orgasm—a clear case of cause and effect. Other times, the positive aspects of fantasy are more subtle but no less significant in our lives.

Annie is a twenty-seven-year-old woman who has been using fantasy to help her sex life ever since she was an adolescent. We met her at the start of chapter 3 when she was twelve years old and bored to tears in the backseat of the family car. She mentally escaped by fantasizing that she was a Pretty Maiden, riding into the sunset on horseback behind a handsome cowboy. Some fifteen years later, Annie is clearly in the driver's seat of her own fantasy experience:

> *Alone with her thoughts and the scenery and still two hundred miles away from a long-awaited rendezvous with her old boyfriend, Annie yawns and opens her car window to let in some fresh mountain air. It's a little cool, but she's warm in her favorite leather jacket. Tired*

of her own singing, Annie lets her thoughts drift toward her imminent reunion with Jake. As she passes a billboard of a rugged guy with a mustache, she smiles to think how Jake would look with more facial hair to match his dark, curly chest hair.

Although she hasn't seen him for four months, since their careers took them in opposite directions, Annie remembers how she always savored watching Jake get ready to make love. She liked to undress first, then lie back to watch his lean, muscular body emerge from his clothes like a gift from its wrapper. In her imagination, his butt starts to look even firmer than it used to in real life. She pictures the two of them naked, and imagines her hands guiding him inside her. Annie sighs, aroused by her increasingly vivid Wild Woman fantasies. She's still not sure where this weekend will lead, but now feels certain of one thing: even if they don't get back together for the long haul, she's looking forward to some quality time in bed with Jake. She lets one hand drop from the steering wheel and tickle her crotch, giving herself a promise of the pleasure to come.

Hours later, when she finally pulls up to Jake's house, she's surprised to see two cars in the driveway. His parents, it seems, have chosen the same weekend for a surprise visit. That night, when Jake and Annie are finally alone together in his king-size bed, she can't stop thinking about his parents sleeping in the next room. But as they start to kiss and touch, distractions slip away. Her thoughts return to the wide-open spaces she traveled through to get here, and she pictures herself and Jake alone in a meadow of wildflowers. As her arousal builds, she climbs on top of him, hugging his body with her legs and burying her fingers in his thick chest hair. As he caresses her breasts, they find their old

*rhythm and gallop toward a mutually satisfying re-
union.*

Annie grew up intuitively understanding that she could use
fantasy to suit her personal and sexual needs. She used fantasy in a
variety of ways to increase her odds of having a positive experience with Jake. First, she fantasized to break the monotony of a
long car trip and revive her flagging energy. She drew again on
fantasy to replay fond memories from the past and rehearse her
hopes for the immediate future. She improved on Jake's looks a bit
in her daydreaming and also turned up the heat of her own desire.
At night, by imagining herself in a different location, she overcame
the distraction of having his parents within earshot and was better
able to function sexually. And she pulled it all off effortlessly,
without even being aware she was fantasizing.

"Fantasy," writes psychiatrist Ethel Person, M.D., in *By
Force of Fantasy,* "is a magic trick that the fantasizer performs
without knowing how he does it."[1]

The ability to fantasize is one of our defining human traits. In
all sorts of ways, we employ fantasy to help us adapt to different
situations. In fantasy we can rehearse for the future, replay the
past, and overcome the limitations of the present. In their day-to-
day lives, women describe weaving fantasies to overcome bore-
dom, soothe frazzled nerves or hurt feelings, practice what to say
in a meeting or how to break the ice on a first date.

Sex therapists have recognized for years that fantasy can be
an effective aid in helping women with sexual performance. They
have frequently recommended the use of fantasies to boost sexual
response, sort of like a vibrator for the mind. One woman, acknowledging that she uses fantasy to help her achieve orgasm, said
her favorite fantasies "are a combination of everything I find most
hornifying." Studies support the wisdom of this approach.
Women with the most active, satisfying sex lives also tend to have
active fantasy lives.

The beauty of fantasy is that we can tap this wellspring of creativity at any time, in any place, with no one else privy to our thoughts. "A major advantage of fantasy as an aid to physical sexual stimulation," wrote Lonnie Barbach, Ph.D., in *For Yourself,* her 1976 classic about female sexuality, "is that it requires no equipment and is always available."[2] Temporarily and vicariously, fantasy allows us to sample highly charged sexual scenarios that exist in a world beyond what real life allows. Not surprisingly, women use fantasy most often to increase sexual desire and to facilitate sexual functioning, especially orgasm.

Besides being effective in turning up sexual heat, fantasies also have an amazing ability to help us cope with the emotional stresses of sex. They offer a way to immediately reduce the biggest block to sexual pleasure: anxiety. Looking more closely at how certain fantasies work, we can discover how they soothe our worries or distract us from concerns that would otherwise get in the way of enjoying sex. By focusing on the steamy images and stories in our minds, we can feel less inhibited and more inspired to be sexually open and expressive. Thus, fantasies often work to increase sexual stimulation while simultaneously decreasing emotional anxiety. When women consider when and why they turn to fantasy, they often mention both sexual and emotional issues.

Usually, we can identify a very specific reason for the fantasies we are most likely to replay. These repetitive fantasies tend to be the ones that we hone, achieving a particular purpose with them. Women describe them as reliable, often adding a comment such as *"It always works."*

The most common functions of women's sexual fantasies fall into nine categories:

1. Enhancing self-esteem and attractiveness
2. Increasing sexual interest and desire
3. Facilitating orgasm
4. Celebrating the present
5. Satisfying curiosity

6. Rehearsing future possibilities
7. Relieving stress and tension
8. Preserving a pleasant memory
9. Coping with past hurts

Many women notice that one fantasy performs a number of functions for them simultaneously. For instance, a fantasy that preserves a pleasant memory may also increase sexual interest and facilitate orgasm. Conversely, fantasies that vary in origin and content can also function in very similar ways. Thus, a humiliating Victim fantasy and a romantic, Beloved-type fantasy can work equally well to facilitate orgasm. We don't have to *like* a particular fantasy in order for it to provide a positive function.

The women who attend Wendy's fantasy workshops often find that paying attention to these functions helps them appreciate the positive help fantasies provide. Many of us will understand more about a certain fantasy of our own by taking this list and checking off any functions the fantasy serves.

FUNCTION #1: ENHANCING SELF-ESTEEM AND ATTRACTIVENESS

Although Margaret and her lover usually have sex in bed with the lights off, in her favorite fantasy she sees herself standing in front of a mirror under bright lights:

"I imagine that I'm in a dressing room at a chic department store, trying on a low-cut silk dress that accents my breasts, hugs my torso, and flares out at my hips. In real life I'd never wear anything so revealing, but I look damn good in this sexy black dress. I spin around slowly, admiring myself from all angles. Then I poke my head out into the hallway and call to my lover. He's been waiting for me patiently while I try on dresses, and I've decided to let him take a close look at this one. I wave him into the dressing room with me, holding a finger to my lips to signal him to keep quiet. Once he's inside the booth, I bolt the door and turn to face him. I can tell he likes what he sees. He lifts me onto a stool facing the mirrors and begins running his hands all over the dress and my body. He reaches under the dress and pulls off my lace panties. Then he ducks his head under the flared skirt and begins to kiss and lick my crotch. My hips start to pump in a familiar rhythm that I know will lead to climax. I watch us in the mirror. Smiling boldly, I decide to buy this dress after all."

Just as a wave of her fairy godmother's wand gave Cinderella a new look for the palace ball, women can use sexual fantasy to help them feel better about themselves and more attractive as a sexual partner. Fantasy enables us to focus on whatever qualities we define as being sexy. We can highlight or even improve on our real appearance in fantasy. Some women imagine looking more like the cultural stereotype of female beauty, perhaps making themselves younger, with fuller breasts or slimmer thighs, longer hair, smoother skin, or stronger muscles. Picturing themselves as more attractive can enhance women's sexual energy or distract them from what they consider to be shortcomings. These imagined changes also help some women feel more deserving of a partner's sexual attention.

As one woman who enjoys a Wild Woman fantasy explained, "In fantasy, I'm thirty with gorgeous, long hair. I'm very hot and sexy, and I love for men to look at me. In real life, I'm fifty and feeling rather repressed sexually. My hair is short, businesslike, and I'm not comfortable when men look my way."

Because our culture relentlessly bombards us with images of perfect female beauty, some women feel undeserving of sexual attention if their real bodies don't measure up to these impossible standards. "In reality," said one woman in her midforties, "my husband can't keep his hands off me. But my body is a real blocker to *me* seeing *myself* as sexual. I cannot imagine that a man would ever respond sexually to this body, these thighs. During sex, I have to imagine myself as younger, more agile, and with a very different physique in order to become more aroused with my partner."

We can effortlessly do away with any perceived flaws in fantasy, thus reducing self-consciousness. Or, we can concentrate on enhancing a feature or quality we do like about ourselves in order to boost self-esteem. Fantasy offers an escape from being our own worst critic. As one woman joked, "In my sexual fantasies, I never have a bad hair day."

Fantasy can also offer an escape from the criticisms of others. In her favorite masturbatory fantasy, for example, a woman named Meg said she imagines herself as a successful, feisty Hollywood screenwriter who is being photographed for an upcoming *Life* magazine spread. The photographer, who bears an uncanny resemblance to actor Al Pacino, follows her around Los Angeles for weeks, keeping his distance while he snaps hundreds of photos. Each time he looks at her through the camera lens with his dark, bedroom eyes, Meg can feel his sexual longing for her and feels more confident about her own sex appeal.

As the fantasy continues, Meg finally makes the first overtly sexual move, inviting him to photograph her on the beach at sunset. As he's studying her through the camera lens, she walks up to him slowly and slips the camera strap from around his neck. Then she takes off his shirt, peels down his pants, and strips off her own clothes while watching his body get increasingly excited by the sight of hers. When they have sex on a beach towel, Meg's lusty fantasy culminates in a real-life orgasm. She knows this would probably shock her ex-husband. Throughout their unhappy, ten-year marriage, he told Meg she was frigid. Now fifty-two and long since divorced, Meg knows from her passionate fantasies that her body is perfectly capable of sexual response. Although she suffers from debilitating arthritis, "I seem to have an incredible amount of sexual energy and stamina in my fantasies," she said.

Imagination can offer women a way to maintain and stay in touch with their inner beauty, strength, and sexiness, even if real life happens to be offering few opportunities for positive sexual expression at the moment. A twenty-eight-year-old woman said she is currently between relationships, "but fantasies offer me a holding place for my sexual interest while I'm technically celibate."

FUNCTION #2: INCREASING SEXUAL INTEREST AND DESIRE

Dorie often turns to fantasy at the end of the day to jump-start her sexual energy. In one of her favorite fantasies, she imagines that as she hugs her partner, a man watches them from a comfortable chair in the corner of their living room. When she unbuttons her lover's shirt and starts to rub her back, Dorie pretends to make eye contact with her fantasy man.

"In my fantasy, he's a straight man getting more and more excited by watching us two lesbians. I imagine that we tease him, saying things like 'Wow, look at that cock. You're getting so hard. You really want to fuck us, don't you? Have you ever had two girls at the same time?' But we also control him. He can't do a thing, he can't even leave his chair, unless we give him permission. His desire gets more and more intense until he's ready to explode." At that point, Dorie usually forgets all about the fantasy man and concentrates instead on mutual stimulation in real life with her partner. Her fantasy has fulfilled its function: to awaken and enhance her interest in sex.

Like Dorie, many women use fantasy to help get them in the mood for sex. As another woman explained, "I turn to fantasy to psych up for sex when I'm feeling tired. My fantasy self empowers me. I can conjure up a fantasy and suddenly feel sexually renewed and hungry."

Some women use fantasy to help them even out a difference in desire within their relationship. When one partner wants to have sex more frequently than the other, fantasy can help boost the sexual appetite of the less interested partner. "I like sex just as much as my husband does," one woman explained. "But it seems like he's *always* in the mood, always ready. Unless I deliberately think about it, I lose track of how much I do enjoy sex. Fantasy helps me remember to think sexy thoughts." Similarly, a lesbian who is in a long-term relationship said she uses fantasy to stir up her own sexual interest enough so that she'll initiate sex with her partner. "We both like sex, but neither one of us is very good at getting things started. Fantasy adds that spark."

If real-life sex becomes fairly predictable, many women turn to fantasy to instantly introduce an element of novelty. They describe bringing fresh excitement to sexual situations by imagining they are having sex for the first time, or at a new location, or in a new way. Many women increase desire by imagining they are having sex in a more romantic place than where they usually make love. Women frequently describe secluded island beaches, remote cottages, or sumptuous hotel rooms where privacy is guaranteed and there are no everyday distractions to interfere with their desire. One woman likes to imagine that her small bedroom is a luxury suite on a train. "I'm turned on by the speed, the rocking motion, and the loud rumbling noises that I conjure up," she said.

For women who might not be enjoying sex in real life because of fear, guilt, or inhibitions, fantasy can emphasize conditions that help them feel more at ease. If they are afraid, they can enhance the safety of an imagined encounter. One woman who feels anxious during sex comforts herself by imagining she's in a stage set with two walls missing, so that she can always picture a way to escape. Another, who used to fear her husband's penis, now thinks of it as her "pleasure toy." If women feel sexually repressed, they can imagine a way for their passions to emerge. One woman said she feels more free to express herself sexually in fantasy than in real life. "My fantasy self is not concerned with social pressures or conventions. She doesn't have to be a good girl."

Sometimes, women take themselves out of the picture altogether in their fantasies to boost their desire. They imagine that they are someone else, or that they are watching as a Voyeur from the sidelines. One woman, for instance, fantasizes about watching through a window while three men take turns having oral and anal sex with each other. "Thinking about these men's bodies, especially their naked, muscular thighs and butts, keeps me from thinking that I'm ugly," she said.

Some women increase desire by focusing their fantasies on their partners' attributes, rather than their own. They might enhance a real partner's appeal in fantasy, giving a man a more attractive penis or a woman fuller breasts. Some women endow their partners with more expressive eyes, a tighter butt, or leaner torso than they have in real life. Others focus more on the non-physical qualities that ignite their desire.

Some women turn to fantasy to increase their own interest in sex if their real relationship is sexually unsatisfying. One woman said that if she didn't engage fantasies about other men to make sex more exciting, "I'd have to admit that my sex life with my husband is dismal and boring." Another woman joked about the advantages of fantasy partners when she said in her Texas drawl, "Fantasies don't fart, suffer exhaustion, or leave balled up socks on the floor." To temporarily overcome the limits of a real-life relationship, some women imagine being in a love scene with a familiar celebrity or a total stranger.

Amy, for instance, enjoys a Pretty Maiden fantasy in which a handsome stranger takes her away for a sexual escapade. She imagines them spending days in bed, feeding one another exotic meals that turn into lovemaking orgies on silk sheets strewn with delicious crumbs. "In real life, my partners have been less wild and adventuresome. The fantasy shows me how a different kind of partner could bring out my hidden, sensuous desires."

A woman who has Beloved fantasies said she doesn't feel as important to her real-life partner as she does to the man she invents. "My fantasy lover treats me special. He really listens to me. He makes me feel as if I'm the only thing that matters," she said, adding with a sly grin, "He also happens to be in great shape and really takes care of his body." In fantasy, unlike real life, women can fine-tune every tiny detail of a setting, activity, or partner to suit their personal pleasure.

If a woman needs a spark of romance, tension, or contrast to get more interested in sex, fantasies can supply the action plot that might be missing in real life. Some women describe their fantasies as sexual thrillers. They get aroused from plots that combine danger or intrigue with sex, turning up the adrenaline and heightening physical responses. Others create imaginary distance or make-believe barriers from their real lovers to make their hearts grow fonder in their fantasy reunions. And while some women get in the mood for sex by imagining more privacy, others deliberately invent fantasy settings where there is a chance they will be seen. They like the increased erotic tension that comes with this element of sexual danger or adventure.

FUNCTION #3: FACILITATING ORGASM

Roberta's fantasy begins with a sweet attraction between soul mates but gets more sexually specific as she approaches climax:

"As our kisses become more aggressive, his mouth leaves mine and trails down my neck to my breasts where his hands are already cupped, gently squeezing and lifting and molding me to his touch. His mouth takes over, sucking, his tongue lapping. Slowly, he makes his way to my clitoris, exploring with his tongue until he finds the place that makes me cry out with pleasure. I can feel his hot breath against my wet genitals. As he takes me to the edge, his hands reach underneath me. When I start to climax the first time, he keeps his face pressed to me and squeezes my ass with each contraction. Then he comes up for air and thrusts himself inside me. I'm ready for him, and we rock together until I climax again. This time he comes with me."

Many women improve sex with fantasies that add the specific kind of stimulation or enhanced sensation they need to reach orgasm. This is one of the most common uses of fantasy among women. As they describe fantasies that reliably take them all the way to climax, they often mention a certain kind of stimulation, explicit body parts, or different ways that fantasy helps them let go. These tend to be women's most goal-oriented, hard-core fantasies, speeding up breathing and heartbeat and increasing vaginal lubrication and clitoral sensation.

In fact, fantasies often make the graphics of sex even more noticeable on a specific sensory level. Fantasy turns up the volume or intensity of the sexual sounds or images women enjoy in real life. A woman who describes her fantasies as "fairly and squarely about a man and woman fucking" said she focuses on high-energy, graphic images of pumping and thrusting to build the excitement she needs to reach orgasm. Women often say they fantasize about "whatever it takes" to get them to climax.

When women use fantasy to increase sensation, they naturally enhance the elements that happen to resonate with their individual erotic preferences. A woman who finds her sense of smell to be especially arousing, for instance, thinks of her vagina as having a "fresh, floral scent" in her olfactory fantasies. Another woman creates very visual fantasies, but only while masturbating. "When I'm with a partner, I have him right there to look at. But when I'm alone, I invent the images I need to see in order to climax," she explained. Some women with visual fantasies imagine exaggerated phallic objects as a way to turn the sexual intensity high enough to peak and release.

A French-speaking Canadian woman who finds sexy sounds arousing fantasizes that she's in a confessional, describing her sexual sins out loud to a priest while she climaxes. To make the fantasy more stimulating, she mentally replays a favorite song by the popular rock group Enigma, complete with ecclesiastical chanting, orgasmic moans, and a woman whispering in French.

Many women fantasize about multiple partners as a way to multiply the sources of sexual stimulation they receive. "How else are you ever going to experience oral sex and vaginal penetration at the same time?" asked a woman who loves her threesome fantasies. Similarly, another woman images herself "in the middle of a sandwich," with male lovers simultaneously entering her from above and below. One woman's favorite fantasy increases stimulation with a scene in which she imagines performing fellatio on a male lover while a woman licks her to climax.

Often, women use fantasy to create the sexual variety that they find missing or in short supply in their real-life sexual experiences. One woman, for example, is married to a man she describes as "loving but sexually repressed." To create the stimulation she wants but doesn't get during real sex, she images being with a series of men of all races, ages, and body types. Each one makes love to her however she chooses and for as long as she likes. She tells them exactly how and where she wants to be licked, sucked, rubbed, and penetrated, and they are happy to oblige. Fantasy gives her all the time and varied stimulation she needs to be sexually satisfied.

Amanda said she creates fantasies that work not only to enhance physical stimulation, but also to help her feel more comfortable about enjoying such abundant pleasure. In one favorite fantasy, she imagines being on her king-size bed with her hands tied to the headboard. Because of the bondage, she has no control over her husband and the two small, beautiful women who massage her with oil and stimulate her with a dildo. She lies back and enjoys while they take turns sucking on her breasts, massaging her clitoris, penetrating her vagina, exciting her G-spot. She said, "I start imagining all the possible combinations of people and parts— mouths, fingers, breasts, penis, vaginas, dildo." In every combination, her own body is the focus of attention. The extravagant stimulation helps her sexual excitement build to climax.

Women sometimes employ disguises in their fantasies as a way of overcoming inhibition so they can enjoy increased stimulation. One woman imagines that she is a sales clerk, minding the cash register, while a man she can't see hides underneath the counter and rubs her genitals. She said, "It's a hands-off thing where I'm not in control of the sex. I just allow my body to be available and enjoy the sensations that result."

Similarly, other women imagine screens, masks, or costumes that keep the overt sexual activity in their fantasies out of their view. Iris, for instance, pictures herself in a restaurant "formally dressed except for one small detail: no underwear. While I'm carrying on a dinner conversation, I feel my legs being pressed apart. I know it's my lover underneath the table. He's free-spirited and playful, but he's only concerned with my sexual pleasure, not his. There's a tablecloth so no one else knows what he's doing. When he eats me, I abandon my self-control and climax over dessert at the Ritz."

While Iris and others enjoy having no control in fantasy, other women reach climax by enhancing their sexual power over others. One woman enjoys a fantasy of being a Dominatrix who orchestrates a group sex scene in which timing is of the utmost importance. She said, "As the one in charge, I can draw out the sexual satisfaction until the very last moment when I give the okay for everyone to experience intense, multiple orgasms at exactly the same time I reach my own thrilling climax."

FUNCTION #4: CELEBRATING THE PRESENT

After a family trip to Disneyland, Emma surprised herself by creating a new sexual fantasy that has brought a heart-pounding thrill into her real sex life:

"When my husband and I are making love, I like to weave in and out of imagining that I am on the Splash Mountain roller-coaster ride at Disneyland. It's a fun way to bring an adrenaline rush into sex. First, there's a slow, steady, winding-around buildup of tension (as we stimulate each other and begin intercourse). Then, a quick and sudden free fall over the top with a wet, exciting climax of physical sensations that make my heart race and take my breath away (as we thrust more rapidly together toward orgasm). Then, a rapid descent and gradual, safe rocking to a resolution (as our genital muscles pulsate and all tension is released). Although I can picture the details of being inside the wooden log, moving along the water canal, up and over the mountain, my focus is not on getting back to the theme park. Instead, I use the fantasy to add a new, exhilarating dimension to the sex that's happening right here and now with my husband."

Although we most often think of fantasy as a temporary escape from reality, fantasy can also enhance our enjoyment of being in the moment during sex. Women sometimes describe fleeting, unscripted fantasy images that help them hold on to the sensory enjoyment and depth of emotion they share during sex with their actual partners. In this kind of fantasy experience, a woman might imagine that she and her lover are breathing as one during sex or that their heartbeats are keeping the same rhythm. One woman said that when she wraps her arms around her husband during lovemaking, she imagines the two of them traveling through space and time together like a rocket ship. She imagines their backs protecting them from the outside universe while their beating hearts create the engine that keeps them going and warms them deep inside.

To enhance the present during sex, one middle-aged woman imagines that she and her partner both have the sexual stamina they felt when they were younger, more energetic, and their love was brand new. A fantasy like this can give present passion a more youthful vigor and urgency. Similarly, women sometimes use fantasy to take what's working in the present into a more spiritual dimension. They might describe a cosmic feeling of merging with their lovers during peak sexual experiences, as if two bodies become one and melt into the pulsing rhythm of all living things.

Because sex is a natural activity, it makes sense that many women turn to images from nature to embellish and highlight sexual activities. Some women use fantasy as a spotlight to make them more keenly aware of all the rich details, textures, smells, and sounds of a sexual scene. In their thoughts, they mentally layer their sense of what's happening in the present moment with images from the physical world. Poet Rochelle Lynn Holt, for example, describes the ecstasy of merging with her lover in sex: "as though you were waves rising and falling / the motion of the sea / as though you were a bird / flying swiftly over the ocean / the moon in the background / a symbol of peace and serenity."[3] Another woman said she fantasized that she and her husband were conceiving a child during lovemaking. At orgasm, she enjoyed an image of the sperm and egg joining together in an ecstatic dance. Similarly, a different woman imagined that her lover's penis was like a flower bulb she planted in her womb.

FUNCTION #5: SATISFYING CURIOSITY

Denise, a twenty-eight-year-old, stay-at-home mother of five children, likes to fantasize that she is a high-class call girl who travels on jet planes with a wealthy businessman:

"The plane is lavishly decorated with a king-size bed. Trays of my favorite foods are always at the bedside. My fantasy partner expects a lot of sex, but I know that he adores me. In fact, I'm his favorite traveling companion." In fantasy, Denise imagines herself as an expert at giving oral sex even though in real life that's something she knows her husband doesn't enjoy.

While some women use fantasy to rehearse for real-life encounters, other women indulge their curiosity about sexual activities they have no desire or opportunity to try in real life. Denise, for instance, said, "I have no desire to leave my family and become a prostitute. I just like imagining the excitement, adventure, and travel."

In fantasy, women can satisfy their desires to know more about activities such as bondage, anal sex, or sex with a friend, neighbor, or animal, even though they may consider those activities taboo or unappealing in real life. Heterosexual women can imagine what it would be like to make love to another woman while lesbians can imagine having sex with a man. Women can imagine sex in public places with no fear of being seen. Fantasy offers a risk-free arena to explore all sexual interests without moral, legal, or physical consequences.

Some women indulge their sexual curiosity as a way to add interest and keep sex from feeling boring. They might imagine changing partners even though they are committed to one partner in real life. In fantasy, they can have the thrill of an imaginary fling with no risk to their real relationship. A woman who works in a television station said, "My new assistant is a really cute young guy who looks just like the boyish actor Michael J. Fox. I'd never want to jeopardize my position or our working relationship by approaching him sexually, but, oh, how I've been enjoying some wild fantasies of him bringing me morning coffee—and more—in bed."

Similarly, another woman in a committed, monogamous relationship said she fantasizes about other partners to add sexual variety and indulge her curiosity. She is certain, however, that she would never want to actually have sex with anyone but her husband. She explained, "In a way, it's like he's the channel through which I get to experience all different kinds of sex. Through him, I'm embracing what I love about all men. And through me, he can connect with womankind."

Women also emphasize that the specific sexual details that pop up in their fantasies as curiosities—such as the gigantic penises that one woman imagined or the double dildos that another woman mentioned—are often things they enjoy in fantasy, but would never want to encounter in real life.

Because they control all the details of their fantasies, women can imagine even potentially dangerous sexual scenarios without any physical risks. Fantasies that involve bondage or S/M, for instance, leave no bruises or rope burns. Similarly, women can fantasize about an orgy or having unprotected sex without risk of sexually transmitted diseases or unwanted pregnancy. Although women have to walk a careful line to avoid danger in their real sex lives, they can temporarily throw caution to the wind in their fantasies.

FUNCTION #6: REHEARSING FUTURE POSSIBILITIES

Caitlin is a twenty-one-year-old virgin whose real sexual encounters have stopped just short of intercourse. Her masturbatory fantasies, however, go all the way, including a hot mixture of images from her own near-sex experiences and scenes from explicit films she has found arousing. She imagines various positions and locations she might like to try someday, such as having sex in the shower or while swaying in the branches of a big oak tree. Her fantasy life is a rehearsal for safe sex; wherever the location, she always imagines slipping a condom onto her partner as part of foreplay. Fantasy also serves as a reminder of the qualities she wants to find in a real partner. Although several men have tried to pressure her into having sex, she's been waiting for the right partner who will let her approach intimacy at a more comfortable pace.

"I hope the next guy I get serious with will treat me the way my fantasy man does," she said. "Then, I'd feel ready and eager to have sex." In the meantime, in fantasy, "I'm maturing as I learn about my own body's responses and invent more ways to please myself and my make-believe partner."

Many women use fantasy to rehearse for a sexual activity they desire, but do not yet feel ready, willing, or able to experience in real life. They may have rehearsed what it would be like to start a relationship with a new partner, or to engage comfortably in a sexual behavior they have never tried before. They may imagine being sexual in a new place they plan to visit, with a new person they've just met (but with whom they hope to become intimate). By rehearsing in fantasy, they can imagine how this experience could be positive and desirable, and thus reduce their anxiety and remain more relaxed, if and when the hoped-for sex takes place.

For Linda, who remembers herself as a late bloomer growing up in a small, rural, conservative community, early fantasy was a place for her to size up potential partners. She crossed off her wish list a man who smoked, for instance, because in her fantasy she imagined how stale his breath would smell. Over time her masturbatory fantasies became more explicit, even though she was quite inexperienced sexually. When she left home in her twenties and rebelled against her strict upbringing, Linda abandoned her fantasies—and lost the benefits they had offered her. "I stopped fantasizing then because I was acting it all out. I'd meet someone at a party and go home to bed with him. I wouldn't rehearse anything anymore in my fantasies. I'd just do it. I took a lot more risks. I wish now I had rehearsed a little more and acted out a little less. I wound up getting pregnant by a guy I met in a bar."

Fantasy can also provide an important rehearsal stage to help women adjust to the challenges that come with age and illness. Evelyn, for example, was afraid her sex life was over at forty when she lost both breasts to cancer. In her fantasies, she rehearsed telling different partners about her mastectomy, "and at first I always imagined they would respond by throwing up." Finally, she risked telling a real-life male friend about her surgery, and he responded with caring and compassion. "After that, I was able to fantasize about giving my little speech and having different men accept me. Only then was I able to fantasize about proceeding with more explicit bedroom activity and regain my interest in sex." For her, fantasy was an important outlet to overcome her fear of rejection and rehearse how she could remain sexual after losing her breasts.

Like athletes who visualize to enhance their performance, women also use fantasy to overcome anxiety and picture a positive sexual experience. Fantasy can be an important way for women to remind themselves, "I can handle this," or to offer an affirmation such as "I'm worthy of sexual pleasure."

FUNCTION #7: RELIEVING STRESS AND TENSION

After an especially demanding workday, Barb reaches for fantasy instead of a glass of wine or the television remote control:

"I often come home with a lot on my mind. If I want to relax, I have to quit mentally reviewing whatever it is I've been working on all day. By fantasizing, I'm suddenly preoccupied instead with sex. Then there's no room to entertain any thoughts about work. I often sit in my favorite sunroom chair and decide which of my old lovers I want to invite into my thoughts. It's like picking a name from a Rolodex. Once I decide on a certain one, I imagine him massaging my lower back and caressing my buttocks until they tingle. Sometimes I stroke my own body in a very soothing way. I'm not really masturbating to reach orgasm, just caressing myself tenderly. I guess I use fantasy the way I often use lavender bath salts: a little something special I do just for myself to help me unwind."

Sexual fantasy offers an easily available tool that women can use to help them relax, escape momentarily from the stresses of the day, or even fall asleep. Fantasies can have a soothing effect, similar to meditation, and may not involve any physical stimulation or the intense excitement of orgasm. Some women use such fantasies to relax or combat anxiety while waiting for a doctor's appointment or sitting through a long plane flight. When used in these nonsexual settings, fantasies can leave a woman feeling calm, centered, and nurtured. Other times, women use fantasy along with masturbation to generate sexual excitement and climax, which then leaves them feeling more relaxed physically.

Along with fantasies that they use to relax when alone, women also employ fantasies during lovemaking to calm down and avoid the stresses that can interfere with sexual functioning. "Instead of thinking about what we need at the grocery store or how I'm going to juggle tomorrow's day care and carpool arrangements, I switch on a fantasy where it's just my husband and me in a hotel room, with no children in sight," explained one young mother. When present circumstances don't feel very sexy, fantasy can create a more soothing ambience to enhance relaxed lovemaking. As another woman said, "I remember the crackling fire and warm comforter from a cabin where we went once on a ski trip, back before we had kids. Then I can relax and concentrate on all the loving touch my husband wants to give me, right here in our messy bedroom with the overflowing laundry hamper."

Many women describe this function of fantasy as a way to take up "air time" in their minds, so that distracting thoughts are preempted by more pleasing and satisfying fantasies. Such fantasies don't really solve any problems, but they can provide a valuable, temporary mental release from daily concerns and cares.

FUNCTION #8: PRESERVING A PLEASANT MEMORY

Gladys is a single, forty-four-year-old woman with a responsible managerial job. She lives quietly at home with her daughter, who's still in college. Until recently, there hasn't been a man in her life. But since she met the free-spirited Monte a year ago, she's become sexually active in ways she couldn't have imagined. "He's a man who loves sex and loves to experiment with me," she said. One of their sexual escapades was so exciting to her that it's become a favorite fantasy she replays when she's home alone:

"In this fantasy, I remember every little detail about the first car trip we ever took together. It was a long drive. When Monte was behind the wheel, I started feeding him a juicy hamburger and fries. He would lick and suck on my fingers as he took the food into his mouth. He kept his hands on the wheel and his eyes on the road, but pretty soon my hands were roaming all over his body. It got pretty hot in that car, and I don't mean the weather. Just after dusk, we pulled over at a rest stop somewhere in Alabama and wound up making love butt naked in a grassy field. Now, if anybody from work ever found out about that wild night, they'd say, 'Dang, girl! Who would have thought it?' That's part of the fun— knowing how out of character this was for me and just how much I enjoyed it."

Fantasy sometimes functions as a repository of women's most important or exciting sexual memories. These mental keep- sakes might include a memory of a first love, a wedding night, or a particularly exciting or novel sexual experience. Women often replay these moments in fantasy to enjoy that pleasure again and remind themselves of the positive sexual experiences life affords. Recalling past sexual experiences in fantasy can reignite the sexual passion a woman once felt and remind her of her capacity for love and intense sexual pleasure.

When women use fantasy to celebrate pleasant memories and treasured moments from their past, they often feel sentimental or proud. For Joni, a widow in her sixties, fantasy has offered a way to hold on to the bittersweet memories of a lost love. It's been more than forty years since she met Lamar in a nightclub where she was a jazz singer and he played the piano. Yet, she vividly remembers their powerful, mutual attraction and how they kept their banter light, superficial, and nonsexual. After all, she was already married to someone else. In the 1950s, society would have frowned on a young, blond newlywed running off with a black man. When Joni's husband was drafted and sent overseas, she put her singing career on hold. "I figured that if my husband was gone, and I was staying out until four in the morning, there wasn't going to be a marriage for him to come home to. And I did love my husband. He meant the world to me. It's just that I loved Lamar, too."

In fantasy, Joni figured out a way to continue her love for Lamar without jeopardizing her marriage. While making love with her husband, she sometimes imagined that she was in bed with Lamar. This fantasy never made her feel as if she was cheat- ing on her real husband. Instead, she noticed that the fantasy sparked some of their most enjoyable lovemaking experiences during their long, faithful, and passionate marriage.

Fond sexual memories we want to cherish are like pictures in an album. But fantasies can also work in another way, preserving sexual memories we'd rather forget.

FUNCTION #9: COPING WITH PAST HURTS

Brett, a thirty-five-year-old seamstress, uses fantasy to keep her thoughts focused during sex so she won't be reminded of the unpleasant sexual touching she experienced as a child. "Although I'd like to be thinking more about my husband and what we're doing," she said, "for now, fantasy is the *closest to the present I can be*. Otherwise, I'd feel out of my body and numb." In her favorite fantasy, she imagines herself dancing with the actor Patrick Swayze in the movie *Dirty Dancing*:

"When I first saw the movie I cried, thinking I'd never be able to enjoy sex. Gradually, though, I convinced myself that I'm worthy of this kind of pleasure. I've been able to imagine myself as the one in his arms. In this fantasy, it's my eyes he looks into. It's my hips moving against his hips."

When women have been hurt in the past, sexual fantasy can work to transform pain, anger, or other negative emotions into something more positive. Fantasy can vent powerful emotions that women may not feel able to express otherwise, or it can block strong feelings that would prevent them from being able to respond sexually. Some women create fantasy scenarios in which they turn pain into pleasure as a way to feel more powerful and more in control during sex, while others put a happier ending on a relationship or sexual encounter that ended badly in real life.

For women who have been betrayed by a lover in the past, fantasy can be a way to block their resulting fear of intimacy. "In fantasy," one woman explained, "my old lover regrets that he dumped me and always insists that he still loves me." Another woman imagines turning a past perpetrator into a kind, gentle protector. The sexual pleasure she experiences as a result of the fantasy also gives her a feeling that she has mastered what has hurt her in the past.

One woman creatively used fantasy to help her avoid the fear triggered by an unpleasant memory. She said, "I was wrestling playfully with my boyfriend one day when he grabbed me by the wrist and held my arm down. He didn't know it, but that gesture reminded me of how an assailant once grabbed me before assaulting me." As a quick solution to feeling fearful, she imagined that she was a champion wrestler. The power of that fantasy role helped her avoid feeling weak or vulnerable as she and her boyfriend shifted from wrestling to lovemaking.

In a different way, a woman named Vicki uses fantasy to cope with past experiences. She channels her anger about a past sexual assault into a fantasy where she is a controlling Dominatrix. Although her current partner played no role in her past abuse, her pent-up feelings of rage automatically boil to the surface when she becomes aroused. She imagines biting and pulling the hair of a "faceless" stranger. Though it doesn't resolve her anger, Vicki's fantasy functions to direct her rage away from her real partner during sex. It also channels her psychological tension into the physiological release and temporary resolution of climax.

When women use fantasy to preserve or contain an unpleasant memory, this process is often unconscious. As a result, they may feel confused or upset by these kinds of fantasies. Sometimes, due to the effects of betrayal, grief, or childhood trauma, a memory can be so disguised that a woman might not readily make the connection between the contents of her fantasy and what really happened to her in the past. A woman named Beth, for instance, was troubled by a sexual fantasy of a woman making children lick her genitals. She had a strong suspicion this was something she had experienced as a child. When Beth confided to her sister how upset she was by this fantasy, her sister told her she remembered their mother forcing Beth and other children to do the same thing. Beth had literally pushed that traumatic memory to the far corners of her mind, disguising it in fantasy until she felt safe and supported enough to let it emerge.

Fantasies can even create the support and comfort that were lacking in the past. Melanie, for instance, created what she calls a "two-part" sexual fantasy. It begins with a graphic Victim scenario that leads to climax, then transforms into a different scene in which she's being taken care of by kind, loving, comforting men. Often, she imagines men she knows and admires in real life in these caretaker roles. In the fantasy plot, she imagines them playing the role of ambulance drivers, hospital orderlies, policemen, or others who rescue or care for her. "The primary caretaker is a man who loves me, nurtures me, but doesn't need anything from me sexually. He's there to hold me, comfort me, understand me, be there for me. He thinks I'm sensational." The caretakers give her the unconditional love, protection, and comfort she yearned for but never experienced as a child.

Fantasies that cope with past hurts are often important reminders of unfinished business. As we'll see in more detail in later chapters, such fantasies may be sounding an alarm, drawing a woman's attention to an issue she needs to address or understand on a more conscious level. Even if she dislikes the thoughts, her fantasy may be serving a positive function for her by containing and preserving the memory of a significant life experience.

᭡

When women describe fantasies that work well, they often relate them with an unbridled pleasure. They can see their fantasies as positive outlets for their sexuality and their creativity. They appreciate their fantasies as their own, ingenious inventions.

Jena, thirty-six and married, said she has come a long way from her first, brief sexual fantasy of nude bodies, at age eleven. "As a young Catholic girl, I thought I surely must be sinning gloriously." As she related her favorite adult erotic adventure story, we listened for all the different ways she now puts sexual fantasies to work:

I am in a favorite ski community and have just finished a hard day on the slopes. My leg muscles burn and my body feels tired, yet supple. I change into a swimsuit and go to a hot tub to soak. I am reading a book of poetry, enjoying the mood created by a passage on desire, when a handsome man walks in. He looks very much like a past lover that I can't get out of my mind. He joins me in the tub, and I begin reading him a passage on desire. I look at his eyes and feel the instant chemistry and passion which is being described in the poem. I draw close to him for a kiss, and his beard is rough enough to chafe my sunburned face. I am helpless with desire. He stands up and I can see he is very excited by the size of his erection. We make love in and around the hot tub, knowing that we are in a public place and anyone could find us here, but our desire to be together overwhelms our caution. Soon after we both have orgasms, a beautiful woman in a bikini comes in and finds us. Rather than being embarrassed, she cocks her head to the side and smiles. We invite her to join us and she gladly obliges. I have always wondered what it would be like to lick a woman to orgasm, and I ask her if she would let me. My partner kisses her gently and tells us how much it would turn him on to see us together. I slowly remove her panties and start kissing her on the thighs. I skillfully use my tongue and finger to bring her to orgasm, and I feel the shudder through her body as she comes. Then I watch as my partner screws her from behind, and I fondle her full breasts as she comes again. We all collapse in a state of exhaustion, then take a cool shower together. We retire to a bedroom, give each other massages, and sleep, cocooning in each other's arms.

Jena said she has enjoyed this fantasy in her daydreams, during lovemaking with her husband, and in masturbation. Listening to her describe it, we could see that she *enhances her own attractiveness* by making herself a little younger and more fit than she is in real life. She *increases her desire* by picturing a partner who is tanned, blond, lean, muscular, with a tight butt and large penis. He also reminds her of a lost love, thus *holding on to a precious memory.* She includes poetry to further enhance her desire by adding auditory stimulation. She *facilitates orgasm* by including descriptions of sexual touch and explicit visual images, including his erection and her female lover's large breasts. Sexual tension is heightened by imagining that they have sex in public, with the risk of being caught. Although she's never been sexual with a woman in real life, Jena *satisfies her curiosity* in fantasy. At the end of her fantasy, Jena carries her thoughts past sexual enjoyment to an imagined state of *relaxation* and satiety.

When the fantasy fades, Jena said it leaves her with "a feeling of being desired and accepted. I enjoy seeing myself having sex with attractive people who take care of their bodies. I feel confident." Indeed, she added, "Every time I think about it, I have a smile on my face and I get a little bit horny."

Jena clearly enjoys this fantasy and the creative sexual outlet it provides for her. Once we identify how we are already using sexual fantasies to help us, we can even intensify these benefits by using fantasies more deliberately for specific purposes.

Sometimes, however, women feel ambivalent or uneasy about a fantasy even if they recognize that it is functioning for them on some important level. As we'll see in the next chapter, instead of feeling comfortable and fun, sometimes fantasies feel more like bad habits or even traps.

CHAPTER 5

Recognizing Fantasy Traps

Sexual fantasies can work for us in many positive ways. But even when fantasies function well on a purely sexual level, leading to heightened pleasure or increased desire, they don't necessarily make us happy or improve our relationships. Sometimes, fantasies can get in the way of intimacy. They can make a woman feel like a victim over and over again. Fantasies can even interfere with our ability to enjoy sex. In the eight dramatic stories that follow, women describe how a sexual fantasy can lose its enjoyable aspects and become serious business when the problems it causes outweigh its benefits.

VICTORIA'S STORY:
"I COULD HAVE BEEN KILLED."

From the street, Victoria can hear the steady beat of rock and roll music and a familiar swell of voices. It's Saturday night in this Midwestern college town, and the parties are in full swing. Victoria, with a tawny complexion and intense, dark eyes, has met many of her former lovers on nights like this. One of her favorite fantasies is to arrive at a party alone, then take her time deciding which man she'd like to take her home. At the doorway, she smooths back her long, shiny black hair and steps inside.

The house is crowded. Victoria jostles her way through to find the beer, pausing briefly to greet friends. She tells them about the part-time job she just started at an adult bookstore near campus and enjoys their shocked reaction. Since she began working there, Victoria has been fueling her fantasies with new ideas she'd like to try. One magazine story in particular, about a sexual escapade between two strangers, really grabbed her attention.

Scanning the room, Victoria spots an interesting-looking newcomer. She can hear the deep tones of his laughter over the music. She works her way closer, within earshot of his foreign-sounding accent. She can't quite place it, but imagines that he grew up within view of the Mediterranean. Maybe in a villa. She imagines him, tanned and bare-chested, diving into warm, aquamarine waters, and pictures herself swimming sensuously alongside him in a string bikini. Although she hasn't spoken a word to him, she boldly studies his face, memorizing every handsome feature.

Later, when Victoria looks for the man on the dance floor, he's nowhere in sight. Too bad. She makes up an excuse about having to get up early and waves good-bye to her friends. As she starts to pull on her coat, she's startled to feel someone's hands at her back, helping her into her jacket. She turns and finds herself face-to-face with the stranger. He smiles, presses a slip of paper into her hand, and leans forward to kiss her lightly on the lips. Without a word, he's out the door.

Victoria, who's used to making the first move in a relationship, is breathless with surprise. Outside, under streetlights, she looks at the paper and sees only a handwritten phone number. Now it's her turn to smile. Her new fantasy seems to be coming true. As she walks home, she imagines his confident hands moving across her skin, finding their way to her breasts. Under her loose-fitting shirt, she can feel her nipples tingle with anticipation of his touch.

Victoria gets home to an empty apartment. Her roommates must still be out. She paces around the small space, too excited to sleep. On an impulse, she picks up the phone and dials his number. He answers on the first ring and says, "I knew you would call." Then he gives her directions to his place, and she's on her way to her car before she can give herself time to reconsider.

As soon as he opens his door, he's kissing her again, this time long and deeply. They pull at each other's clothes. When they're both naked, he sweeps her into his arms and carries her into his bedroom. The sex feels wild, unrestrained. He seems to know exactly how she yearns to be touched. She climaxes twice before he enters her, then they come again, together. She falls back on the bed, exhausted and satisfied, and curls up against his warm body.

Suddenly, she feels his weight shift and opens her eyes to see him kneeling above her. He holds her down with his full weight, pinning her arms over her head. She can't move. Victoria looks into his eyes and sees a crazed look, as if he has turned into someone else. Her heart pounds, but not from sexual excitement. "Now," he says slowly and deliberately, *"I'm going to kill you."*

Victoria realizes in a flash that no one else knows where she is. She still doesn't even know this guy's name. Why on earth did she get herself into this situation? She could disappear or die, and no one would know where to begin looking for her.

She gives herself two choices: scream and plead for mercy, or play his game. She decides that crying and tears would probably only make him more aggressive, so she cranes her head forward to kiss him. Unlike their earlier kisses, which were passionate and full of sexual longing, this one feels desperate. She begs silently for her life and hopes she's made the right choice. He at first seems surprised by her kiss, then pleased. "You aren't very strong," he says, easing his weight off her arms, "but you sure are beautiful."

They have sex one more time, but Victoria feels none of the earlier pleasure. Now her body feels cold, tense, tight. She fakes her way through, pretending to come when all she can think of is her terror. Finally, he climaxes and rolls off her. His breathing becomes slower, and Victoria is pretty sure he has fallen asleep. She gets up from the bed carefully, trying not to make a sound, and pulls on her clothes in the living room. As she flees, shutting the door behind her, Victoria realizes that following her fantasy has almost cost her her life. She vows never again to let herself fall into this kind of trap.

❦

For Victoria, the problem wasn't the content of her fantasy. Indeed, many women enjoy fantasies about having sex with a handsome stranger. Rather, Victoria got trapped when she became seduced by excitement, threw caution to the wind, and acted out her fantasy on impulse.

Certain fantasies are best left as fantasies. Just because a dangerous sexual scenario has been pleasing in fantasy is no guarantee that it will work out in real life. By acting out an arousing but risky fantasy, a woman ignores the potentially negative consequences to herself or to others. Elements of the taboo or the forbidden can make a fantasy more exciting, but engaging in such behavior in real life can lead to extramarital affairs, unwanted pregnancies, exposure to sexually transmitted diseases, or experiences that are humiliating, damaging, or even fatal.

KATE'S STORY:
"I'M A SLAVE TO MY OWN FANTASY."

A thin woman with delicate features, Kate looks younger than her thirty-six years. Something about her seems fragile and vulnerable. At church functions, more matronly women are always trying to feed her or fix her up with their eligible sons. Her office colleagues know her as a serious, reliable worker, but also as a quiet, shy person who avoids socializing after hours.

Her acquaintances would be surprised to learn that Kate feels as if she's leading a double life. When she's alone at home, certain fantasies creep into her thoughts like invaders, and she feels powerless to stop them. As soon as a fantasy kicks in, her hands move automatically to her genitals. She masturbates compulsively, greedily demanding more and more pleasure from her own body. While she's touching herself, she imagines that she's "taking a time out from God."

Lately, Kate has noticed that her fantasies have even started creeping in when she's away from home. She was at an evening church meeting recently when she let her thoughts wander. She felt the familiar pull of fantasy, taking her out of the present and making her feel flushed with sexual desire. Kate was so upset that she rushed out of the meeting, claiming illness. Even before she arrived home, she could feel the heat spreading into her genitals. She raced into her bedroom, threw herself down on her bed, and let the fantasy run its predictable course.

Although the setting can change from one fantasy to the next, the characters in Kate's mind are always the same. A powerful, sexually aggressive woman, who often looks like the actress Holly Hunter, seduces a younger, more vulnerable woman. They might be on a scientific expedition to a tropical rain forest, or maybe actresses on a Hollywood set. There's usually some adventure and excitement to draw the two women together, and the older one pounces like a sexual predator. Although the younger woman doesn't look exactly like Kate, she recognizes their similarities.

When she climaxes, Kate feels all of her troubles temporarily wash away. She doesn't feel so anxious anymore. While in real life she often feels lonely and awkward around other people, Kate soothes herself with fantasy. She depends on her fantasy life so much for comfort that she often wonders if this is how it feels to be addicted to drugs.

When her fantasy fades, though, Kate feels shame and confusion flood in from all sides. She considers herself deeply spiritual but keeps returning in her mind to this secret, underground world. She feels trapped there, enslaved by her own fantasies. More and more, her fantasies seem to be taking over her life. She feels as if fantasizing is wasting her time, affecting her decisions, and limiting her activities.

Kate's fantasies even interrupt her sleep. She awakens several times a night, trying to avoid the fantasy but then giving in to it so she can get a few fitful hours of sleep. One night as she tosses and turns in bed, trying to keep her erotic thoughts at bay, Kate realizes that, for several years, no one has touched her outside of her fantasy world. While she longs for closeness and comfort, she channels all of her sexual feelings into her secret life. For the first time, Kate really sees how her fantasies have taken over her life. They have become driven and compulsive. In search of a few moments of pleasure and release, she's been trapped into behavior that is rigid, ritualized, and out of her control.

❦

Kate is not alone with her obsessive fantasies. Many women describe recurring, intrusive fantasies that feel beyond their control. One woman said, for example, "When I experience my abuse fantasies, I feel like I'm on a food or alcohol binge."

Some women describe going into a trance state when a fantasy begins at the start of lovemaking, daydreaming, or masturbation. Others feel triggered into a particular fantasy when they reach a certain point of sexual arousal or response. When fantasies become so predictable and driven, they no longer work well to satisfy curiosity or express playfulness about sex. Instead of being enjoyable outlets for sexual energy, these kinds of fantasies feel like burdens. Obsessive fantasies often relate to unresolved emotional conflicts. Kate, for example, was neglected by her mother when she was a child and started turning to fantasy for the comfort missing from her real life.

Generally, women want to be in the driver's seat of their own fantasies. We don't want to feel as if we've been taken hostage by thoughts that flood in, against our will, taking us places we don't want to go. Intrusive, out-of-control fantasies can leave a woman feeling victimized by her fantasy life or angry at her inability to break free of these powerful sexual thoughts. Sexual pleasure may become overshadowed by feelings of helplessness and shame.

MAGGIE'S STORY:
"I HATE BEING TURNED ON BY
SUCH REPULSIVE THOUGHTS."

Maggie spends her working hours as a marriage counselor, helping couples talk out their differences and find common ground on which to build a relationship. Her kind eyes convey her genuine compassion for other people, and she speaks with intelligence and a commitment to her work.

At night, as soon as she turns out the light, she feels her husband move closer to her in bed. She knows that he wants to make love, and she feels a cold sense of dread come over her. She doesn't want to push him away again. And yet, even with all her communication skills, she doesn't know how to tell him how upset she gets by the thoughts she has during sex. When Maggie takes a deep breath, her husband thinks she shares his passion. Really, it's a sign of her resignation: she feels no choice but to use the awful fantasy that always helps her get through sex.

As soon as she and her husband begin their usual sexual routine, Maggie (a Christian in real life) imagines herself as a young Jewish woman held captive in a Nazi concentration camp. She is strapped to a table, and a soldier in jackboots walks efficiently around the room, making notes on a clipboard. As he leans closer to tighten the leather straps holding her to the table, he stares at Maggie with cold, uncaring eyes that remind her of a snake's. Nauseated, she looks away and sees the swastika on his armband. The same symbol is worn by the other short-haired soldiers who watch from behind a glass partition. She hates the very sight of them, but can't get them out of her mind. When Maggie's husband massages her clitoris, she imagines it's the Nazi's hand on her crotch. When he sucks her breast, she imagines the Nazi clamping a torture device onto her nipples. Finally, when she climaxes, Maggie feels a rush of power. She imagines herself delivering something that the Nazis really want. Because she can climax so easily, she is the one they have picked to escape the gas chambers.

Maggie is pulled out of the fantasy when she hears her husband's voice. "What did you say?" she asks him. He repeats, "You seem so serious. I wonder what you're thinking about when we make love."

Maggie turns to him in tears. How can she tell him that she's been fantasizing about Nazis in order to get turned on for the last twenty years? She can't even remember when she first invented this story. She does recall trying hard to change it, but every fantasy that arouses her seems to weave together the same threads of surrender, and power, and sex. She doesn't know why, but the very fantasy that she hates most in the world is also the only one she can count on to bring her to climax.

❧

Women who are disturbed by the content of a particular fantasy say that certain sexual thoughts leave them feeling upset, ashamed, or cut off from their real partners. They may feel disgusted and fear that the disturbing content makes them "perverted."

The content of fantasies can make women feel bad about themselves because they realize they are turned on in fantasy to images that turn them off in real life. These images can be serious and heavy like Maggie's, with such depictions as rape, violent sex, sex with children, or other forms of exploitation. For other women, the content can be less intense, but still quite upsetting. One woman, for instance, was distressed by a recurring fantasy about having sex with her large French poodles.

Women said they resented the dissonance created by fantasies that are at odds with their personal values. One woman, a prominent feminist, said she felt trapped because the images she naturally finds most erotic go against the conditions of equality she works to achieve in the rest of her life. "I hate these fantasies that are politically incorrect, even if they're juicy," she said. Similarly, other women described feeling trapped by fantasies that are against their religious beliefs. A Catholic woman, for example, was disturbed by an intruding fantasy of having sex with a priest. Sometimes, women are concerned when fantasies seem to run counter to their sexual orientation.

Left alone with their upsetting, even nightmarish thoughts, some women spend years feeling isolated, ashamed, and at fault. They may not make the connection between the content of their fantasy and a painful or traumatic experience they may have suffered in the past. Once they make that connection, however, these fantasies seem more understandable.

Instead of blaming ourselves for upsetting fantasies, we can learn to see them as reminders of some confusion about sex that has never been resolved. For Maggie, fantasy was a way to contain the painful dynamics of her childhood. She grew up with a father who controlled her life as if he were a prison warden. In her fantasy, she found a way to imagine herself as having sexual power over her captors in order to ensure her survival. Whenever she accommodated her husband's desire for sex, without really being interested, she used this reliably arousing fantasy to get herself through sex. Until she worked through the connection between her fantasy and her childhood, Maggie was stuck blaming herself for having erotic thoughts she found repulsive.

In addition to replaying past events, unwanted fantasies can also lock into a woman's arousal patterns the powerful, pornographic images she may have first seen at a young age. If a woman has made an early association between sex and violence, for example, she may fantasize about violent acts during the most tender lovemaking. Whether the fantasy is a trap or not depends on whether she considers it more arousing or more upsetting. Women who truly feel trapped by the content of their fantasies often describe them as essential for arousal or orgasm, but humiliating or disgusting to think about after having sex.

GERI'S STORY:
"MY FANTASY WAS GETTING IN
THE WAY OF MY RECOVERY."

Although she's been sober and drug free for eight years now, Geri spent much of her twenties in a drug and alcohol daze. She had dozens of lovers during those years and often felt like she was selling her body for drugs. People who knew her when she was using wouldn't recognize her now. She used to wear heavy makeup and tight, low-cut tops, trying to attract men's attention. Now, she wears her auburn hair short and neatly styled, dresses in attractive but rather conservative clothes, with just a touch of lipstick to offset her naturally pretty features. Back when she was using drugs and booze, she recalls, "I let men use me, too, over and over." Fantasy is what kept Geri in blinders, preventing her from seeing the harm of her behavior.

When she was high and having sex with a man she had just met, Geri would pretend that he was her knight in shining armor, riding up on a white horse to save her. She pictured him rescuing her from life on the city streets and taking her away from the seedy drug houses she frequented. She imagined them starting life over in the country where the air smelled fresh.

Even before she got clean, Geri began to see how fantasy was keeping her from facing her problems. She seldom enjoyed sex, yet craved intimacy. She realized the sad sexual bargain she was making again and again: the man got to have his orgasm, and she got to be held afterward. That's all she really wanted, those few minutes of being held and warm and safe.

One night, Geri was in bed with a man she had just met. "He didn't know me well enough to love me. I suddenly realized that, even though he was holding me then, he wouldn't even be here next week. There was going to be no commitment, no rescue." She was overcome with sadness, realizing the huge distance between her fantasy world and her real life. In that moment, Geri recognized the trap she had fallen into with fantasy. "I was devastated, and knew I couldn't hold on to that romantic fantasy any longer. It was keeping me in a life that offered no lasting satisfaction."

❧

For some women, a particular fantasy can maintain or reinforce behavior that interferes with recovery from drugs, alcohol, or other addictions. Geri, for instance, kept herself from facing the consequences of her addiction by kidding herself with her rescue fantasies. Her Pretty Maiden fantasies were quite similar to ones that many other women describe. Yet, they became a trap for Geri because she used the fantasies to block her awareness of the harm she was doing to herself. Once she faced her addiction, she realized that she would have to rescue herself from the life she was living. With that new awareness, her old white knight fantasies no longer fit.

Other women have come to a similar conclusion about fantasies that they seem to outgrow when they make a major life change. One woman found that her Victim fantasies were replaced by Wild Woman fantasies after she divorced an abusive husband and landed a high-paying job. She said, "I changed my life, and my fantasies changed with it."

For other women who are in recovery, sexual fantasy can

pose a challenge for a different reason. For them, fantasy may feel like a rewarding behavior that they engage in secretly—much like their old addiction. They may use fantasy to escape or numb out, just as they once did with drugs or alcohol. If their fantasies feel at odds with the healthy, honest, caring approach to life they're taking in recovery, such thoughts can generate shame. This shame can then threaten a relapse into the addictive behavior they're working so hard to overcome.

For women who have taken to heart the Twelve-Step slogan "You're only as sick as your secrets," the realm of fantasy can feel like a giant, sick secret. As writer Guy Kettelhack points out in his book *How to Make Love While Conscious,* it's the secretiveness, not the content of fantasies, that is most problematic for those in recovery. "It's only when we become convinced that fantasies are our only way out, or our only way of dealing with certain difficult feelings, that we get into trouble. Then we treat fantasies like we used to treat drugs and alcohol: as our only possible escape."[1]

For women who are recovering from sexual abuse, fantasies can be a constant reminder of the past. They can perpetuate a negative view of sex that a woman first learned during abuse and reinforce arousal patterns to a type of sexual interaction she does not want to be in. One woman, for example, had been sexually abused earlier in her life and was working hard to build a new relationship on a foundation of trust, communication, and mutual caring. In a recurring fantasy, however, she would imagine a gang of men taking turns raping her. She pictured the leader and most brutal member of the gang as her current lover, who in real life was tender, caring, and respectful. Because her fantasy perpetuated a secret image of her boyfriend as a violent rapist, it prevented her from developing a deep sense of emotional trust and safety with him.

By becoming more conscious about their fantasies, women in recovery can enjoy more choice and control over which sexual thoughts they really want to entertain and which ones might be trapping them into unwanted behavior patterns.

SOPHIE'S STORY:
"I HAVE NO RIGHT TO DO THIS TO HIM."

Although they've only been dating for a couple months, Sophie and Joe have just moved into an apartment together. At forty, with a willowy build and strikingly good looks, Sophie has never had trouble meeting men. Her sex life has been active and exciting. Yet, something about Joe touches her deeply. He's sweet and gentle—so different from the men she's dated in the past who have been mostly interested in sex. Joe seems more genuine and eager to really get to know her.

Sophie feels ready for what she hopes will be a long-term relationship. She has decided it's time to settle down. In the past, her sex life has involved a lot of fantasy play. She's been with many men who have enjoyed playing the role of her sexual submissive. They've had fun acting out fantasy scripts, such as one in which she has played a stern teacher, spanking an errant schoolboy as part of foreplay. Unlike former lovers, Joe seems to know nothing about the sexual lure of dominance and submission. Sophie has decided not to tell him much about her past lovers or the "dominant female" scenarios she has found so pleasurable.

During their first sexual encounters, Joe's tender lovemaking had seemed sweet. Sophie enjoyed this "vanilla sex." It was so refreshing and relaxed. Having Joe caress her body and look deeply into her hazel eyes felt different from the way she had experienced sex in the past. When Joe said, "I love you," she believed him.

Since they've begun living together, though, Sophie has started to miss the sexual tension she used to enjoy with other men. She wants to make sex with Joe more exciting and has decided to take more initiative. Recently, she has started to teach him about the erotic thrill of dominance and submission. Using certain gestures and phrases during sex, she has been gradually introducing him to the scripted fantasy world she first learned about as a young woman when an older man gave her a copy of

The Story of O, an erotic novel about bondage. Now during love-making with Joe, she sometimes takes charge and speaks in a commanding voice. When he gets an erection, she pretends to spank him on the behind with a silk scarf, saying, "Look what a big, naughty boy you are." Amused, he plays along.

After a few subtle hints in lovemaking, Sophie becomes more bold. One day, she playfully tells Joe he will have to strip off his clothes and clean the bathroom if he wants to have sex. Although she doesn't explain the details to Joe, Sophie knows this fantasy script by heart. She has played it out in the past with plenty of other willing men. It's been months since she's staged a full-fledged sex script, with costumes, and Sophie is excited. After giving Joe a few minutes to get started, she puts on a black push-up bra, garter belt, and stockings that she knows will turn him on. Then, she opens the bathroom door and finds him right where she wants him: on his knees, sponge in hand, scrubbing the hard tile floor. The bathroom is sparkling, clean enough to pass any white-glove test. According to this fantasy script, however, Sophie has to find something to nitpick. That's part of the game that gives her more sexual control.

"You're so sloppy," she starts in, "so lazy. Can't you see you've done a very poor job here?" Getting more aroused by her controlling fantasy role, Sophie struts into the bathroom, spewing more comments about his failed performance. According to the script, Joe's supposed to beg her forgiveness and ask to make it up to her. Eventually, when Sophie gives the go-ahead, they'll proceed with sex.

But in the middle of her make-believe tirade, she sees him looking up at her. He seems stunned and confused, and she sees a pained look in his eyes. Joe's genuine emotional response doesn't match Sophie's fantasy script. Horrified, she blurts out, "My god, what am I doing?" She drops her fantasy role and realizes how much she is humiliating Joe by treating him as her sex slave. She pulls him to his feet and says, "Please forgive me. I don't have the right to treat you this way." In that moment, it becomes clear to Sophie that she needs to give up her rigid fantasies if she's going to allow her new relationship with Joe room to grow.

❧

For Sophie, her familiar fantasy role became so predetermined that it was robbing her new relationship of the chance for real intimacy or spontaneity. In the past, the Dominatrix role had offered Sophie the control over men that she wanted in order to feel safe during sex. She took the role on as a reaction to early sexual experiences she had, in which she was overstimulated and felt out of control about sex.

As a child, Sophie had overheard her parents having sex as many as "a dozen times a night." Her mother had told her that it's a woman's duty to satisfy her man's desires. In the Dominatrix role, Sophie turned those gender roles upside down and gave herself supreme authority to say when and how a man could let go in sex. She sought out partners who wanted to be controlled, for reasons of their own. With Joe, however, Sophie realized that her old role didn't fit the dynamics of her new relationship. What's more, the rigid fantasy role didn't allow room for her and Joe to explore the erotic potential of their relationship as it evolved.

Taking a need for control to an extreme, a woman might get carried away with a fantasy and actually coerce or manipulate her partner into acting it out with her. She might turn lovemaking into a predictable ritual, always performed the same way so that nothing will interrupt the flow of her favorite fantasy.

A woman's strong attachment to her fantasy can also lead her to initiate sexual activities her partner dislikes. One woman, for instance, set up a threesome sex scene in a hotel room as a birthday surprise for her husband. She didn't realize until it was too late, however, that her favorite group sex fantasy was repulsive to him. Another woman started to make love to her boyfriend

in a car, ignoring how ill at ease he felt about the risk that someone would see them. Because of his anxiety, he was unable to
perform sexually, and they were both disappointed.

Even the language of lovemaking can become problematic if
it expresses one partner's fantasy at the sake of another's comfort.
"I wanted my lover to talk dirty to me," one woman explained. "I
liked him to call me a bitch and a whore. I found that exciting, but
he didn't tell me until we broke up that he hated the way that
made him feel."

If a woman's fantasy makes her unaware of her partner's real
needs and desires, or if it reduces the partner to a sexual performer,
the fantasy becomes a trap that can hamper the development of
real intimacy. The partner can wind up feeling used, uncomfortable, or turned off, and the relationship can suffer as a result.

JOSIE'S STORY:
"MY FANTASY MAKES ME AFRAID OF SEX."

Josie and her lover, Nell, awake in each other's arms on a bright
spring morning. Because it's Saturday, neither of them has to be
anywhere for hours. For the first time in days, they have a chance
to enjoy each other's company without interruption. Nell offers to
give Josie a back rub, and she eagerly rolls onto her stomach. She
can feel Nell's strong fingers kneading the tension out of her muscles and lets out a low groan of pleasure. In the next instant,
though, when Nell's hands move down her back and onto her
buttocks, Josie tenses up.

The last few times they've tried to make love, things have
gone poorly. Josie has either started a fight to break the mood or
wound up in tears after sex. It's not really the sex that has her so
upset, but the violent fantasy that always seems to come with
arousal. As soon as she feels anything but numb, the fantasy slides
into her thoughts and jerks her out of the present. In the fantasy,
she pictures herself in a room that looks like a dungeon, where

faceless strangers tie her up, pierce her chest with thick needles, and take turns licking her to climax.

As Nell starts to kiss her neck, Josie suddenly pulls away and tries to jump out of bed. "I'll make some coffee for us," she offers in a voice that's artificially cheerful. Nell grabs her arm and pulls her back to bed. "What's wrong?" she asks Josie, searching her face for an answer. "You can tell me anything. Let's just get it out in the open." Josie shakes her off and stands up. As she leaves the room, she says curtly over her shoulder, "All I wanted was a back rub." Inside, though, she's hurting. She knows that not dealing with her fantasy is destroying their chance to enjoy the closeness they both want.

❧

Although fantasy can be an effective tool to turn up sexual desire and enhance functioning, some women consider fantasy their biggest obstacle to enjoying sex. If unwanted fantasies threaten to flood in when they become sexually aroused, they may shut down or numb out in order to stop fantasizing. Some women avoid sex altogether as a result. As one woman said, "I stopped having sex with other people several years ago. Now I'm even celibate with myself."

Fantasy can disrupt sex at different stages in the sexual response cycle. One woman, for instance, relied on a particular fantasy to become aroused. She would imagine herself as the star of a porn movie she had watched with her husband. "I become that coldhearted, manipulative bitch who knows how to arouse men. There's no sense of caring. I see myself on top, with my breasts swinging. I get aroused, but then this feeling of disgust comes over me. Usually I stop having sex. It's just too upsetting. There's none of the human connection that I really want."

Another woman was troubled by an image of her past rapist whenever she climaxed. As a result, her orgasms became muted and unsatisfying. For another woman, fantasy interfered at the end of sex. Instead of relaxing in her husband's arms after love-making, she was plagued by a fantasy that he would leave her for another woman. As a result, she felt anxious and stirred up every time they had sex.

MAI'S STORY:
"I'VE ABANDONED MYSELF."

The moment Mai slips into the cool water at her health club, she automatically lets her mind wander. As she pulls herself through the pool and finds a comfortable breathing rhythm, she mentally shifts into one of her favorite sexual daydreams that have always made her swimming workouts fly.

In this fantasy, she imagines herself running laps at a nearby track. She sees her body as slim and athletic, set off by form-fitting Lycra tights. Her own baby boy is nowhere in sight in this fantasy, but she recognizes his pediatrician working out at the track. He runs a few laps alongside Mai, then they stretch together and begin talking. He can't seem to keep his eyes off her. He invites her back to his apartment, and they ride together in his white Porsche. As soon as she walks into his place, she notices the chrome and glass furnishings, the modern art, the Stairmaster, the white carpeting, all the hallmarks of a rich doctor's home. She could get used to this luxury. Mai decides to take a shower, and the doctor paces around the apartment, getting more and more aroused while he waits for her. Unable to control himself, he bursts into the bathroom while she's washing her long blond hair, and they have soapy, slippery, wonderful sex on the shower floor.

Mai's fantasy fades as she climbs out of the pool and dries her body off with a towel. As she enters the locker room, she catches a head-to-toe view of herself in a mirror. Unlike the tiny, lithe, blond-haired, blue-eyed jogger of her fantasies, she is a tall, rather heavyset woman with shiny black hair, dark eyes, and the distinctively beautiful facial features she inherited from her Asian-American parents.

For the first time in months, she really looks at herself in the mirror. She's been struggling with her weight ever since her baby was born. She tries to imagine what it would be like to see her real self in her own fantasies. If a man like the doctor ever saw her naked, she imagines he'd run in the other direction. Even when she's making love with her husband, who constantly reassures her of his love, Mai keeps the lights off and her eyes shut. She can't accept her own body, so why should he? At that thought, Mai's eyes cloud with tears. She realizes she doesn't even find herself good enough for her own fantasies. She moves away from the mirror, feeling left out and unworthy.

❧

If the contrast between how a woman sees herself in real life and in fantasy is too great, it can keep her from acknowledging her own unique beauty and sexual attractiveness. While some women use fantasy to fine-tune their self-image to correct perceived flaws and overcome self-consciousness, others feel as if they go too far, obliterating their sense of self. By radically changing who she is in fantasy, a woman can be trapped into feeling undeserving of sexual pleasure and attention in real life.

This problem with fantasy can be worsened by a woman buying into cultural stereotypes of what a beautiful female should look like. If she thinks a sexy woman must have Barbie-doll features and a *Playboy* physique, she's likely to be disappointed by her own face and body. Mai, for instance, didn't think she was attractive because of her size and racial background. As a result, she denied her innate beauty and felt undeserving of attention. Other women describe going to extremes in a quest to become their fantasy ideal, submitting to endless rounds of plastic surgery, liposuction, and dieting. They spend a fortune on hair coloring, curling, or straightening, or erase all signs of their original, natural self in a head-to-toe makeover.

Although many women enjoy fussing over their looks, this quest for perfection can become a trap if a woman goes too far in trying to live up to her fantasy image. She risks losing her identity in the process.

Desiree, for instance, has tinkered with her body for years, trying to reshape it into what she thinks men most want. Her brown hair has been dyed blond so many times that it's brittle to the touch. She has paid surgeons to make her breasts larger and her nose smaller. When men act turned on by her, she knows they're reacting to the body she has created, not her authentic self. "I usually date selfish, macho guys who get off on being with a woman who looks like me," Desiree said. "I just started a new relationship with a nice guy who has really taken time to get to know me, but I'm having a hard time being with him. He says he loves me for who I really am, but after all I've done to myself, how can I believe him? I wonder what he'd think if he ever saw the real me."

MARY'S STORY:
"I'M SICK OF BEING HIS FANTASY GIRL."

After a long day at work, Mary barely sets foot inside the door of her apartment when Lan, her lover, is pawing at her clothes, unbraiding her hair, and pulling her toward the bedroom. She tries to be playful, tickling him into letting her go. "Let's go out for dinner," she suggests, stepping back from him. "I'm starved."

"I'm starved, too," he says, unbuttoning her shirt, "but not for dinner." He fluffs her long hair so that it cascades onto her shoulders. "Forget the ponytail," he says. "You know I like your hair down."

Mary, who was still a virgin when she and Lan met a year ago, can scarcely believe how adventuresome her sex life has become. Lan can never seem to get enough of her. In the last several months, he's had sex with her in more positions than she believed were humanly possible. Once, he even had her perform oral sex on him when they were speeding down the freeway.

Right now, though, Mary's not really in the mood. She's feeling sore from having such frequent sex. When she complains, he tells her, "It only hurts if you're uptight. You need to loosen up more."

From the very first time they had sex, she's been responsive to his touch, nearly always climaxing. Lan says he loves that about her. It reminds him of the sexually hungry women he has seen in porn movies. Sometimes during sex he holds her head a certain way to duplicate a film scene. Then, he calls her his *"fantasy girl."*

"Come on, baby," he says now, "we can make each other feel so good." He kisses her face softly, the way he did when they first met, then takes her shirt all the way off and drops it at her feet. She knows this is her cue to strip the rest of the way. She leaves a trail of clothing on the floor as they work their way into the bedroom. When she lies back on the bed, she's wearing only the red silk panties that he gave her. Then, without any more foreplay, he's on top of her. When they have sex this time, though, she's too uncomfortable to respond. As soon as Lan climaxes, he storms out of the room. "You don't know how to have a good time anymore," he tells her angrily.

Mary is still hurting a few minutes later when she goes to take a shower. She panics when she sees a bloody discharge and realizes she doesn't even know a gynecologist to call. She phones her older sister, Jill, and blurts out the whole story. Jill reacts with anger. "You mean he wants you to perform like those women who get paid to fake it? If you won't listen to reason," Jill adds, "listen to your body. It's trying to tell you to stop being with this guy. He's hurting you with his warped fantasy world, and he doesn't even care. This isn't the way love should feel."

That hits home. Mary realizes she has been turned into Lan's sex doll, jerked around like a puppet on a string. She realizes that their sexual problems are not her fault, but rather a result of Lan imposing his pornographic fantasy world on her.

✿

Like Mary, other women get trapped by their partners' sexual fantasies. Especially if a woman is young, sexually inexperienced, or feels she is responsible for other people's happiness, she can wind up with a partner who plays off her insecurities and treats her as an object.

Some women realize they are caught in this kind of trap when they feel upset or uncomfortable about a partner's specific sexual request. One woman, for instance, said her lover at first suggested then begged her to wear a black garter belt and a silver-studded neck collar. His insistence made her feel less important than the items he wanted her to put on. Another woman said she reluctantly accommodated her husband's long-standing fantasy to have a sexual threesome. "I did it only to please him, and it was horrible. We invited my best friend to join us in bed, and it ruined my friendship with her forever."

Similarly, other women described feeling uncomfortable because of partners' suggestions that they have sex in a public place or in a position that they don't like. "At first, when my boyfriend would suggest these daring sexual escapades late at night, it was kind of exciting," said one woman, who had sex with her boyfriend in public rest rooms, drive-in movies, and dark alleys. "But after a while, the sex began to feel driven and uncomfortable. I didn't want to be pulled into that any longer."

Sometimes, acting out fantasies together can be a positive, fun experience for a couple. When the fantasy is mutually pleasing, a woman willingly chooses to make her partner's fantasy her own. If a woman is made to feel uncomfortable, humiliated, or threatened into participating in her partner's fantasy, however, it never feels authentic to her. Instead, she can wind up feeling used.

Serious consequences can result if a partner's dangerous fantasy is allowed to go unchecked. One woman said her husband's sexual energy became gradually more abusive during their fifteen-year marriage. In part because of their shared belief in Christian fundamentalism, she assumed it was her wifely duty to accommodate him in bed. He had always been forceful, holding her arms over her head when they had sex and insisting on being on top. One night, he shocked her by tying her arms to the headboard with ropes. When she cried, he told her, "It's your job to make me happy in bed." Instead of trusting her instincts that his comment was a danger sign and seeking outside help, she tried bargaining with him, offering to let him tie her up once a month. Sex became increasingly violent, sometimes leaving her arms and breasts bruised for days afterward. She took on his abusive fantasy as her burden to bear, not facing the seriousness of his behavior until he was caught tying up and raping their niece.

❧

The problems women describe as a result of fantasies range from mild to terribly serious. Many women notice that these problems seldom occur in isolation. Often, one troublesome fantasy poses a number of concerns. The content, for example, can be upsetting and the experience of the fantasy can feel out of control. Certain fantasies can reinforce a negative view of sex and lead a woman to do things she doesn't really want to do. One partner's strong attachment to a specific fantasy might interfere with the couple's communication and get in the way of more honest intimacy.

While troublesome fantasies can cause serious concerns, no fantasy trap has to be permanent. In later chapters, we'll describe the success women have had with changing, eliminating, or healing fantasies that caused serious problems. For most women, the first step in healing is to become more conscious about the traps fantasies are posing.

Because evaluating fantasies is a subjective task, each woman has to judge for herself how a particular fantasy may be working for her and against her. Often, the understanding that a fantasy is problematic comes about in a moment of realization when a woman sees that the scale has tipped, and the drawbacks now outweigh the benefits of a particular fantasy.

In Wendy's fantasy workshops, she often uses a checklist to help women evaluate their own fantasies. Similarly, we can ask ourselves the following questions to help evaluate whether, and to what extent, a particular fantasy may be causing problems:

- Does the fantasy lead to risky or dangerous behavior?
- Does the fantasy feel out of control or compulsive?
- Is the content of the fantasy disturbing or repulsive?
- Does the fantasy hinder recovery or personal growth?
- Does the fantasy lower my self-esteem or block self-acceptance?
- Does the fantasy distance me from my real-life partner?
- Does the fantasy harm my intimate partner or anyone else?
- Does the fantasy cause sexual problems?
- Does the fantasy really belong to someone else?

Fantasies work best for us when they feel optional. We like to know that we have a choice about what goes on in our minds. One woman said she compares sexual fantasies to the offerings in a video store. She wants to be able to choose which video store she frequents, which tape she rents, and when she watches it. Most of us can probably relate to her analogy. In fact, we may realize that we also want to be the one who holds the remote control: turning a fantasy on or off to suit ourselves, fast-forwarding through sections we don't like, and replaying scenes we really enjoy.

As we listen to women evaluate their own fantasies, we gain a new appreciation for the power these erotic thoughts have to affect us. They aren't just idle daydreams, randomly flickering through our consciousness. Although fantasies can vary widely, they are generally good for us when they stir desire in ways we like, not when they make sex unappealing or get in the way of intimacy. Nor are fantasies necessarily an indicator of what we should do in real life. For the safety and pleasure of ourselves and our lovers, the line between fantasy and reality needs to remain clear, not blurred.

Whether our fantasies are a cause of problems or a source of delight, we have good reason to explore them more deeply. As we'll see in the next chapter, going further with our exploration gives us a chance to learn even more about ourselves through our fantasies.

CHAPTER 6

Deep Discoveries

It doesn't take much prodding for women to start examining their fantasy lives more closely. Because of women's natural curiosity about their own fantasies, our interviews often lasted much longer than we expected and took us in directions we didn't anticipate traveling. It was as if each woman intuitively knew that her fantasies had a message worth hearing. "My fantasy tells me to be free and creative in life," one woman said. Suggested another, "My fantasy tells me I am capable of loving myself despite my shortcomings, and that someone else will love me, too."

If we take only a superficial look at the meaning of our fantasies, we might conclude that fantasies are good at telling us things we already know. Maybe we yearn for a vacation to a tropical island. Maybe we'd feel more amorous if we had no deadlines to meet, a partner who could last all night, and no kids asleep in the next room. The message of a fantasy isn't always profound or complex.

Beyond these surface messages, however, deeper discoveries await. Women who take the time to describe the contents and functions of their fantasies, then trace how these private thoughts overlap and interweave with their real lives, are often amazed at how much more they can learn. "Fantasies are like gifts, waiting to be unwrapped," one woman said. "Fantasies are one of the best resources I can think of for tapping into my own mind," another added. "Fantasies are marvelous doors to walk through," said a therapist who appreciates the opportunities fantasies offer us to look inside ourselves.

Like their fantasies, the discoveries that women can make by looking closely at them are highly personal and intensely individual. In general, we can turn to our sexual fantasies to give us information in three important realms of our lives: sex, relationships, and personal growth. Fantasies can help us to see these three areas more clearly and in greater detail.

In this chapter, we'll hear from three women who have made deep discoveries about themselves by reflecting on how their sexual fantasies connect and intersect with other aspects of their lives. Gale has learned more about what she needs to have a satisfying sex life with her husband. Jane has gained an understanding of what she really wants to find in a lasting relationship. Brynn has acquired a stronger belief in herself and her inner strength with the help of her active fantasy life.

At different times in their lives, their sexual fantasies have left these three women feeling surprised, bewildered, turned on, turned off, empowered, helpless, delighted, and, finally, amazed. Only by seeing the wonderful complexity of their fantasy lives have they been able to finally make sense of them and fully appreciate fantasy as an expression of their own creativity and wisdom.

GALE'S STORY:
A PATH TO BETTER SEX

Outside the community hospital, foot traffic is heavy on this spring afternoon. Clusters of nurses walk briskly, heading for their afternoon shifts. Gale, dressed in workout clothes, trots down the steps and waves to several of her coworkers as she heads in our direction. She's a vibrant thirty-year-old with a crown of dark, curly hair and an olive complexion. She's suggested we join her for a walk along one of her favorite riverfront trails where she likes to relax after her high-stress work in the intensive care unit. "We'll have plenty of privacy," she promises as she leads the way. Indeed, all the other walkers and runners within earshot are wearing headphones.

Gale decided to meet with us after her marriage counselor mentioned our research. "Sexual fantasy is what got me into therapy a few months ago," she explains now, "and I still find it too hard to talk about in any detail with my husband, my girlfriends, my counselor, or just about anyone else. I hope maybe I'll learn something reassuring from your research."

Gale and her husband, married nearly nine years, are childless by choice and spend their free time enjoying mutual interests in the outdoors. "We've always been close, and I'm sure that I love my husband," Gale says, "but for the last couple years, our sex life has been rocky. I've been avoiding sex for months now, and I haven't been able to tell Darren why." If he reaches for her in bed, even if it's just for a good-night hug, Gale finds herself swatting his hands away.

What Darren doesn't know is that Gale can't get interested in sex unless she fantasizes that another woman is making love to her. She especially likes to imagine scenes of oral sex and gets turned on by imagining a partner with a perfect body, "someone like Cindy Crawford, although I don't pay much attention to her face. I imagine a flat stomach and the curves of her breasts and hips." The same fantasy comes up if she masturbates and reliably leads to orgasm. Because she's so confused about what the fantasy means, though, Gale has been trying to avoid getting aroused.

"It's been a terrible struggle to figure out what's going on with me," she says. "Am I gay? And, if not, why can't I get turned on by realizing I'm in bed with Darren? Just the thought of staying in the present with him during sex terrifies me." Indeed, the last time they made love, Gale pulled a pillow over her face so she wouldn't see Darren. "I guess my body enjoyed it, but I totally blacked out in my mind. I was so upset afterward that I haven't been able to have sex with him since. That was two weeks ago."

Although they haven't yet talked directly about Gale's fantasies, she and Darren have acknowledged their bedroom crisis. Before they went to a counselor, they tried reading sexual enrichment books together. Gale was afraid to look at the drawings, though, for fear that she'd get turned on by the images of women's bodies. So far, she hasn't been able to explain her confusion to Darren. "He's such a gentle, sweet guy, and he so wants to please me. He's willing to hear any suggestions about what I want to do in bed," Gale says, but she has trouble talking openly. She used to enjoy oral sex, for instance, but now resists letting Darren stimulate her that way. "I can't get past my fears to really open up with him. I'm afraid what he might think of me."

Before we talk more specifically about her fantasies, we ask Gale to tell us more about her sexual history, especially anything that might have been a source for her persistent erotic thoughts about women.

"I grew up in a Florida beach town, and I guess I've always enjoyed looking at women's bodies," she begins. "I loved walking up and down the beach. I remember the smell of suntan lotion in the air. There was incredible sexual energy, with everyone wearing only these skimpy bathing suits. There were plenty of cute guys, but I focused on the women's bodies. Who had a better figure than I did? How did I compare? That was my main worry as a teenager."

In her high school locker room, Gale remembers stealing looks at other girls' bodies, comparing their anatomy with her own. "It was a pretty WASP-ish community, and I have a rather dark complexion. I noticed that I was the only girl with dark nipples, and wondered what was wrong with me."

At home, sex was never a topic, Gale says. "My dad was an

alcoholic, and my mom was uptight about sex. She always said it was just for sluts." She remembers how her body made her feel like the odd one in the family. "My two sisters were close to my age, but they were kind of skinny, boyish and flat-chested, like my mom. I was the only one with much of a bust, and my whole family always made comments about my body. When I was little, I remember my dad pulling down my swimsuit so my tan line would show and calling me his Coppertone girl."

In her teens, as her figure developed, Gale's sisters warned her she was getting fat. "As my hips got wider and my waist smaller, they told me I had a big butt." Gale has looked at photographs of herself from that time and can see now what an attractive, hourglass figure she had. "But I was so critical of myself. To this day," she says, shaking her head in resentment, "my family still makes the biggest deal over my weight. If I lose ten pounds, they all mention it."

In high school, Gale would often sneak out with friends for evening beach parties that included beer and marijuana. "I got drunk for the first time when I was in the fifth grade, and I tried pot in the eighth grade. By fifteen, I was stoned all the time. Pot created kind of a fantasy for me, where I didn't feel like I was in my body. I could enjoy feeling sexual and attractive, and didn't feel guilty about it." Gale remembers how her defenses melted away when she got stoned. "I'd get relaxed then, and could enjoy making out with boys. It was pretty innocent at first, just kissing and petting with our clothes on."

At sixteen, Gale fell for a man she had met on the beach. He was in his twenties. "I went to bed with him because I wanted him to love me, too. I didn't enjoy sex with him, but I was afraid he would leave me otherwise." In fact, he did leave as soon as he learned that Gale was pregnant. When her mom discovered that Gale had had an abortion, "she chased me around the house and called me a slut." What Gale didn't discover until years later was that her mother's first child—Gale's older sister—had been conceived out of wedlock.

After her abortion, Gale avoided relationships for a couple years. If she was stoned and lonely, she often had Pretty Maiden fantasies in which she would imagine being wooed by a man who "looked like Prince Charming." Then, at eighteen, she met a new boyfriend, Steve, who was handsome and sexually adventuresome. He liked to have sex in places where they might be seen, such as the back room of the store where Gale worked. And, unlike anyone she had met before, he was fascinated by sexual fantasies.

"The first time I ever fantasized about a woman was a result of Steve. That was one of his fantasies, for him to watch me make love with another woman. We never acted it out, but he would talk me through the whole fantasy while he and I were having sex. He would tell me everything that he would be seeing in his imagination. He imagined that he would be sitting in a big chair, watching me and another woman give each other oral sex. He'd get so turned on by that idea."

Gale found herself getting turned on, as well. "It felt like we could trust each other, because he was sharing so much with me," she remembers. Yet, Steve wanted even more from her. "He was always pressing me, trying to find out what else he could do to please me. I was so inexperienced. He was only the second man I'd ever slept with. I was embarrassed to talk about sex. I just said, whatever you're doing feels great. And it did. I looked forward to having sex with him. I felt really passionate."

When Steve kept pushing her to open up more, she related an incident to him that she had never shared with anyone. "I told him about a girl in eighth grade who had touched me sexually one night when I was sleeping over at her house. I pretended to be asleep and not know what she was doing, but really, I was excited. It felt good."

A few months later, when Steve and Gale broke up, he used that secret against her. "He told me I was gay. He said that was why I didn't know what I wanted in bed, and that was why I had liked it when that girl had touched me. For months, he had been feeding me fantasies about me and another woman. Then, he twisted everything all around and threw it back in my face."

Shortly before she broke up with Steve, Gale had a second abortion. "I remember exactly when I got pregnant the second time. I didn't have any birth control with me, and neither did he. We had gone to this crescendo of passion, and I just went with it. I said to him, 'Don't worry about it.' He assumed that meant I was on the pill, but I wasn't. I was completely in the moment. I remember making eye contact with him throughout sex and really enjoying myself. I was totally present." When she learned she was pregnant a second time, however, Gale plummeted into a major depression.

Her father, who by then had been sober for several years, helped get her into a drug treatment program. Gale began attending AA meetings and started to feel that she was turning her life around.

Yet, although Gale felt like her life was improving, her sex life has never been the same. The last time she ever felt like she could let go in sex was when she got pregnant. "When I have sex with my husband now, I feel like I'm hanging back, on my guard. I'm afraid to feel passionate. I'm terrified to look Darren in the eye, because I'd be acknowledging that I do want to have sex. Just the thought of that makes my heart pound," she says. She chokes up, stops walking, and drops onto a park bench. "I'm terrified of getting pregnant again," she says between sobs. "And the last time I was completely into sex, I got pregnant. I can't let that happen, not ever again."

As she regains her composure, we talk with Gale about what her erotic fantasies of women might mean. One observation draws her full attention: a woman can't get pregnant from oral sex, or from having sex with another woman. "That's it!" Gale says. "That makes so much sense." Suddenly, she can see how her same-sex fantasy protects her from her fear of another unwanted pregnancy. As we talk further, Gale sees sources for her female fantasies dating back to her teens, when she had a natural interest in the beauty of the female body. At eighteen, when she was having her first orgasms, Steve introduced her to his lesbian sex fantasy. She can see how her early erotic associations were shaped by Steve's fantasies about oral sex between women. She adds, "It makes sense, too, that a woman would know best how to give another woman oral sex. Here are all these possible reasons for my fantasy," Gale says, "and not one of them seems to point to my orientation."

When we leave Gale for the afternoon, she promises to keep us posted on any changes in her fantasy life. She also mentions that she and Darren have recently decided to take a deliberate vacation from sex, while they build a new foundation for intimacy. At their counselor's suggestion, they're going to start using some sex therapy exercises that gradually progress from nonsexual to more erotic touch and teach couples new skills for communication.[1]

About four months later, as promised, Gale phones with an update. She sounds excited.

"Darren and I have made wonderful progress," she begins. During their agreed-upon break from sex, they have learned to touch one another in new ways that help them appreciate and explore each other's bodies. Gale finds that she loves to touch her husband's smooth, hairless chest. "I've realized just how muscular and masculine he is," she says. "Before, when I was thinking about women, I never really appreciated his body." At night, they often fall asleep entwined in each other's arms.

Gale has also learned how to start talking with Darren more directly about sex. In turn, she has listened to Darren express his own concerns about being sexually inexperienced. "I was so terrified to tell him about my fantasies," Gale adds, "but I finally worked up my nerve. When I told him I get turned on by watching women's bodies, he just grinned and said that he does, too."

During their several months without sexual contact, Gale felt herself growing hungry for Darren's touch. Kissing became a major turn-on for her. "Darren began showing up in my dreams, and I would wake up aroused and wanting him," she explains. After a dream she had last week, she finally decided she was ready and eager to resume having sex with her husband.

"In my dream, Darren and I were on a vacation in Paris. I had wandered alone down this boulevard, and found my way into a dress shop. I was standing in front of the mirror, admiring myself in a beautiful French gown that really showed off my body. I looked up, and there was Darren, watching me from the street." In her dream, Gale waved her husband inside the shop and asked him, "How did you find me?" He said, "I thought I might find you here." Then, Darren held out a delicious-looking French pastry, a long, chocolate-covered, cream-filled éclair. Gale took her time, licking her lips and savoring each bite while maintaining eye contact with her husband. "I woke up feeling so happy that he had been part of my dream," Gale says, "and I knew that the éclair represented something more than just fine French pastry."

When she told Darren about her dream, she was able to explain to him how her fear of pregnancy had made her afraid to really receive his sexual attention. She also told Darren that she had been bottling up her own passion, and that she was afraid of overwhelming him with her sexuality. "He told me, not only could he handle it, but he was looking forward to sharing it," Gale laughed. "He said I made him feel like a stud."

Soon after that, Gale and Darren made love again. "I didn't try to avoid my old fantasies," she says, "but they just didn't come up this time. Darren reminded me to breathe and stay present. When it was over, I realized that all I had been thinking about while we made love was the two of us."

JANE'S STORY:
A PATH TO A SATISFYING RELATIONSHIP

On a Sunday in autumn, Jane is enjoying a rare afternoon at home by herself. Her son, in his early teens, has just left for a movie. She waves us to a seat in her living room where books from this semester's literature classes are piled into precariously tall stacks. As she puts on hot water for tea, Jane explains that a friend from college told her about our fantasy research, and she decided on an impulse to share her story. She enters the room with a tray of steaming teacups, drops onto a large floor pillow, and yawns. "I'm a little tired today," she says, stretching out her long legs. "I'm almost thirty-seven years old, a single parent, and here I am back in school. My son and I race to see who gets to use the computer first at night. I'm working so hard, but this is exactly what I want to be doing with my life right now."

Jane has traveled far from her childhood in Boston, where she attended parochial schools, wore neatly pressed uniforms, and grew up with the message that even thinking about sex was bad for the soul. "The nuns used to tell us we were accountable for our thoughts. We were not supposed to have sexual pleasure, even in our minds." Now, here she sits in her favorite blue jeans and a colorful, snug-fitting T-shirt that shows off her womanly curves, about to divulge her favorite masturbatory fantasies. "Pretty ironic, huh?" she laughs.

As she begins to tell her story, Jane explains that she can't relate how much her fantasies have taught her without also describing the different kinds of relationships she has had with men. Although it's taken her years to solve the riddle, fantasy has been giving her important information about the qualities she yearns to find in a life partner.

Jane pulls a dog-eared scrapbook from a bookshelf and thumbs through to find a picture of herself as a shy-looking teenager. Puffy, blond bangs hang low on her face, almost hiding her wide brown eyes. Although her face looks young, her body is quite mature. In the picture, taken in front of her suburban home, she's arm in arm with a taller, older, and very muscular boy.

"I will never forget Ed, my first boyfriend from when I was about fourteen. He was so good-looking, I couldn't believe he was interested in me. I was only a freshman, and he was a senior. After we'd been going out for a few weeks, I told my mom I was thinking about having sex with him. Actually, it was Ed's idea. That was all he ever talked about. My mom freaked out. She said, no, don't, it's horrible. Then she described her honeymoon night to me. It was basically a rape scene. I was too young to hear that, especially when she told me that was the night I was conceived. That blew my mind, hearing that I was the product of marital rape."

Soon after that conversation, Jane's boyfriend told her he was tired of waiting and forced her to have sex in the back of his car. She didn't dare tell her mother how she had lost her virginity. Instead, she dried her tears and took to heart the message she had been hearing at home and in school: "Men are animals. They can't help themselves, once they get aroused. It's a woman's duty to accommodate men's sexual needs, but she shouldn't expect to like it."

Not until she was eighteen did Jane have her first experience with an explicit sexual fantasy. Although she'd had a series of lovers by then, she had never climaxed with any of them. The only kind of sex she had experienced was fast and rough, like her boyfriends.

"Then I met a new guy who was really into masturbation. He did it all the time, and he said it turned him on to watch me touch myself, too. I figured out that my thoughts had a lot to do with stimulating my body. If I just sat there and touched myself, it would take a long time to climax. But if I started thinking stuff, I would get aroused much faster." She focused on the only kind of sexual imagery she could imagine: male genitals. "I pictured a man getting hard, and that would turn me on." Yet, even though she climaxed as a result, Jane felt as if she was performing for her boyfriend, not for her own pleasure.

Gradually, though, Jane began experimenting with touching herself when no one was watching. "That was the real birth of fantasizing for me. It was a big step, just letting go of guilt long enough to have my own fantasies. I finally realized, I can think whatever the hell I want to think, and it doesn't hurt anybody. That helped me get past the guilt."

She also discovered that expanding her thoughts could increase her sexual pleasure. Although she was still having sex with a partner who rushed through the act, she could imagine slowing down the stimulation in her fantasies, giving herself the time she needed to get aroused. "My orgasm would spread and encompass more of my body, not just my clitoris. I'd feel things more deeply, sometimes all the way to my arms and head and toes, and I liked that." She started locking herself into the bathroom at home for long, relaxing baths, so she could have the privacy to explore her body and experiment with different fantasies. An early favorite was imagining that she was on a honeymoon in Hawaii, spending hours playing with her fully erect husband.

Jane flips forward several pages in the scrapbook to find her wedding picture. She's twenty-two and barefoot, wearing a flowing, embroidered cotton dress and a wreath of wildflowers in her long hair. Her husband, Mark, is tanned and rugged from working outdoors. They're standing in front of their new home: a cabin in the woods of the Pacific Northwest, near the logging camp where Mark led a work crew. The polished chrome of his motorcycle glistens behind them in the afternoon light.

Looking at the photo, Jane is flooded with memories from a troubled marriage that lasted most of a decade. "I was so young. Like all the guys I seem to attract, Mark was pretty rough around the edges. We met in a pool hall where we used to party, drink beer and dance to rock music. I had left home, traveled across the country, and was barely scraping by as a waitress. I thought Mark was my ticket to happiness."

Instead, she found herself in a marriage that echoed her parents' unhappy relationship. Like Jane's father, Mark was critical and demanding. "He never hit me, but he beat me up verbally all the time. He said awful things to me. When he got annoyed, he called me a stupid, ugly bitch. He made me feel like I never did anything right. And he was insanely jealous. If any other guy so much as looked at me, Mark would blow up. At first, I thought that was a sign of how much he loved me. After a while, though, it wore me out."

Their sex life was active, but unsatisfying to Jane. "Like all the other guys I've been with, Mark made love hard, fast, and often. I've had a lot of sex, but I've never had what I consider to be a good sexual relationship with a man. I seem to attract these hard-core guys like a magnet. I've wondered if it's something I project." During her marriage, Jane's fantasies were unscripted and visually graphic, usually focused on male anatomy. She always relied on fantasy to get her to orgasm.

Their son was born a couple years into the marriage, and Jane tried to make the relationship work for his sake. "As bad as things were with Mark, our marriage was the best relationship I'd had up to that point in my life." Gradually, as she became more interested in reading about philosophy and spirituality, Jane started imagining a different kind of life for herself and her son. "I started thinking, maybe if I could value myself more, maybe then I could attract someone who's nicer, kinder, more spiritually oriented. Someone more like I am."

After she and Mark broke up, Jane decided to give herself some time without a partner. She moved with her son from their rural home to a larger city and started taking women's studies classes at a local community college. "And around that time," she recalls, "my fantasies began to change. I don't know where this came from, but I started thinking a lot about women's bodies. I got much more turned on than with my old fantasies of men's bodies." Although she was a little uncomfortable with these images at first, her new fantasies did not cause Jane to question her orientation. "I understood, somehow, that it was like a celebration of being female for me. I felt like I had entered a new phase of honoring my own femaleness, bathing in the beauty of full breasts, soft, round bellies, and the mysterious crimson folds of the vaginal lips. I knew I still liked men's bodies. But I realized, if I'm giving myself pleasure, it helps to think about what makes a female body feel good. I don't understand what a man feels, but I do know what a woman needs to feel good."

Until two years ago, Jane avoided any new relationships. "I only had sex by myself, with my new female-focused fantasies and my vibrator." During this period of celibacy, when she was also beginning full-time studies at a university, Jane tried to make time for enjoying her fantasy life. At night when her son was asleep, she sometimes turned her bedroom into a fantasy stage, lighting scented candles that added to the sensual mood. She smoothed lotion onto her bare skin, enjoying the soft, silky feel of her voluptuous female body. "It took me years to expand past my early, quick fantasies about men's bodies. These more gentle, sensuous thoughts helped me learn to slow down."

Then, after a time of being away from men, Jane started having occasional, casual sex with a good male friend. "I knew I wasn't going to have a long-term relationship with him, but he wasn't like a stranger, either. Every few months, we'd just go to bed together. He had a sweet, gentle side that appealed to me, and sex was different with him than with the men I used to sleep with. Before, it was always the man getting his needs met then rolling off me. Those guys wouldn't object if I had a good time, but they never bothered to help me out much, either. This man, though, was a sweet lover, very patient and gentle. That felt really different for me." In retrospect, Jane sees that her female sexual fantasies had helped prepare her for being able to enjoy a different style of lovemaking. "I felt more deserving of his touch and attention to my body. For the first time in my life, sex really felt mutual."

Several months ago, however, Jane decided to stop sleeping with him, despite the great sex they had enjoyed together. "I was surprised and hurt one day when he began critiquing me. He told me I was fat, that my breasts sagged, and that he preferred women who had firmer bodies. I've gained a little weight during my thirties, and I've tried hard to stop beating myself up for the way I look. So he really hurt me." What she realized later, however, "was that he didn't crush me. I thought, wow, I must be getting a better sense of myself as a person, for me to be able to hear this and not just crumble. I also realized that he doesn't have such a great body himself. He's sort of a toothpick. He's not at all well built, like the men I've been with in the past. Of course, I'd never say that to him, but I also know I'll never sleep with him again. No way."

Jane has noticed her fantasies changing again as she gives more deliberate thought to the kind of partner she wants to spend the rest of her life with. "I've moved on to imagining myself in a sexual relationship with a different kind of man than the ones I used to be with. I'll pick out someone wonderful, like an actor, and attach all my feelings to him in fantasy. It's such a crush. When I imagine having sex with him, it's like we're really in bed together. I can feel him on top of me, penetrating me, wrapping his arms around me."

Jane turns a few more pages in her scrapbook and points to a picture of one of her favorite crushes: the actor Patrick Swayze. "He has such a great body, and I've always been attracted to good-looking men," she says, "but that's not what really draws me to him. It's the kind of *person* he is." Jane flips through stories she has clipped out of magazines, reading snippets that reveal Swayze's sense of humor and tidbits about his family life. "He seems like such a genuine, sweet man, really devoted to his wife," she says. "And from what I see in the pictures, she's not a Hollywood bimbo."

Just last night, Jane reveals, she had a dream about the actor. "He was miraculously single and dancing seductively with me. I had a wonderful orgasm. What's great about dreams, of course, is that I'm so free. There's no guilt, no second thoughts about whether I'm a worthy partner. I'm just there with him, enjoying his sexual attention."

Although she's a free spirit in her sexual dreams, Jane sometimes notices self-doubts creeping into her fantasies, just when they start to get steamy, and ruining the mood. She still struggles with the idea that the kind of man she wants to be with would find her desirable, just as she is. While her erotic dreams usually take her all the way to orgasm and feel delightful, her self-critical fantasies can interrupt her sexual response, leaving her depressed.

Lately, Jane has been experimenting with a new fantasy script. Instead of fantasizing about an actor she's unlikely to ever meet, she's been imagining a relationship with her English professor. She finds him incredibly intelligent and attractive. Although he's never made a sexual overture toward her, she said, "I can totally imagine the warmth of his body in bed next to me. He has these wonderful, caring eyes, and it feels like he's looking right into my soul." However, in real life, Jane has decided she would never want to have an affair with him. "Because he's my teacher, we could never truly be peers." Through fantasy, she's been able to figure out that she wants a real relationship where both partners feel like equals.

As she closes her scrapbook, Jane turns her thoughts on the future instead of the past. "Where I want to go next, in my life, is to find a real partner who is able to appreciate my sensuality, the beauty inside this body of mine. I don't want to have to measure up to some standard of what a perfect female looks like, or feel like I have to act a certain way for someone else to get excited about me." Fantasy has given her a sense of what it would feel like to let a man truly get to know her, body and soul. Jane sees that, even the fantasies she has rejected as too far-fetched, starring Patrick Swayze or her gorgeous English professor, have been paving the way for a healthy relationship in real life. She feels more confident about what she has to offer a partner, and more deserving of the kind of mutual caring that has so far eluded her in real life.

A month before our interview, Jane started getting better acquainted with Todd, a philosophy student about her age who also is rethinking his dreams and hoping to find a meaningful relationship. So far, they've gone on some long walks and have enjoyed talking over coffee until late at night. Their kisses have been sweet, and Jane especially likes the way Todd greets her with a big bear hug. Yet, she feels in no hurry for their relationship to become more sexual. For once, she says, "I've promised myself to take my time." When she feels sexual tension building, she uses fantasy for release and as a place to rehearse the kind of sexual interaction she'd like to enjoy with Todd, eventually.

"I'm slowly building a picture in my mind about the experience I want to share with Todd. I imagine candlelight and music. My room would be neat and tidy instead of cluttered. We'd talk, and we'd have sex, and we'd have more conversation, and lots more holding and cuddling, and more sex. I can picture all that happening with him, and I can believe that I really deserve it."

In fact, Jane has to wrap up our interview because she's meeting Todd tonight for dinner. As she puts her scrapbook away, she turns with one last thought. "It's going to be a committed, long-term relationship for me next, or nothing. I've had plenty of casual sex, and I don't want that again. I want to find someone who accepts me, just as I've learned to accept myself. And I want to share all my sexuality with only him. I don't want to dilute my energy with more than one person. There's no other way we could truly be partners. I have so much to give."

For Jane, fantasy has been like a mentor, teaching her to better understand and appreciate herself. Almost by chance, she discovered early in life that she was turned on by visual images of male bodies. As she later sought to enrich her sexual experience, she wove more sensual, female imagery into her erotic thoughts. That phase in her fantasy life helped her accept and honor the beauty of her own body and made her realize she was deserving of a loving partner's attention. Now, she understands that she wants a partner in life whose love will be passionate but will also go well beyond sex. When she takes that step, she'll be turning the best of her fantasies into reality. "What's amazing," Jane adds, "is that all this knowledge has come from inside of me. Fantasies have given me access to my own inner wisdom."

BRYNN'S STORY:
A PATH TO INNER STRENGTH

Brynn walks briskly into the waiting area, offering a warm smile and a firm handshake. "Sorry my hands are so cold," she says. "I guess I'm nervous about this." On the way to her office, where she counsels women who are getting out of prostitution, we walk past a bulletin board. Here, her clients post messages to one another, spreading the word about dangerous johns who shop for sex on the streets of this large East Coast city.

"WATCH OUT for Dave—about 30, tall, with a gold tooth and dragon tattoo. Drives a black Lincoln. Talks sweet, but he's mean," reads one note written in an urgent hand. Another, penciled onto a dog-eared scrap of paper, warns women to be wary of a white police detective with a paunch and a thin mustache: "He'll use you, beat you, and then deny it. A woman hater. BE CARE-FUL."

Brynn, forty-seven, with curly, brownish hair turning gray at the temples, knows from experience that there's neither romance nor a Prince Charming waiting for women on the streets. The popular film *Pretty Woman* got it all wrong, Brynn insists. "From all that I've seen, the whole sex industry does terrible harm and violence to women." Although it's been more than twenty years since she stopped selling her body, she remembers in chilling detail how much danger she faced every time she took money for sex.

Settling into her office chair, Brynn says she's been giving careful thought to the evolution of her fantasies. In some surprising ways, she credits fantasy with helping her become a stronger, healthier person. However, she's also wary of exposing her most personal thoughts in an interview. "I wouldn't want some perpetrator to read my story and use it to jerk off," she says. She refuses to let herself be used, ever again, for the sake of satisfying a male sex fantasy. She takes off her glasses, rubs her eyes, and gathers her thoughts. After a moment, she takes a deep breath and begins to tell her story.

She got started in prostitution in her late teens by following the lead of an older woman. "I had just left home, after a horrible childhood. My dad had died when I was ten, after being sick for years. It had always been my job to be a good, quiet girl and help take care of him. There was never any joy in my life. Then, after he died, my stepbrother started sneaking into my room at night and molesting me. By the time I was a teenager, I felt like such a piece of shit. I'd often masturbate, using fantasies of sexual violence. On the streets, I met a woman who's Jewish, like I am, and a junkie, and a prostituted woman. And I thought to myself, 'Oh, boy, I'm finally coming home.' I had never felt more connected or safe with anyone. She wasn't really a pimp, but she guided me into the life."

In much the same way, Brynn says, pimps continue to prey on women who look like they're hurting. "Women walk into the bus station with their shoulders hunched, their heads down, carrying some terrible weight, and you know they haven't been loved much. Pimps will come in with this promise of love, and that's how so many young people get pimped. They wind up living the fantasy that someone will love them."

Brynn worked in a strip club in the Southwest from her late teens to her early twenties. She remembers it as "a sleazy little place in the back of a porno shop." Before she went to work at the club each night, Brynn used to sit around and get loaded on drugs with the other strippers. "We were all into downers," she recalls, "any kind of downers. I shot heroin for a while. I was always so wrecked." Between porn films, the women would take turns on the dance stage. With her inhibitions loosened by drugs, Brynn wiggled and writhed in ways she had never moved her body before.

Although her body felt loose, her mind clamped shut. "I closed all my fantasies off. I was in so much pain during those years that I disconnected from everything, even my own thoughts. I was just fucking so much, I didn't have time to fantasize about sex, you know?"

It's not that she was unaware of sexual fantasies during those years. "The manager encouraged us to watch porn, so we'd know what men's fantasies were like." Indeed, she now realizes, her head was so full of male fantasies, she had no time to entertain her own sexual thoughts. "That's what happens in prostitution. It's a male fantasy, and women get hooked into it. Acting out their fantasies was my job. I didn't have the slack time to make up any new ones for myself."

When it would be Brynn's turn to dance, she recalls, "I'd have the length of one song to take off all my clothes. Maybe three minutes. Then, I'd be the only naked woman in a room full of drunk men. Talk about vulnerable."

Although the customers were supposed to keep their hands off the women, Brynn says, "that was a big joke." When she wasn't stripping, she averaged two or three customers an hour. "I was giving fifteen blow jobs a day, easy, and being penetrated a couple times a day. Some men think, if they pay you, they can penetrate you with their penis, their gun, their boot, or whatever else they damn well please. Every once in a while, somebody would rape me at knife point. I don't know how I made it out alive." She adds bitterly, "I never enjoyed sex with any of those men. Never."

In the years since she left that life, Brynn has realized, "you have to be in touch with yourself somewhere, on some level, to even have fantasies. And I wasn't." Many of the women she counsels now, who are taking their first steps out of prostitution, are as shut off from their own thoughts as she once was. "To be a prostitute, a woman has to be cut off from herself. She can't let her heart get involved. It's a desperate life, and a woman has to stop herself from feeling in order to survive it."

Brynn pauses for a moment, and the glad shrieks of children at play drift down the hallway from an office day-care center. Her walls are colorful with the bold crayon drawings made by her clients' children. She leans forward to pick up from the floor a pair of red arm pads she uses to practice kung fu and other self-defense moves. Then, she continues her story.

For Brynn, healing from a lifetime of abuse and trauma didn't begin until long after she stopped working the streets. Her family got her out of prostitution by having her committed to a mental hospital, against her will, where she was given shock treatments and more drugs. "I was numb the whole time I was institutionalized. I don't remember having one fantasy while I was in that hospital."

Eventually, though, she moved into a halfway house where her recovery began in earnest. With the help of a psychiatrist, she broke through the wall that she had built up around her. "I learned how to communicate again, to stop feeling numb. For the first time, I stopped seeing life through wounded eyes. I think of that time as the start of my liberation from a life of abuse."

With her therapist's help, Brynn was able to see how she had developed sexual arousal patterns to thoughts of violence and exploitation. That new awareness helped her understand and accept her old Victim fantasies without shame.

And almost overnight, her fantasy life began anew. "It was different now, though. Always before, I had been the loser in my fantasies. I was always getting hurt or raped or penetrated. Now, I saw that I had other choices."

Tapping into her long-dormant imagination, she began creating romantic fantasies about being loved and expressing tenderness with a woman partner. She came out as a lesbian around that time, and her new fantasies celebrated a feeling of connection with other women. As she started enjoying real sexual experiences with other women, her same-sex fantasies became more explicit and erotic. "Suddenly, I was feeling turned on everywhere in my life. I started to feel whole again."

In the years since then, Brynn has used fantasy more deliberately to stay connected with her deepest feelings and resolve issues from her troubled past. One recurring fantasy, which she is working to change, offers her a way to cope with the painful memory of her stepbrother's abuse.

"In this fantasy, I replay the moment when he's coming into my room late at night. I'm supposed to be asleep. I feel that excitement from the attention that he gave me during the abuse, and an adrenaline rush because I know something's going to happen. As awful as it feels, I know that this fantasy helps me get more conscious about that piece of my history. I understand now that my body responded during the abuse, while I pretended to be asleep, and that I felt horrible about that. Fantasy gives me a place to keep working on my healing, where it's safe and where I'm in control." Eventually, when she feels ready, Brynn wants to try changing her fantasy script so that she imagines herself sitting up in bed and yelling at her stepbrother, "What the fuck are you doing in my room?"

Another occasion when fantasy delivers a message is when Brynn visits her family. "When I go home, I have trouble feeling powerful and whole. Consequently, a certain rape fantasy always comes up. I even look forward to it and set the stage for it to unfold."

Brynn breaks into a broad grin, shaking her head as if amazed by her own reaction. When she starts talking again, she can't stop smiling, even though she knows it seems incongruous with her story. Usually, this fantasy begins when, in real life, she's lying on the beach in a bathing suit, feeling the warmth of the sun. "I imagine that this gang of men comes up to me on the beach. They say mean things to me. Then they hold me down and all take turns raping me." In this Victim fantasy, Brynn is replaying the old arousal patterns about violence that she learned earlier in life.

Instead of feeling helpless or overwhelmed, though, "when I have this fantasy now, I turn onto my stomach on a beach towel and masturbate against a hard lump in the sand until I climax."

In her work as a counselor, Brynn hears horror stories every day from women who have been sexually victimized. Those true stories never turn her on. Only in fantasy, where she pulls all the strings, does she let herself get aroused by thoughts of being sexually dominated. "In my beach fantasy, nothing feels brutal. Although I'm being attacked, I feel powerful because I survive what they do to me. They think they're controlling and hurting me, but I'm really using them to get off. It's just exciting, terribly exciting." She thinks for a moment, then adds, "Perhaps this fantasy is my sweet revenge against everyone who's ever used me."

Brynn's favorite recurring fantasy doesn't appear to be sexual at all. Yet, it delivers incredible, erotic pleasure. Unlike her Victim fantasies, which often coincide with masturbation, this one is a sexual daydream without any accompanying stimulation. It often percolates into her thoughts when she's out for a walk.

"I imagine that I'm walking through a park. A strange man approaches, and I can't really make out his face. In fact, in all my fantasies, it's only my stepbrother who has a real face. So, some faceless man comes at me. All sorts of things might happen next, but I'll tell you about three possible endings. In one, I make eye contact, but he keeps coming at me. So I make a loud, sudden noise, and he's startled and runs off. I feel powerful."

In another version, Brynn explains, she tries talking to the attacker in her counseling role. "I say things like, 'I know you've probably been hurt. You must be feeling powerless, too, and that's why you're doing this.' I flood him with compassion, telling him that hurting me will only shut him off more from his best humanity. He listens to me, and then walks away. That ending feels good to me, too, but it's not my favorite."

As she tells the third version of her fantasy, Brynn is almost out of her seat with excitement. She talks fast, gesturing wildly with her arms as she describes the ensuing battle. "In my very favorite version, the man comes at me, and I use all my self-defense moves. I rip at his face, scratching his eyes. When he bends down to grab his face in pain, I knee him in the head. I do a headlock and pull him to the ground. I keep going, until he's literally lifeless, facedown in the dirt."

Brynn's fantasy gets more complex when she imagines the police arriving on the scene. As their sirens blare and lights flash, she tells them how the man attacked her and how she fought back. Instead of standing hunched over like a frightened victim, she walks tall, aware of her strength. "They don't even think of charging me with murder. Instead, they call the media. I'm a hero."

In the final scene of her fantasy, Brynn poses for the television crews. She stands victorious over her attacker, who turns out to be a notorious sex offender. She imagines herself with her foot on his back and one arm raised high in the air. "I have this amazing sense of justice. I feel a glow all over my body. I'm flushed with it. I feel sexually charged and very, very alive."

Brynn's strongest erotic associations still relate to violence and power. But in her favorite fantasy, she's no victim. She's a fighter and a valiant protector of other women, just like the strong person she has become in real life.

❦

Gale, Jane, and Brynn have all discovered that sexual fantasies are a valuable resource, worth listening to throughout life. Not only have they gathered important insights about themselves by reflecting on their fantasy lives, but they have gone on to consciously apply what they have learned. If we choose, all of us can similarly benefit from putting the messages of our fantasies to work.

Reflecting on our own fantasy lives involves thinking about all the different fantasies we've created, noticing how they change with new experiences and how we've used them at different stages of our lives. It's as if we're taking a seat on a garden bench and gazing at the inner world our unconscious mind has created. As we look over this landscape with an uncensoring eye, we can ask ourselves some questions to help us detect patterns and connections, such as:

- How have my sexual fantasies evolved over time?
- How do my sexual fantasies relate to the real sexual experiences I've had?
- How have my sexual fantasies influenced my behavior in intimate relationships?
- What types of sexual stimulation occur regularly in my fantasies that I'd like to experience more in real life?

Because these are *sexual* fantasies, after all, it's only natural that we can use them to enhance our sex lives. Some women make quick but important discoveries about their sexual styles by identifying which sensory modes and character roles are most prevalent in their fantasies. Then, they use this information to experiment with new ways of enjoying sex, highlighting the sensory styles and relationship dynamics they naturally love best.

One woman, for instance, has discovered that the visual graphics of fantasy are what take her to climax. Her favorite fantasy involves an erotic striptease scene. Now, instead of always having sex in the dark and relying on the fantasy to get her aroused, she sometimes turns on her bedroom lights and keeps her eyes open while she and her lover slowly undress. Another woman has realized that she often takes on the fantasy role of a Wild Woman who seduces a stranger. Her real sex life has become more exciting since she started trying on the more assertive qualities of her favorite fantasy character when making love with her husband.

In the same way that fantasies give us useful information about sex, they also deliver insights we can bring to our relationships. Some women realize, for instance, that there's a certain level of excitement in their fantasy relationships they would like to add to their real relationships. Studying the contents of fantasies can also help women recognize unresolved grief from old relationships that they need to address so they can more fully enjoy their present relationships.

In addition, we can look closely at our fantasies to understand how we feel about ourselves sexually. If our fantasies give us a model of a woman who openly embraces her sexual energy, then we can be inspired by it to feel more deserving of the same pleasure in real life.

Once we've surveyed the big picture of our fantasy lives, we may feel intrigued. We may be curious about the meaning of certain fantasies. Next, we'll describe some tools and techniques that can help us get a better view of a particular fantasy. As we'll see in the next chapter, zooming in for a close-up look at a fantasy often leads to even more surprising and significant personal discoveries.

CHAPTER 7

Guided Explorations

Exploring sexual fantasies often leads to what we call "Aha!" moments, when we make an important connection between our fantasies and the rest of our lives. Sometimes, these epiphanies offer us key insights about ourselves that we can then use more deliberately to enhance passion and pleasure.

We don't have to wait for these breakthroughs to happen on their own. A more direct and active approach to exploring the contents of our sexual fantasies can help us bring new insights to light.

One guided exploration technique that many women find helpful is to imagine putting a particular fantasy on stage. It's no accident that we've used a theatrical metaphor for examining the contents of our sexual fantasies in a more deliberate, conscious way. After all, it was a woman named Anna O., one of the first patients to undergo psychoanalysis, who first described her fantasy life as a "private theater."

She coined a lasting phrase that all women can benefit from using. We *are* the playwrights of our own sexual fantasies, selecting the plot, themes, characters, and setting, all for the most personal of reasons. Sexual fantasies tend to build in tension toward a climax and resolution, just like a well-crafted play. And by imagining our own fantasies on an imaginary stage, we also get a chance to envision the particular kind of theater that best matches our unique imagination—whether it's a laser show, pulsating with lights and sounds, or an Elizabethan stage where the characters speak in poetry.

By choosing to explore the stories and sensations that play out within this theater of the mind, we can tap into a rich resource for learning more about our sexual styles and deepening our self-understanding. In some cases, this guided exploration may also lead to emotional healing. While we all can benefit from learning how to take a closer look at our sexual fantasies, it's up to each of us to decide whether to let our fantasy life remain mysterious and unexplored, or whether we want to open the curtain on a specific fantasy and thoroughly examine what's on stage.

This guided exploration is designed to isolate specific aspects of certain fantasies so that we can examine the details of plot, theme, character, and setting, one at a time. Because fantasies, like dreams, often come richly layered with symbols, the meanings may be disguised or, at least, not obvious. By taking one particular fantasy and looking at the contents from many different angles, we have more opportunities to coax out important and maybe even hidden details.

This active approach often feels like solving a mystery. We hunt for clues that help explain the workings of the erotic imagination. We can ask ourselves nosy questions designed to detect the source of sexual heat in a particular fantasy image, scene, sensation, or theme.

Decoding the contents of our fantasies is something that no one else can do for us, because there is no template or master key to translate these highly personal symbols. Making sense of fantasies requires that we trust our own intuition and not rush to judgment.

Although putting our fantasies on stage can be an effective

way to coax out the details, there's no guarantee how we will feel once we understand all these intricacies. As we'll hear in the following stories, some women are delighted by what they discover. Others are relieved. And some are upset. In analyzing our fantasies so closely, we run the risk of losing the very mystery that has made some fantasies so sexually arousing. At the same time, however, we gain self-knowledge that can help guide us in creating an even more satisfying fantasy life and, perhaps, also improve our sex lives. If we have unwanted sexual fantasies, we can use this same approach as the groundwork for future healing.

※

Karen, a thirty-seven-year-old physical therapist, was motivated to explore her fantasies more thoroughly because she finally felt as if she had found a soul mate in a kind, caring man named Thomas. "I really wanted this relationship to last," she said, "yet I could feel it coming to a head again, just like all the other ones." Because of her confusion about her sexual fantasies, she had been avoiding sex with Thomas even though she longed to feel his touch. "I ate that up. I loved for him to hug me hard, tickle me, and massage my body all over," she said. "But as soon as it got sexual, I shut down to keep my fantasies away." For years, in fact, abstinence had been Karen's only surefire solution to keep her disturbing fantasies out of her head.

Before she met Thomas, Karen kept telling herself that the right man would solve her problem with fantasy. "I kept kidding myself by thinking I'd meet some special guy. We'd be able to make love, and every time it would be wonderful." With the right partner, she hoped to be able to focus on the present during sex, "and stop going off into this other world in my mind where things were going on that felt like the exact opposite of what was really happening in lovemaking."

Once she met Thomas, though, Karen finally realized, "another person can't make my fantasies go away. I have to face them myself." What's more, she decided that her secret fantasy life made her feel dishonest, "even though I always said I wanted to be honest in my relationships."

This time, Karen was determined not to let her fantasies cost her another partner. On the brink of a crisis, she decided to start being more open with herself about the sexual fantasies that had confused her since she was a little girl. She set out to discover exactly what was playing in this private theater of her mind.

WHAT'S THE PLOT?

We can understand what a particular fantasy has to say by exploring the plot or story line. The plot is often the foundation on which we add many other significant details and layers of meaning.

Although fantasies often feel fleeting and transitory when we experience them, we can capture these thoughts by writing them down or recording them on audiotape. Just by getting the story out in this concrete way, we can remove some of the mystery from our fantasy lives and feel empowered to do more in-depth exploring.

As an important technique for better understanding her fantasy life, Karen decided to keep a journal. By writing down her fantasies, she hoped to reveal the full story of what she was thinking about so often during sex. "When I experience fantasy, it feels like I'm in an altered state," she explained. "It's all feelings and sensations. Nothing happens in words. Because of this, I didn't know how to even begin to search for meaning. I wanted to write it down to get the story out where I could look at it."

Karen's first effort was to write down a vague memory of a fantasy that involved an orgy scene at a stranger's apartment. She started with just the bare thread of a story, but as she continued writing, more details emerged on paper. Sometimes she paused to close her eyes and encourage her memory of the fantasy to unfold.

She kept asking herself leading questions, such as "And *then* what happens?" When she finished, she was surprised to find that her fantasy read like a script, with a plot running from beginning to middle to end. "I'd never been aware of this structure in my conscious thoughts before," she said.

Once Karen wrote out the synopsis of her orgy fantasy, she had a text she could start dissecting. Her next step was to underline the parts of the story she found most arousing, as a way to help identify what function the fantasy was serving for her. Then, she decided to give her fantasy the title "The Apartment Mix-Up." Here's how it read:

> *I'm planning to visit my aunt, but <u>by mistake I knock on the wrong door of an apartment house.</u> A man wearing only a towel answers the door. He's delighted to see me and pulls me inside. Right away, I realize I've entered a wild bachelor party. The host <u>mistakenly assumes I'm a stripper,</u> hired for the evening like another woman I spot across the room. She is already engaged in a group sex scene with several other guests. The man tells me he's been waiting for me, hands me $600, pulls up my sweater, and begins fondling my breasts. <u>I don't have a chance to say a word.</u> Because he's wearing only the towel, it's easy for me to notice his prominent erection. <u>By chance,</u> I'm wearing some sexy new lingerie under my conservative clothes, a fashion statement that the man finds delightful. As the other male guests notice me, they pull me into an orgy scene. The sexual energy reaches a frenzy with men stimulating me from all angles—sucking my breasts, screwing me from behind, grabbing at my butt—until I climax. Then, abruptly, my fantasy stops.*

Once she had captured her "Apartment Mix-Up" fantasy on paper, Karen was surprised to find that she felt different, seeing it in this tangible, black-and-white format. She wasn't so judgmental or ashamed of her fantasy now. It didn't upset her in the way it always had before, when it barged uninvited into her thoughts during sex. Like women who have shared their fantasies at workshops or in interviews, Karen now felt no more embarrassment than if she were pondering a strange dream.

When she thought about what made the fantasy so erotic, Karen recognized how much sexual stimulation her character was receiving from all the men. For the first time, she realized that the visual graphics of sex also played a big role in arousing her. Looking more closely at the story line, she recognized that her character was swept away by the men's desire for her. The woman, a Pretty Maiden, didn't intend to become sexually involved. It just happened, before she could even think of protesting. The parts of the story Karen had underlined as being the most erotic, in fact, all had to do with the chance circumstances that had led up to the sexual encounter.

"Even though this is something I would never choose to get involved in, I see how it's incredibly exciting in fantasy. The beauty of it is that it's all circumstantial," Karen said. "The girl walks into this scene, totally unaware. She didn't set it up, or know what she was getting into. She just knocked on the wrong door. She's not guilty or responsible for getting mixed up in this scene." Once she understood her fantasy in this way, Karen was able to see that it was, in fact, sort of clever. The content had functioned well to help her enjoy sex by taking away guilt feelings about being sexually stimulated.

Karen's fantasy took on the shape of a narrative when she put it into words. When our fantasies are more unscripted, we can write down our impressions of this sensory experience. We might ask ourselves what the sensations feel like, what makes them so erotic, what other experiences they might resemble, or whether the sensations always unfold in a particular way. Once we think about an unscripted fantasy in this way, we may discover that it does unfold along a time line, or at least have a beginning, middle, and end that mimics our sexual response cycle.

One woman, for example, captured the essence of an elusive, sensory fantasy by describing it on paper this way: "When I search for words to describe it, I sense that my lover's kisses fall on my cheeks like <u>big raindrops</u> on a <u>moist summer day. Heat rises</u> in waves through the <u>wetness.</u> My body pulses with energy and the <u>hot blood of desire.</u> As I start to become aroused, these sensations of <u>heat and moisture</u> intensify. I realize that I like sex best when it gets really physical, even a little <u>sweaty.</u>"

By creating this kind of written record, a fantasy becomes less fleeting and easier to examine away from a state of sexual excitement. The writing process also brings fantasies more under our deliberate control. This can be especially helpful for exploring fantasies that feel intrusive or out of control. Karen, for example, had chosen when she wanted to sit down, open a journal, and tune into her own fantasy life. Seeing her fantasy as words on paper, in a contained space, made it feel benign and less threatening. In this form, her fantasy didn't look like something that would have the power to control her. After telling the story of her fantasy, Karen was eager to learn what more she might discover by probing even deeper.

WHAT'S THE THEME?

Next, we can look for a theme or common thread that makes particular fantasies erotic. Even if the specifics of the plot change from one fantasy to the next, or evolve gradually over time, women often discover that their fantasies share a familiar flavor. We often find the themes of our fantasy lives by stepping back from the details and looking for broad patterns and similarities in the content. Power dynamics, for example, may recur in a predict- able way. Characters may look or behave the same way from one fantasy to the next. A particular fantasy role, such as Pretty Maiden, Wild Woman, or Voyeur, may be strongly favored. To appreciate the significance of a recurring theme, we can ask ourselves how it makes us feel, why we find it erotic, and how it may relate to other issues in our lives.

Karen, for example, compared her "Apartment Mix-Up" fantasy with others that she also wrote down in her journal in order to find a theme. "In all these fantasies, no matter what the setting, the girl always gets a lot of attention, even though the men exploit her in the process. In my real-life sexual experiences," she reflected, "I used to let high school boys be sexual with me because I craved their attention. With Thomas, my current partner, our sex life has been the best for me when he has been really attentive. If he takes the time to stroke my hair, cuddle me, wrestle with me, all of that, then I know I'm going to get more pleasure out of the sexual experience." By seeing this pattern, Karen realized that a desire for attention was a common theme in her fantasies, and in her real life.

Heidi, a businesswoman in her twenties, figured out that her fantasies always involve some kind of deceptive sexual activity between an older man and a high school girl. The man might be a teacher and the girl a student whom he keeps after class. "And always, he can't help himself once he is alone with the girl. She is so desirable, he just has to have her. The fact that it's taboo makes it all the more exciting."

For Heidi, the dominant theme of sexual deception occurs on another level, as well. The girl only appears to be innocent so that she can inflame the man's desire. Examining her own role in the fantasy, she saw herself as a Wild Woman, disguising herself as a Pretty Maiden. In real life, she identifies closely with the girl. "I love to lead a man along sexually, letting him think it's all his idea. Really, though, I have everything planned. I always know what I want, and I'm always in control."

After considering the theme of her fantasies, Heidi realized that they reflect her desire to be a sexual adventurer in real life. "I didn't want to turn into my mother, who always seemed uptight and repressed. I never saw her as a good model for how to enjoy sexuality. As a result, I've deliberately gone in the other direction," she said, "seeking out sexual encounters to enjoy."

Patti, a thirty-five-year-old Sunday school teacher, looked at the variations in several fantasies that she at first thought had nothing in common, only to discover that they shared a common theme. Her fantasies also involved deception between a man and a girl. Unlike Heidi, though, Patti had fantasies of being a true Victim. She felt repulsed by seeing herself in this role, even though her fantasies offered a reliable route to orgasm. In one fantasy, Patti would imagine a little girl whose mother has just died. She comes home from school, and a man is there to comfort her. He puts her on his lap and they watch television together. Instead of her favorite cartoon shows, though, they watch pornography. In another fantasy, the little girl and the man are having a picnic on the kitchen floor. It begins playfully, with delicious food and card games, but becomes sexual as the man begins to stroke and touch her genitals. All the while, he whispers encouragement to her. In yet another, Patti fantasizes about the girl taking a bubble bath with the man. Once again, it starts gently and playfully, then leads up to genital touching. "Now we're going inside," the man tells the girl and slips his finger into her vagina.

When she looked at all of these fantasies together, Patti could see the pattern emerging. "The man always pretends to be offering the girl tenderness and kindness, but his caring is just a pretense. It's trickery. He uses it as bait to build up to abusing her," she explained. "The girl really is innocent. She doesn't want sex, she just wants kindness." Patti was able to see that all of her fantasies had been about betrayal, echoing the theme in the books and films she had always found most erotic. Until she described this theme in words, though, she never realized how unfair these scenarios were to the girl. "The girl needed to be protected, and instead she was always getting betrayed and used," she said. For the first time, Patti decided, "This man in my fantasy has no right to keep using the girl this way." The discovery of this theme convinced her that she did not want those thoughts in her head any longer.

Instead of telling the story in detail to understand all about the erotic elements, some women are able to detect the major theme in their fantasy lives by condensing a fantasy to its bare essence. "It's an erotic thriller," one woman explained after she had used this discovery technique, "with the thriller dimension adding to the heart-pounding sexual excitement." Another woman said her favorite fantasies were "like something you would read in a romance novel. It's always about a meeting of two hearts, two souls." A woman whose fantasies end with her becoming a Dominatrix, getting pleased the way she demands, says the theme "is about getting what I want, sort of my sexual coming-of-age drama."

Women often discover that the major theme in their fantasy lives relates to a core issue about being accepted, loved, cared for, or desired, reflecting common human needs. Adrienne, for instance, had a recurring fantasy in which she imagined she was performing an erotic dance for her ex-husband on a kitchen drainboard while he did the dishes. The fantasy bothered her because she feared it meant she still wanted to have sex with her ex-husband. Since her divorce, she had married another man she considers kinder and more compassionate. She would rather that her sexual desires focus on her new husband, instead of her former spouse.

When Adrienne put this fantasy into words, she realized that her character was playing a Dominatrix role, ordering her former husband not only to do the chores but also to perform oral sex on her while his hands were deep in soapy water. She wrote:

> *I imagine that my ex-husband has cooked a wonderful dinner, and I come to the table wearing a topless outfit. My breasts are very large, and he can't take his eyes off them. I tell him he can look at me, but he has to do the dishes first. As he stands at the sink, I get up on the*

drainboard on my hands and knees with my butt toward him. I begin to dance and strip out of the skimpy costume I'm wearing, and he's begging me to let him touch me. I tell him he must finish his work first. While he keeps washing dishes, he tells me how beautiful my cunt is. Finally, I let him go ahead and eat me.

When she compared this fantasy to others, Adrienne realized that they all involved doing something to draw a man's attention. In another fantasy, for instance, she imagined being in an auditorium with bright spotlights shining on her and rows of men watching her give a sales presentation. Instead of paying attention to her presentation, though, the men stared at her large breasts and long, shapely legs.

Considering why she might crave male attention, she blurted out an answer that surprised herself. "I always felt invisible to my father. My mother was a powerful force in my life, but my father was about as engaging as a table. It was like he never even saw me. He was like a piece of furniture in our house." Thinking more about her drainboard fantasy, she suddenly realized how strongly her ex-husband resembled her father in looks and demeanor. Neither man, she also realized, had been able to give her the nonsexual attention she wanted. Yet, in her fantasy life, she had found a way to use her sexual energy to get back at men and temporarily satisfy the need for male attention she had always craved. After this buried message became conscious, Adrienne noticed her reliance on the fantasy gradually diminished. Her new, more appealing sexual thoughts involved sharing a Beloved-type relationship with her current husband.

WHO'S ON STAGE?

Next, we can take a closer look at the characters we fantasize about. It's as if we shine a spotlight to illuminate everything about them and hold up a microphone so we can hear their motives for appearing in our fantasy lives. This way, we gain a better idea of the qualities that are most significant in the characters we have cast in our fantasy scripts.

When Karen looked more closely at the characters in her "Apartment Mix-Up" fantasy, for instance, she realized that no one in her story had a clearly defined face. Although she identified closely with the woman who entered the apartment by mistake, she said, "I realized she's not really me. It's as if I'm watching this woman and feeling whatever she feels. I'm more of a Voyeur. When the woman gets to feel sexual, so do I."

Although Karen could discern very few details about the men's faces, she observed that they all shared a high state of sexual excitement and an attitude that it was okay to use women for their sexual pleasure. In fact, Karen realized, the men's sexual appetites reminded her of her older brother and his interest in pornography. When she was a young girl, her brother often lured her into their basement with his secret stash of skin magazines. Looking back, she recognized those episodes as the start of her fantasy life, and could see how the kind of male sexual energy she first experienced as a girl had been kept alive by her fantasy cast of horny bachelors. These men, like her brother, seemed to express their sexuality off in a separate world, where the normal rules governing behavior didn't apply.

It took some detective work for Karen to flesh out the anonymous men in her fantasies. Other women may more easily recognize the people in their fantasies, but need to dig deeper to figure out why they are there. A young woman named Carla, for instance, didn't have to wonder who was in her favorite fantasy. She knew it featured herself and five of her closest acquaintances. She decided to take a closer look at these characters to see if she could find out why they always appeared in the same sensory-type fantasy.

Carla wrote down a quick summary of her fantasy right after

masturbating, before the details would have a chance to fade from her conscious thoughts:

> *I am myself, on a bed or the floor. This room I'm in is quite dark, although there are candles flickering. Around me are five people, all pleasuring me in different ways.*

Carla then realized that she seldom fantasized while making love with her boyfriend, with whom she enjoyed an active sex life. They had recently moved into an apartment together, and were making long-range plans as a couple. In her masturbatory fantasy, Carla imagined herself receiving sexual pleasure from all five people. She continued describing the fantasy:

> *What's important isn't the setting or plot, but the emotional relationships I have with these people. They are all my closest friends and lovers. One is my current boyfriend, with whom I hope to make a life together. Another is an ex-boyfriend, with whom I had a wild and steamy sexual affair a couple years back. Another is a woman friend who is sex personified, a woman I consider to be a goddess. The fourth is an incredibly sexy and beautiful male poet who is more of a platonic friend (although we did kiss once). The fifth is my best girlfriend from seventh grade. She and I did some sweet sexual exploring together when we were much younger. And me? I am a dead ringer for Kim Basinger in the movie 9 1/2 Weeks, my favorite erotic thriller.*

On one level, Carla's fantasy was boldly erotic, with the five characters all contributing to her sexual pleasure. "They are five sets of mouths, hands, genitals, all at my bidding. They know just how I like it." While she could see how the fantasy functioned to turn up the sexual heat by providing all sorts of physical stimulation, she sensed that it also contained an important emotional message. Each character, Carla realized, contributed one key aspect of what she considered to be an ideal relationship. Each one added a significant piece of the whole.

To figure out what these five special people had to tell her, Carla imagined asking each one to speak to her. Their fantasy monologues proved enlightening. Her current boyfriend said, "I offer you deep love and partnership." Her ex-boyfriend told her, "I give you permission to enjoy wanton, wild sexual pleasure." Her beautiful woman friend said, "I am the kind of sensuous, sexual woman you also want to become." The poet said, "I remind you of the sweet, pure pleasure of friendship." The girlfriend from junior high said, "I teach you about feminine nurturing and tenderness and inspire an adventurous attitude about sex." When Carla imagined giving herself the microphone, she pictured herself saying, "I like sex. In fact, I'm insatiable."

As she thought more about this fantasy, Carla also realized that *she* was the common thread pulling all the other characters together. "These are all people I've had real-life experiences with. In one way or another, each has helped make me into the sexual woman I am today." Furthermore, each character offered Carla something precious that she didn't want to lose or forget. "At this point in my life, when I'm building what I hope will be a lasting relationship with one man," she explained, "I am reminded of all the facets of emotional and sexual connection I want to cultivate in my life."

Instead of wanting to change the fantasy, Carla looked forward to experiencing it again. Now that she understood the multi-layered meaning better, she could imagine enjoying the fantasy on a sexual level, while also continuing to learn more about herself and the emotional connections that are most important to her.

For Elaine, in contrast, the identity of a male lead in a hot Beloved-type fantasy wasn't obvious. It took more detective work to figure out, but left her pleasantly surprised. Married, in her forties, and busy with a professional career, Elaine had been fantasizing during lovemaking "about a young, tall man with a beaded headband and long, dark hair. He lay back on a bed and stared at me as I walked naked before him. What I saw in his eyes was not so much sexual lust, but a deep love and desire to be close to me. Somehow, he knew me. It was a wonderful, erotic fantasy, really pleasurable to experience. This smiling guy, with a noticeable erection under the sheets, was obviously turned on by his love for me. But I was unaware of his real identity. He looked like a cute hippie from the seventies."

As she described her mystery man in more detail, with big, shining blue eyes, full lips, and dark brown hair that fell at a certain angle across his forehead, it dawned on Elaine that she was describing how her husband (now a clean-shaven, well-groomed, balding, gray-haired businessman) had looked when they first met. The most erotic part of the fantasy, when she studied it, was how sexually turned on she became as the man expressed his open, unbridled passion for her. In real life, she was a little afraid of being so open with her own feelings. She had been hurt badly in a previous relationship, when she was younger and very open sexually, and had been afraid to risk being so vulnerable again with her husband.

"I realized that I had disguised my husband in my fantasy," Elaine said. "Falling in love with him *was* a real turn-on, but it had felt scary to bring that out in the open. When I realized who I was fantasizing about, I knew I could no longer fool myself. I didn't need to hide how I truly felt. Showing him openly how sexually excited I can feel toward him is a little scary. But now, after all these years together, I realize I can safely express my love and desire for him. I told him about my fantasy. He was delighted. Since then, we have both been more expressive about our sexual feelings for each other."

We can also make discoveries by looking beyond the fantasy characters' obvious identities. Many of us, for instance, fantasize about famous people we've never met in real life. Perhaps we think we know them from the roles they play in movies, the songs they sing, or the speeches they make in political or religious arenas. By exploring who these people are, who they remind us of, and also what qualities we find most erotic about them, we can sometimes decode more subtle messages and meanings in our fantasies.

One woman, for instance, developed a powerful attraction to the great Italian tenor, Luciano Pavarotti, around the time she was going through a divorce and a sexual dry spell. When she was alone and listening to his recordings, her sexual fantasies would take flight. "He seems so masculine to me, such a man," she explained with a sigh. When she learned that Pavarotti was scheduled to perform near her home, she broke her budget to buy a ticket, then dressed for his concert as if she were primping for a date. "After the concert, as he stood up onstage signing autographs for his fans below," she recalled, "I positioned myself where he would get the best view of my low neckline. Standing there, I remember sending him an urgent telepathic message: Look at my breasts!" In this fleeting, playful fantasy, she was not only celebrating the tenor as a masculine symbol, but acknowledging the vitality of her own female sexuality. Although she was temporarily celibate and fast approaching middle age, she understood that she had plenty of passion left to enjoy.

We can discover more about the characters in our fantasies by imagining which actor or actress we would assign to play the leading roles, as if we were a casting director. To help focus our thinking, we can deliberately prod ourselves with questions that get to the heart of character traits and special qualities. We can consider, for example, whether the blond female lead would be played better by an innocent, silly Meg Ryan, or a bold, sexy Madonna. We can ask ourselves whether the male stranger would more closely resemble a kind, intelligent Denzel Washington, or a comical but profane Eddie Murphy. Then we can go on to consider: "What is it about this actor that makes him right for my fantasy? Who would I rather cast for the part?"

A woman named Juana was bothered by a fantasy in which a

waitress was badgered and pawed by a persistent, aggressive male customer. "This sleazy, manipulative man in my fantasy reminded me of Jack Nicholson—egotistical, leering, and sex-crazed. I would have had a whole different feeling about the fantasy if the man behaved more like Nicolas Cage."

WHAT'S ON STAGE?

As the playwrights of our own fantasy lives, we get to decide not only which story we're telling, but exactly how it will be staged. Often unconsciously, we select the props, costumes, stage lights, and backdrop. When we decide to look closely at all these elements, we may be amazed by the detailed choices we've made and how attached we are to them.

In Karen's "Apartment Mix-Up" fantasy, the setting proved to be an important element that made her story more erotic. She envisioned herself arriving at a row of numbered apartments and knocking on the wrong door. "Instead of knocking on door #96, where I was intending to go, I knocked on door #69. I had read the numbers upside down," she said. That mistake was part of what made her entry into the bachelor party an honest goof, and took away her guilt. Yet, the very numbers "69"—slang for oral sex—also proved symbolic. Later in the fantasy, Karen imagined herself willingly giving blow jobs to several of the men. She also imagined the men dressed only in towels, a detail that made it easier for her to notice their prominent erections and become more aroused by the visual graphics. All of these details, Karen realized, helped the fantasy build up to its climax, and her own.

For a woman named Hannah, the details in a familiar fantasy took her by surprise, once she looked more closely. She knew that her most persistent sexual fantasy involved being with an old boyfriend on a crowded dance floor. In the fantasy, she imagined him unzipping her velvet dress and unhooking her bra as they danced closely together. Once she pictured herself completely nude and swaying against his body, she would climax. Then, her fantasy would fade away.

As she thought about the fantasy in more detail, however, Hannah noticed that the music was so clear, she could hear the jazzy whine of saxophones and clarinets. She could feel her clothing slide across her bare skin. She could see the pattern of light created by the rotating mirrored ball suspended from the ceiling.

Curious to see what else she might be able to recall about the fantasy, Hannah took out some paper and began sketching the setting. Although she was a woman in her thirties, she drew a nightclub scene from the swing era, complete with big band and long dance floor, lined with tables occupied by well-dressed couples. As she kept doodling, Hannah considered who might be sitting at these tables. "I imagined most people looking friendly and having a good time. But then, I drew a few people who looked uptight and disapproving," she said. To her shock, she realized that these uptight people in the audience included her older sister and brother-in-law at one table, a church elder at another, and her parents seated right next to the dance floor. Not until she had sketched in all of the scenery did Hannah think to identify these "extras" in her fantasy plot. They weren't leading roles or characters she interacted with in the fantasy, but more like props in the background.

For Hannah, who had grown up in a sexually repressive home, this elaborate fantasy scene became a place where she could boldly own, and even flaunt, her strong sexual energy. She recognized that this fantasy had functioned well to help her overcome earlier shame and enjoy her sexuality. Yet, as she thought more about the details of the fantasy, she realized it made her uncomfortable to know that her family members were sitting in the audience. Knowing who was watching robbed the fantasy of its erotic potency. As her own fantasy maker, she decided to transform the people who resembled her parents and other family members into unrecognizable strangers. By imagining a more anonymous setting, she felt more comfortable seeing herself in an exhibitionist, Wild Woman role.

As we tune into the details of our sexual fantasies, we may notice dreamlike symbols.[1] Sorting out what these symbols might mean is something each of us needs to do within the context of our own lives. When we hit on the right interpretation, we'll have a "felt sense" of our hunch being correct. For example, Hannah had also noticed that her father, an alcoholic in real life, was clutching a highball glass in her fantasy.

Another woman wondered why her most erotic fantasy always seemed to take place inside a car. When she closed her eyes and tried to bring back all the details from her fantasy, she realized she could smell the distinctive scent of a new car. She could feel smooth, cool leather upholstery under her thighs. When she thought about where she was in the scene, she realized she imagined herself in the front passenger seat, and that the car was parked. She noticed that the windows were fogged up from heavy breathing in a small space. It dawned on her that the car resembled the one her high school boyfriend used to drive. They had spent hours kissing and petting in those bucket seats, maneuvering feet and knees around the phallic gear shift knob. She also remembered how she had enjoyed her first orgasms in that car, even though she and her boyfriend hadn't dared to "go all the way," as they used to say back when she was a teenager. Later, after she lost her virginity, it took her years to be so sexually satisfied with a partner again. Now, she could see how her fantasy was replaying her sexual awakening and supplying the extended foreplay and petting that was often missing from her current sex life.

Another woman, Fiona, gained a surprising insight about one of her recurring fantasies when she carefully diagrammed everything she could remember about the setting. In the fantasy, she imagines herself as a teenage patient at a doctor's office. The doctor becomes sexually aggressive, undressing her and making lewd comments about her body. When Fiona drew a bird's-eye sketch of the office, noting exactly where the exam table was in relation to the window, desk, and chair, she recognized the setting as a replica of her father's medical office. That information made her think more closely about her relationship with her father and realize how uncomfortable she had often felt when he talked brazenly about his sexual conquests and made lewd comments about women's bodies.

As an adult, Fiona could see that her father had poor boundaries and little consideration for her needs as an impressionable adolescent. Realizing that the imagined setting was really her father's office helped her break open the disguise of her fantasy. The man in her fantasy symbolized her father, even though he didn't look like him. Since her teens, she had been eroticizing her father's inappropriate sexual comments and sexualizing his arrogance.

If we feel disturbed by the symbols or settings in fantasies that seem bizarre, it's comforting to remember that we created everything this way for a reason. Joy, for instance, realized from exploring her sexual fantasies that she often transports herself to a different time, place, even planet. In a favorite fantasy, she imagines that she is an astronaut who lands on a planet populated by alien females. All of the aliens find her sexually desirable, and she engages in a sexual frolic with one woman after the next. A twenty-three-year-old who grew up in a conservative, religious household, Joy only recently came out as a lesbian. For her, the extraterrestrial setting for her imagined sexual adventures and the warm welcome she receives from the alien females are far removed from the real world, where she has had to endure harsh family criticism about her orientation.

For women who experience fantasies as a burst of sensation instead of a scripted story, symbolic meaning can become more clear if they try to spell out what's behind their strong sexual feelings. Examining the props in a sensory fantasy can offer a helpful way to peel back another layer of meaning. We may arrive at new insights by using the process of free association in connection with the props or other elements in our fantasies.

A woman named Nora, for example, wondered why she enjoyed an unscripted fantasy about mangoes. As she became sexually aroused, she would imagine her senses flooded with the scent and taste of tropical fruit. To figure out why she might have chosen a mango as a fantasy prop, she asked herself what mangoes reminded her of. At first, Nora thought about the physical qualities of mangoes—their distinctive color and shape, and the way they smell, taste, and feel. Then, as she continued to make associations, she arrived at another level of understanding. "When my boyfriend and I first fell in love, we took a trip to Hawaii. For those two weeks, we spent every minute together. We had incredible sex. The first time I ever tasted a mango was in bed, on that trip. One morning, my boyfriend woke up early and brought a tray of food to our room for breakfast. It was such a thoughtful thing for him to do. We ate the sweet, sticky fruit with our fingers, feeding each other and covering ourselves with juice, and then licking each other clean into oral sex. Once we got back to the mainland and got busy with our day-to-day lives, he never brought me breakfast in bed again. I guess I had forgotten all about that morning, except in the sensations of my fantasy."

A woman named Mattie found that her unscripted fantasy made more sense to her after she looked at the meaning of the props it involved. By exploring the props, she also learned why this strange sensory fantasy had always left her feeling so anxious and upset.

Right before orgasm, Mattie would experience an overwhelming sensation, as if her whole body was infused with what she called *"the essence of Coke.* It was as if I could smell Coca-Cola, and hear it fizzing," she said. When this sensation came up during sex, Mattie would feel confused. "The strange thing is," she explained, "if I continued having sex, the feeling would go away as soon as I had an orgasm." This sensory fantasy seemed to be tied to a specific point of high arousal in her sexual response cycle. Whenever this fantasy flooded into her thoughts, Mattie noticed a wave of emotional emptiness and abandonment. These strong emotions also mystified her, especially since they felt so at odds with her current satisfying relationship.

One day, Mattie visited her boyfriend at the gas station where he worked. High on a window ledge, a dusty collection of old soda bottles caught her eye. Mattie couldn't explain why, but she felt unnerved by a distinctively shaped Coke bottle from the 1950s. When she asked her boyfriend to hand it to her, she was astonished to find that her hand shook with fear as she took hold of it. As she struggled to understand the importance of this symbol, Mattie remembered where she had seen a bottle like this one before. When she was a little girl and her father was in the army, their family had lived on a military base overseas. The biggest treat any kid on the base could ask for was a bottle of Coca-Cola.

Eager to learn more, Mattie talked about her strange reaction and "essence of Coke" fantasy with a therapist. Gradually, by exploring more about her past, she was able to recollect the rest of her story. "As a little girl, living on that army base, my father would often get me out of bed late at night and have me come sit with him in the living room. He would fondle and stimulate me until I reached a state of high arousal. Then, while he jerked off, he gave me a Coke to drink as my reward," she explained. In her adult fantasy life, Mattie had been holding on to this buried memory. In her mind, she had linked up a state of high sexual arousal with her memory of the soft drink her father used to give her as a "reward" for "cooperating" with him. Because she didn't climax during the abuse, her sensory fantasy about Coke stopped as soon as she moved toward orgasm. That part of her sexual response cycle had not been contaminated by sexual abuse. By exploring a mysterious fantasy sensation, she had discovered an important clue about her sexual history.

❦

After we take time to explore the plot, theme, characters, and symbols of our fantasies, we often wind up feeling that we have gained concrete, useful information. Once we have brought these unconscious thoughts out into the open, we have new information about ourselves that we can choose to bring into our sex lives, relationships, and more general personal growth.

Once Karen worked her way through the who-what-when-where-why of her fantasy, she realized she had extracted an enormous amount of detail about her "Apartment Mix-Up." She understood that her fantasy offered her a way to experience sexual energy without feeling guilty for being so responsive. She saw that her own erotic style was strongly visual, and that she was turned on by seeing men's genitals. She also realized she liked a lot of physical stimulation and emotional attention during sex, and that she enjoyed giving oral sex. Karen also made an important connection between the faceless men in her apartment fantasy, who operated on their own rules, and the brother who had pulled her into his secret, pornographic world when she was a girl. Since childhood, when she had been introduced to sex under the guise of secrecy, she had been feeling guilty about her natural sexual response. Now that she was an adult, she realized she could let go of those outdated feelings and begin accepting her sexual excitement with her new boyfriend, Thomas.

Karen decided to talk more directly with Thomas about sex. She told him that she had been avoiding sex to avoid her fantasies. They began talking about what she needed to enjoy sex more. In many important ways, exploring fantasy had taught her to pay attention to the lovemaking techniques she found most erotic.

Eventually, Karen was able to extract the most positive aspects of fantasy and began weaving them into her present-day lovemaking. She explained, "One afternoon, Thomas and I were relaxing in our backyard hot tub together. He was paying me a lot of attention, talking quietly and stroking my hair. I loved that, and told him so. I started to get aroused and suggested that he might want to get out of the water and wrap up in a towel. I had bought some thick, white bath towels that looked similar to the ones I had found sensual in my apartment fantasy. When Thomas was wearing only the towel, I invited him to sit on the edge of the hot tub. He was eager to see what I had in mind, and I was eager to see what was under his towel. When I started to give him oral sex, he continued stroking my hair and face and whispering sweetly to me. Meanwhile, the jets of the hot tub were hitting my genitals, giving me the extra stimulation I know I need to climax. Throughout lovemaking, I was able to stay present with him. It was a great afternoon for both of us."

This guided exploration of specific fantasies will bring many of us as far as we want to travel into the meaning of our fantasies. We have lots of new insights now to help us feel more relaxed about our fantasies and more prepared to create better sexual experiences. However, this active exploration can also lead us to a determination to make changes and heal from any fantasies that remain troublesome.

❦

CHAPTER 8

Healing and Changing Unwanted Fantasies

For complex, personal reasons, we may feel imprisoned by our fantasy lives. Women sometimes describe feeling overly dependent on certain fantasies, controlled by them, or sickened by their contents. Even if fantasies offer a reliable, surefire route to orgasm, they don't necessarily lead to satisfying or lasting sexual pleasure. As we've seen, erotic excitement may be overlaid with feelings of discomfort or even disgust. Fantasy traps can harm self-esteem and, in some cases, promote negative sexual behaviors. If we feel that the pain caused by certain fantasies outweighs the sexual pleasure they create, or if negative fantasies get in the way of intimacy, we may become motivated and courageous enough to want to make changes.

Yet, without resources available to help guide healing, many women have met with dead ends, frustration, and grief. On their own, some women have tried addressing concerns with fantasy by keeping journals or engaging in more general recovery work. These steps can often lead to new insights and better self-awareness, but they seldom help us get to the root of a problem with sexual fantasy. As one woman explained, "I worked hard on recovery from sexual abuse, I worked hard to improve my self-esteem, I faithfully kept a journal. Yet, until I worked directly on my sexual fantasies, they never changed."

Similarly, other women have reached a dead end either by trying to run from their troublesome fantasies or by intentionally experiencing them more intensely. Some women have tried "numbing out," avoiding sexual feelings to shut off their fantasies. But this approach has led to increased feelings of sexual frustration, sadness, or damage to relationships or self-esteem. Other women have tried forcing themselves to think about the fantasies they hate, hoping this mental "flooding" will exhaust their interest in them. Instead of healing, though, they have wound up feeling overwhelmed and even more ashamed and uncomfortable.

In a desperate attempt to overcome the pain of their unwanted fantasies, some women have even acted them out, hoping to master them. A few women we interviewed described taking part in "dungeon" fantasy scenes, where violent sadomasochistic sex was played out against theatrical backdrops, in an effort to heal unwanted fantasies. A woman who had participated in S/M sex that involved body piercing and whipping said, "I wanted to walk back through the fire and know that I could survive." She understood that her violent fantasies resulted from sexual abuse she had endured as a child. "As an adult, I wanted to prove to myself that I had become strong enough to handle it," she said. Another woman who was an abuse survivor said she was attracted to acting out S/M fantasies because she so often felt numb during sex and wanted to experience more intense sexual sensation.

Even with the best intentions, however, acting out violent or dangerous sexual fantasies is a misguided path to healing. It can lead a woman to retraumatize herself, harm her own body, and reinforce arousal patterns that may have been learned during prior sexual abuse. It's another dead end to healing and lasting sexual joy.

How can we more effectively heal or change the fantasies we dislike? Through her workshops, research, and clinical practice related to fantasy, Wendy has developed strategies that work for healing and changing unwanted sexual fantasies. Women who have suffered with intrusive fantasies for years have succeeded in healing by employing a variety of these techniques that deal directly with fantasy concerns. Many of these women said that their healing began when they first heard the reassuring message that change is indeed possible, and that specific tools and techniques are available to help them.

Although this special healing work differs from one woman to the next, it usually involves making changes in sexual thoughts, as well as sexual behaviors. As we've seen in previous chapters, our sexual fantasies are intricately related to our sexual activities. They can both *reflect* and *affect* what we do sexually. Thus, to heal, we need to go beyond solving the riddle of what an unwanted sexual fantasy means and employ additional strategies that deal with the intrusive and habitual ways fantasy can function. By using behavior-change strategies at the same time that we gain more understanding about a fantasy, we can reduce the likelihood that an unwanted fantasy will recur and bother us in the future.

This type of healing can be difficult to do alone. Few women have the resources available to tackle in-depth psychological work and acquire new insights about sexual behavior. As a result, when healing unwanted sexual fantasies, most women need the help and support of a therapist trained to address these issues. Professional help is essential if a woman is involved in any potentially dangerous, addictive, or high-risk sexual behaviors. All of the in-depth stories shared in this chapter have come out of Wendy's work with individual clients or from women who have attended her fantasy workshops.

STRATEGIES FOR HEALING

Although the healing process is unique for each woman, there are four broad approaches that can help address what we may dislike about our fantasy lives. When used to create a personal healing plan, these approaches can work together in powerful ways to positively influence both our sexual thoughts and our behaviors. These strategies for healing unwanted fantasies include:

- Going deeper to find the meaning
- Reducing the need for the fantasy
- Disrupting the function of the unwanted fantasy
- Transforming the fantasy into a more positive experience

This is not a step-by-step program for healing. Rather, these four approaches, and the specific, therapeutic techniques they contain, are meant to be undertaken separately or in conjunction with one another to fit a particular woman's needs.

GOING DEEPER

In this strategy, a woman looks closely at the contents of her fantasy from many angles and sometimes plays with the story until she finds what core confusion or unresolved emotional issues it represents. For many women, going deeper for meaning is the primary and most interesting approach they take. Because it is designed to uncover the complex issues that lay hidden and disguised within our unwanted fantasies, this approach generates much useful information for healing. Many women begin with the guided exploration techniques, described in chapter 7, to plumb the contents of their fantasies. This can be a good first step, because it reveals the basic plot, characters, setting, or feelings contained in the disturbing fantasy. A woman can then build on this knowledge with a variety of additional discovery techniques that reveal even deeper layers of meaning.

Because going deeper involves consciously examining and dissecting an unwanted sexual fantasy, it helps to do this work in a nonsexual setting. Having gained some distance from the sexual heat of a fantasy, we can analyze it without arousal, fear, excitement, or the other emotions it typically inspires. A woman can also reduce the charge surrounding a fantasy by imagining that the fantasy is contained within a Plexiglas cube or inside a dollhouse, or that it is recorded on videotape and is playing out on a television screen.

Exercises for going deeper include such activities as drawing and diagramming a specific fantasy on paper. When drawing a fantasy, it can be helpful to make stick-figure drawings of the characters. Stick figures consist only of lines and circles, so they don't require the artistic talent needed to create full-figure drawings. In addition, stick figures are more schematic than erotic, which can help us examine them more comfortably. Women can expand on the stick-figure exercise by drawing dialogue balloons, then writing down the characters' conversations or thoughts inside the balloons, as if they were comic strips. These dialogue balloons can help draw out what the characters are thinking, feeling, and saying to each other.

Making a bird's-eye view diagram of a fantasy enables us to see where all the characters or props are in relation to one another, and can include traffic patterns and movement. One woman with vague memories of having been molested discovered that the floor plan she drew of her rape fantasy matched exactly where the window, door, dresser, lamp, and bed were located in her grandfather's spare room.

We can also probe deeper in an unwanted sexual fantasy by writing a more detailed journal description of it, or using three-dimensional objects to stage it, or engaging in role-playing to expand on our understanding of the characters.

Techniques for going deeper work best when they honor a

woman's personal talents and styles. If a woman is more visual, then she will more likely benefit from drawing pictures or using artistic modes in therapy. If she is more verbal, then she may learn more easily by role-playing dialogues or analyzing words for meaning. Similarly, if she is more tactile, she might benefit from using three-dimensional objects such as dolls or figurines as therapeutic aids.

Once a woman gains a clearer view of the details within the fantasy, she can ask herself even more questions to reveal the deeper meaning of these contents or sensations. A woman who fantasized about being penetrated by a baseball bat, for instance, kept asking herself what this sensation reminded her of from an earlier time in her life. She discovered in therapy that her sensory fantasy was disguising a painful memory about childhood sexual abuse.

We can often get at the intent and core issues of negatively charged characters in scripted fantasies by role-playing a dialogue with them, or even pretending to interrogate or confront them about their actions. In a Victim fantasy, for instance, a woman can imagine what the response would be if she asked the perpetrator such questions as "Why are you doing this to her?" "Where did you learn to act this way?" "Do you realize the harm you're causing?" "What is it you *really* need?"

Our feelings about a fantasy can change dramatically if we imagine expanding on the time frame of a particular fantasy story. If we think of a fantasy as a video, we can imagine rewinding or fast-forwarding the tape to see what happens in the plot before and after the fantasy itself. By extending the story, we can learn more about a character's background, intentions, and true desires. This technique can make the characters seem more complete and less mysterious. Imagining that the action continues can help us to see the emotional fallout and other consequences of the sexual acts in the fantasy. We can conjure up new endings that make the fantasy less erotically charged. One woman's fantasy of a sexual assault lost its power when she imagined the assailant being caught by police and sent to jail.

Similarly, the introduction of a new character can help us understand the complex dynamics that give the fantasy its erotic charge. For example, a woman who has fantasized about a girl being sexually victimized can imagine how the fantasy would change with the arrival of a child-advocate character who addresses underlying emotional needs. The new character could stop the abuse and remove the victim from harm. If the woman created this fantasy because of her own abuse history, she could look to the advocate character for help with her recovery. The advocate might deliver nurturing messages the woman needed to hear when she was younger, such as "It wasn't your fault. You're safe now. Your body belongs to you." One woman, for example, imagined an advocate rescuing her from a sexual torture chamber, wrapping her in a warm quilt, and delivering reassuring messages while they sat together alongside a peaceful riverbank.

Women who go deeper into their unwanted fantasies often discover that these kinds of fantasies have less to do with sex and more to do with an unresolved emotional hurt from a confusing or otherwise traumatic past sexual experience. Thus, when we lift the disguise of these fantasies, unravel the contents, and get at the very core of meaning, we find nothing inherently sinister or perverse about our true sexuality. Rather, we often discover universal human needs for love, protection, safety, attention, or compassion, which we needed and deserved at an earlier stage in our lives.

Reducing the Need

Another strategy for healing unwanted sexual fantasies is to identify and practice those things that make us less susceptible to the fantasy's intrusion. We figure out how to prevent and become less dependent on the fantasy.

Unwanted sexual fantasies tend to occur more often when a woman is under stress, feeling pressured to perform sexually in a certain way, or not receiving enough other forms of sexual stimulation. Thus, a woman can reduce the need for an unwanted fantasy by reducing the stresses that might trigger or encourage the fantasy and also finding new ways to enhance sexual arousal.

Women can use this approach before sex, by changing the setting and situation in which sexual activity takes place. One woman realized that she was more likely to have a negative fantasy if she was masturbating in the dark. Turning on a soft light and playing some music helped her stay in her body and in the present moment. Another woman found she could reduce her need for fantasy by having sex in the shower instead of in bed.

Changing the time of day for lovemaking can also be helpful. One woman, for example, realized she was most inclined to rely on an unwanted fantasy if she had sex at night when she was tired. As a child, she had been sexually molested late at night, when she was sleepy. A state of sleepiness became a trigger for her fantasies. She and her husband decided to make love only during the daytime, when she had more energy. Her intrusive fantasy disappeared.

Women can also reduce sexual stresses by increasing the amount of time they set aside for lovemaking and avoiding the feeling that they are under a time pressure during sex. They can take steps to ensure that they feel safe during sex, such as locking doors, communicating more with a partner, or securing privacy.

Unwanted fantasies can also be reduced by reassuring ourselves that we don't have to climax every time we have sex. Instead, we can focus on the pleasure of feeling sensation, self-caring, and emotional connection and closeness with a partner. These deliberate changes in attitude can help reduce the need for a particular fantasy by decreasing anxiety about having to respond and perform sexually.

During sex, women can reduce their need for a certain fantasy by experimenting with different sexual positions or kinds of stimulation, in order to change sexual habits. "Being on my back always makes me feel like the Victim in my old fantasy," explained one woman, who reduced the intrusion of this fantasy by switching to a side-by-side position during sex. Another woman found that she could change her reliance on an unpleasant masturbatory fantasy simply by switching which hand she used for self-stimulation. This changed a specific sexual habit that had always accompanied the fantasy in the past.

Many women report that it helps them avoid a particular fantasy if they concentrate on their own breath and body sensations. They may also focus on their partner by making eye contact and talking during lovemaking. Or, they may slow down their sexual relating to include the time and stimulation they need to build arousal without the unwanted fantasy.

Because unwanted sexual fantasies serve positive functions by increasing arousal, we can reduce reliance on them by employing new forms of sexual stimulation. One woman, for example, had made an effort to heal from her unwanted Voyeur fantasies that related to past sexual abuse. In examining her fantasies, she realized that her old fantasies were providing a lot of visually erotic stimulation. She experimented with keeping her eyes open during sex, to help her avoid fantasy, and discovered that watching her husband's body move rhythmically, "like a Calypso dancer," provided the turn-on she needed to climax in the present.

Other ways to increase stimulation include taking a hot bath before sex to increase blood flow, using a vibrator, using a personal lubricant, concentrating on the most sensitive areas, such as the clitoris, breasts, lips, and G-spot (in the vagina), and letting ourselves make noise during sex. Relieving the need for an unwanted fantasy means we need to give ourselves permission to indulge in the joys of sexual sensations and be proactive in expanding our repertoires of activities for increasing sexual excitement. To help discover new ideas, some women find it beneficial to read sexual enrichment books and articles on increasing sexual pleasure, such as those often found in women's magazines.

DISRUPTING THE FUNCTION

In this strategy, a woman does what she can to upset the un-wanted fantasy's ability to enhance arousal, facilitate orgasm, and generate sexual feelings. By disrupting the reliable functioning of a fantasy, she makes it a less desirable and less attractive alternative. A variety of behavioral techniques support this approach to heal-ing.

Disrupting the function is an approach that is used primarily during sex. The most commonly used technique in this approach is called "stop thought." As soon as a woman notices the unwanted fantasy, she can consciously decide to stop it and think of some-thing else. We can stop a fantasy by imagining we push a "pause" button on a tape control. This stop-thought technique improves with practice. At first, it may be difficult and not work every time. Gradually, however, it may prove helpful as we learn to stop reinforcing unwanted fantasies with sexual pleasure. By gaining and exercising some conscious control over an unwanted sexual fantasy, we shrink its influence and give ourselves time to develop patterns for sexual response that are linked with more positive thoughts and feelings.

A variety of metaphors have helped women understand this stop-thought technique so they can apply it. One woman, who had unscripted fantasies that welled up like a wave of terror when-ever she felt sexual arousal, said she imagined taking a broom and sweeping this unwanted sensation from her mind. Another woman pictured her unwanted fantasy as if it were lint accumulat-ing on a screen in a clothes dryer. "Each time the fantasy comes up, I stop having sex and imagine that I'm pulling off more lint," she explained. Another woman compared stopping a fantasy to "pulling it off the airwaves." She said, "I tell myself that this show has been canceled."

It helps some women to temporarily stop a fantasy if they focus on present sensations, such as their breathing or their part-ner's breathing, or the emotional connection they share. If having a fantasy makes them feel as if they are in an altered state, or temporarily out of their body, they can pay attention to the physical reality all around them: the furniture in the room, the ticking of a clock, the feel of their skin moving against a sheet, or the scent of their lover's cologne.

In order to train themselves to stop a fantasy, women may need to pause physical stimulation, as well, even if that means the sexual excitement will temporarily drain out of the moment. A woman can reassure herself, and her partner, that nothing bad will happen by slowing down, taking a break, and remaining calm. Similarly, if a fantasy comes up during masturbation, a woman can choose to stop, take a break, and let the fantasy fizzle. "I just get up and have a cup of tea, instead of moving toward climax with a fantasy that I know I'm going to hate," one woman said.

Partners can be a source of comfort and support in stopping an unwanted fantasy, as well as disrupting the negative feelings of shame, anger, or disgust that a fantasy can cause. "When my old fantasy comes up, I tell my partner I need to stop. He just holds me then, and tells me he loves me," one woman said.

By shifting in and out of an unwanted fantasy during a sexual encounter, some women find that they can gradually reduce the amount of time they use it, yet still fulfill a specific function. Because the most common functions of sexual fantasy are to increase arousal and achieve orgasm, for example, a woman may decide to use fantasy only during the parts of her sexual response cycle when she needs a boost. She may use fantasy to build up to a certain level of physiological excitement, then shift from fantasy to an awareness of being in her body, and enjoy present sensations as she continues with sex. One woman described "tossing my fantasy," when she got to a certain plateau of sexual excitement. "I've worked at tossing it earlier and earlier, so that I can enjoy more of sex in the present."

Another woman found that focusing on her partner's face helped her move from the fantasy to the present experience. She explained, "I still use my old fantasies to get aroused, but just as I'm about to come I switch to making eye contact with my partner. That way, my orgasm isn't just connected to my fantasy, but it includes him, too. It seems more emotionally close and real than when I used to stay in fantasy all the way through sex."

Eventually, by shifting in and out of fantasy, women can decrease the use of a fantasy considerably and even make it disappear from their thoughts during sex. This gradual weaning away from the fantasy is preferred by some women because it provides lots of time to develop new skills for arousal. Using this combination of tolerance, conscious restraint, and patience, they can slowly retrain themselves to find other routes to sexual pleasure. Shifting in and out allows them to harness the power of the fantasy as they work toward eliminating it.

TRANSFORMING THE FANTASY

The fourth main strategy for healing unwanted sexual fantasies involves transforming a particular fantasy into a more positive experience. This approach draws on a woman's innate creativity to adapt and revise her fantasies, so that they better fit her current needs and desires.

We can transform a fantasy in a nonsexual context by writing down a different version of it in a journal, or enacting different fantasy plots with three-dimensional objects. Or, we can transform a sexual fantasy during sex, while it is actively "running" in our mind. By becoming more conscious of when we are engaging in fantasy, and reminding ourselves that fantasies are our own creations, we can deliberately bend or shape the contents of our fantasies to positive images and depictions of healthier interactions, while maintaining or developing some erotic elements to keep them sexually exciting.

We know that unwanted sexual fantasies are often upsetting to experience because they eroticize abusive or harmful relationship dynamics. To change a fantasy toward healthier sexual dynamics, we can ask ourselves, "What might I change to make my fantasy feel safer, or to have the characters relate in situations of consent, equality, respect, trust, safety, and mutual pleasure?" By incorporating these conditions for healthy sex, we can remove the abusive quality of an unwanted fantasy, yet retain the specific sexual stimulation or other erotic charge it might be offering.[1]

This technique often works by making gradual changes in the contents of fantasies. Instead of completely revising them beyond recognition, we can change what's disturbing about them in smaller steps so that we don't lose their erotic power. Tory, for instance, who had experienced recurring fantasies about sex between an older man and a little girl, was able to imagine changing the characters' ages by a few years each time she used the fantasy until it no longer resembled her own childhood sexual abuse by an uncle. Over time, the man got younger and the girl aged. Eventually, they became two adults—both mature enough to consent to sex. In its new form, the fantasy still aroused her. She had reinforced it with sexual pleasure each time she made a change in the contents.

A woman named Janette changed the plot of her fantasy to make it feel less bothersome, but held onto what made it hot for her. In her old fantasy, she had imagined a traveling salesman taking advantage of a young farm girl's sexual curiosity and naïveté. She shifted the plot to focus instead on a traveling salesman and a young rural woman. She imagined them meeting, falling in love, and becoming sexual. This new fantasy still had pastoral scenery, with warm summer sun falling on grassy fields and helping her feel relaxed during sex. It also included the sexual attention that the salesman paid to the woman's body, such as the breast and clitoral stimulation that she found so pleasing. But now, her own arousal and excitement unfolded within the context of mutual exploration, not deception or trickery.

Some women find it helpful in healing to change specific settings, props, and other details in their fantasies to reduce what they consider to be negative or unpleasant elements in the scene. One woman had fantasized about being chained to a table by faceless strangers who took turns having sex with her. She was able to revise the scene by imagining loosely tied silk cords instead of metal handcuffs on her wrists. Then, she imagined pulling her hands free of the restraints and transforming the scene so that the faceless men left and her real lover arrived. Eventually, she was able to shift to an image of her lover gently holding her hands over her head during sex, which she still found intensely erotic but not upsetting.

※

Regardless of which strategies we choose to blend into our personal approach to healing or changing an unwanted sexual fantasy, certain reminders can be helpful. First, we need to remember that we do have choices, and that healing is possible. There are so many specific things we can do, even while having sex, to control, diffuse, transform, or eliminate fantasies that may have disturbed us for years. It may take some experimenting to discover which techniques work best.

It also helps to remember that this path leads to a more satisfying sex life. Many women find that they change the very way they think about sex, once they have done some healing work to get rid of unwanted fantasies. They often develop a more relaxed approach to sex, in which they take time to honor their more natural sexual rhythms. As one woman explained, "I could climax in two minutes with my old fantasy, but I hated how I felt afterward. Without it, it takes me longer to become aroused, and I know I may not have an orgasm every time, but when I do climax, I feel like I can really own the pleasure fully, as mine."

Throughout the healing process, we can continue to offer ourselves compassion and respect our own needs. Instead of getting angry if unwanted fantasies continue to come up, or if they return during periods of stress, we can learn to view a relapse as a signal that we still have more healing work to do. It's not a sign of failure. Our goal doesn't have to be eradicating unwanted fantasies completely. Rather, we can work toward gaining more control of our fantasy lives and learning to use sexual fantasies to help us create the kind of sexual experiences we truly desire.

For Judy, Renee, and Kris, healing has been a process of both change and empowerment. All three women discovered that they had the power to break free of disturbing sexual thoughts. They learned they could take their newfound knowledge and use it to more fully enjoy sex. They also discovered that their sexual fantasies didn't have to feel like traps anymore, but could be valued as incredible resources that they had been carrying inside themselves all along.

PROFILES OF HEALING

When Judy, a single woman in her early thirties, arrived at a sexual fantasy workshop and saw a roomful of other nervous women, she was reassured to learn that she was not alone in feeling as if her fantasies had taken control of her sex life.

"I didn't always have fantasies," Judy explained, "but once I hooked into them, that was the only way for me. For at least fifteen years now, I've felt like I can't have an orgasm without a fantasy." Because she had been reinforcing these fantasies with sexual pleasure for so many years, Judy now felt as if they were wired into her sexual response.

At the workshop, Judy began with an exploration of a typical fantasy. Calling her story "Pleasure and Pain," she wrote this description of the plot:

> *I imagine myself as a naive girl of about fifteen, walking into a massage parlor where I've arrived for a job inter-*

view. The room is curtained, with a chair and a massage table in the center of the room. The proprietor is a handsome man in his thirties. He asks me to take my clothes off. I'm reluctant, but I do it anyway. Once I'm naked, I cross my hands over my chest so he can't see my breasts. I'm really bashful, but he's encouraging and patient.

He asks me to come closer to him. Even though I'm embarrassed, I start becoming more sexual and precocious. I sit on his lap. Somewhere along the line, I've put on a G-string. I'm straddling his knee and rubbing my clitoris against him. He asks me to put some lipstick on my nipples to make them red. I ask him to help me. He does, then I cup my breasts and put them into his mouth. I want to show him that I can be sexual, so he'll hire me.

He asks if I like to be spanked, and I say yes. He puts a pillow on his desk and I lay atop it with my bottom in the air. He pushes a button and the curtains open to reveal a bunch of men watching from behind a window. I don't want them to watch, but I don't know how to say no. He spanks me with his hand, and there's something erotic about the skin on my bottom turning red. I can see this happening to me as if I'm a Voyeur, watching the action. He says he'll always spank me if I ask him to. I want him to again, but he says I need to ask for it. I don't want him to stop, but I don't want to ask, either.

Finally, I do ask him to spank me again. He tells me he will. He also tells me it's okay to climax this time. He says I need to make a lot of noise so the men behind the window can hear me. "They'll like that," he says. "Put on a show so they can see you come." I want this job, and I'm feeling really aroused, so I go ahead and let go. Then I come, and the fantasy immediately ends.

After Judy had her fantasy down on paper, she could see how it functioned for her in a number of ways. It included a lot of sexual attention and physical stimulation of her breasts and genitals, which added to her arousal. When she experienced the fantasy, she watched the sexual action unfold as if she were offstage. This Voyeur perspective had let her watch the details she found visually exciting, such as her red nipples, the G-string, and her skin turning red when she was spanked. She also noticed the auditory stimulation in her dialogue with the man and the sounds she made at orgasm.

In another exercise, Judy traced when the fantasy routinely came up in her thoughts. She could see that it clicked on when she got in bed for sex and lasted all during her sexual response cycle, from arousal until orgasm, when it vanished. The only time Judy didn't need her fantasy was in the resolution stage, as she rested after sex and her body became calm.

By analyzing the theme of this fantasy, Judy saw that it was about a woman gaining the permission to be sexual. She saw her fantasy character as someone bashful and embarrassed about sex, who needed permission to let go and enjoy sexual energy. Indeed, the man encouraged her to "put on a show" and "make noise" when she climaxed and assured her that the other men would like that. At the massage parlor, Judy realized, it was literally a woman's job to perform sexually for men. She asked herself, "Is this how I really want to think about sex, that it's something women can only enjoy if men give us the okay?"

Although Judy could see that the fantasy fulfilled important functions for her, she still wanted to loosen the hold that her fantasy life had on her thoughts during sex. She wanted to stop seeing herself as a bashful, sexually inexperienced girl who needed reassurance and permission in order to feel sexual. "I want to be able to enjoy sex on my own terms, without feeling shame, getting punished, or needing a man's permission," she said.

As she did more exercises to help her trace the history of her fantasy life, Judy could see that these recurring sexual fantasies had been holding on to the confusion she had felt about sex at a younger age. At the workshop, Judy did some role-playing to get deeper into her character and to add to her understanding of what the girl in her fantasy really wanted and needed. "When I think about that girl in the massage parlor, I see someone who's curious but embarrassed about sex. She finds boys her own age kind of scary. She wants to become a sexual woman, but she's not sure how. The man gives her permission to be sexual, but he treats her like an object. He controls the show and tricks her into asking for sex. There's no love, no emotion at all in this sexual scene. He acts nice, but he looks like someone who could get violent if he didn't get what he wanted."

Looking back, Judy realized that she had started having sex at about fifteen—the very age of the girl in her fantasy—because she assumed that was what boys expected of her. She felt powerless to control sexual energy and didn't allow herself permission to set limits. Because she was sexually active at such a young age, she had missed opportunities to experiment with less overtly sexual relationships. "I didn't have boyfriends who just wanted to be friends and make out playfully. I missed those safer opportunities to let things unfold more slowly. I went out with guys who wanted sex, and I didn't realize that it was okay to say no. I didn't feel like I had any control."

The role-playing exercises at the workshop helped Judy understand that, as she had become more mature, her early confusion about sex had persisted. Instead, in the fantasies that she honed and repeated, she had been reinforcing her view of herself as someone naive, inexperienced, and unsure sexually, even though that view didn't mesh with reality any longer. Her fantasies felt out of sync with her life. "I got rid of my clothes from high school decades ago," she realized, "but I'm still wearing the same old fantasies."

By the end of the workshop, Judy felt as if she had experienced a breakthrough in understanding. She saw that her fantasy life had gotten stuck at the very age when she felt most confused about sex. With the other women in the group, Judy brainstormed about what she had missed learning about sex when she was younger. They came up with a long list of ways she might have let her budding sexuality unfold more slowly, such as dancing, holding hands, petting, kissing, and mutual exploring that stopped short of intercourse. Everyone laughed when one woman recalled the pleasures of "outercourse" as a way for an adolescent girl to get used to her sexual feelings. As she brainstormed with the group, Judy felt as if she was filling in some important developmental gaps.

By exploring her fantasy in such detail, Judy also learned what it had to teach her about the kind of sexual stimulation she naturally found most erotic. She felt empowered to create a more playful, less goal-oriented approach to sex. In self-stimulation, she could imagine practicing this new route to pleasure, in which she could remove the pressure on herself to "perform" and enjoy indulging in the heat and undulating rhythms of her own sexual energy. She gave herself permission to seek out new inspirations that reflected her natural erotic interests. When she was younger, she had loved romance novels. Now, she decided to check out the new generation of romance writers who featured smart women boldly enjoying sex. Judy also realized she had the right to speak up more in lovemaking and ask partners for the kind of stimulation she needed to enjoy sex.

Judy left the workshop hopeful that her insights could help her change the way she relied on fantasy for arousal and orgasm, and open a new door for creating more satisfying sexual experiences. Instead of viewing sex as a job women performed for men, Judy felt free to begin enjoying her sexual energy for herself.

❧

Although Renee had shared a home with her boyfriend, David, for about eight years, she had never told him the details of her fantasy life. Lately, though, her recurring Victim fantasies had become more upsetting than ever. More often than not, she was avoiding sex with David to avoid fantasy. He complained about how unavailable she was, and how distant she seemed on the rare times when they did have sex. Worried that David might leave her, Renee started addressing her concerns about fantasy.

Renee's fantasy had evolved over the years, but it typically involved a girl in her late teens being held down by a group of men and raped by their leader. When she wrote a summary of her fantasy plot, she called it "Don't Be Scared—You'll Like This."

> *A man brings this beautiful, innocent-looking girl into a bedroom, or sometimes to a restaurant after hours. A group of men and I are waiting for her. The men and I tell her we're going to teach her about sex. We restrain her with our hands, and she's scared. She says, "No." We tell her this won't be rape, because she'll like it. We'll be soft. We'll teach her how to have an orgasm. I'm the one telling everyone what to do, the Coach. As the men hold the girl down on a bed or table, I stand near her head, whispering, holding her hand, comforting her. I tell her not to be scared. I tell the men where they can touch her. I thank the leader for bringing her, and he becomes the main one who has sex with her. It can be oral sex or intercourse. When she's getting aroused, I tell her to tell us when she's about to climax. When she comes, I come, then the fantasy goes away.*

To explore the fantasy in more detail, Renee diagrammed it on paper with stick figures and then verbally described all the characters. Once Renee used this exercise to make the details of her fantasy more conscious, she was able to make some surprising comparisons between fantasy and real life.

The Victim, Renee realized, represented herself. "She's like my replacement, someone who can feel the sexual pleasure for me. She's also beautiful, like an advertising image of what a young woman should look like. That's why the men want her. When she's excited, I'm excited. When she climaxes, so do I. In real life, though, I have a hard time being aroused if I stay present."

The woman she labeled as Coach was also a character Renee identified with. In fact, Coach looked just like Renee, at her current age of thirty. Again, she noticed important contrasts between fantasy and reality. "In real life, I don't have any voice in sex. I never speak up, even though I know where and how I want to be touched. In the fantasy, it's interesting that I'm the Coach, giving everyone instructions and asking questions."

The Rapist, the main perpetrator, looked just like David, Renee's real boyfriend. "Although I call him a rapist, he's really gentle in the fantasy. He either does oral sex or has intercourse with the Victim, to make her come. He does whatever the Coach tells him to do. In real life, David is controlling about sex. We always have to do it the way he wants, and when he wants. If I try to initiate sex, he ignores me. Sometimes he wants me to look at his penis, even though that upsets me. But in the fantasy, his goal is to please the girl, to teach her how to have an orgasm."

Renee imagined the other men in the fantasy surrounding the Victim and restraining her, with a different man holding down each arm and leg. They also caress her, adding to the stimulation. "She's trying to say no, which I also find arousing. In real life, I can't be aroused if I'm saying yes."

In Renee's stick-figure drawing, the girl's mouth was divided in half. On the left, it was drawn as a straight line, representing silence. In the fantasy, the girl didn't speak, mimicking Renee's silence in real life. On the right side of the stick figure, Renee had drawn the girl's mouth open, as if she were talking or screaming.

Renee drew a big circle for a dialogue balloon beside each stick figure's mouth. Then, as if they were cartoons, she filled in what they were saying and thinking in the fantasy. This exercise also turned up some surprising details.

Renee wrote the words that she imagined the girl was thinking. She pictured herself telling the Rapist: "I'm confused about you. I feel betrayed. You win. You disgust me, but also make me feel good. I'm scared. Why are you doing this to me?" Then, writing more boldly, she imagined the girl wanting to shout, "Leave me alone! Let me go! I hate you! I want to fight you." After she added these final, angry words, Renee drew tears coming from the corners of the girl's wide eyes.

The Coach, positioned in the drawing next to the girl's ear, was drawn with her mouth open. Renee wrote one dialogue balloon to capture what she was saying to the girl: "I'll help undress you. Don't be scared. You'll like this. Can you feel it? We'll teach you." To the men, she had the Coach saying, "Do it this way. She'll like this. Touch her here."

The Rapist figure, who was positioned between the girl's legs, was saying to her, "Do you like this? Do you feel this?" At the same time, he was thinking to himself, "Surrender. I can make you feel good. I can make you do what I want."

When she thought more about the other men in the scene, Renee saw them as faceless, powerless, and confused. She labeled them "Stupid Things." They were saying, "We don't make decisions. We're friends of his [the Rapist]. We're excited. We want to do more, but we can't." Meanwhile, they were thinking, "We hate the girl. We use her."

Once she had used the stick-figure exercise to reveal all these details, Renee talked about how she felt, now that she had so much information about the fantasy. She realized that she felt bad about casting her boyfriend in the role of a perpetrator. Even though he was controlling about sex, she didn't want to think of him as a rapist. She also realized she felt betrayed by the Coach, who pretended to befriend the girl, but ordered the men to hold her down and sexually abuse her. The Coach had told the girl it wasn't rape, but really, it was.

In real life, when Renee was about eight years old, her mother's boyfriend had tickled and fondled her, then performed oral sex on her. In looking for connections between real life and her recurring fantasy, Renee realized she felt betrayed in her fantasy, and she also felt betrayed by her mother in real life. She had blamed her mother for not protecting her and for allowing the boyfriend to abuse her. In the relationship between the Victim and the Coach, Renee now saw that she had re-created the relationship dynamics between herself and her mother.

By going deeper into her fantasy, Renee had brought the fantasy characters out of the recesses of her mind and fleshed them out so that she could learn more about them. This process gave Renee a new feeling of control over her fantasy life and reminded her that these were characters she had created. She now saw that she had the power to change them, or challenge them, or learn from them. Renee understood that she could make choices about her own fantasies. She wasn't stuck with the same recurring plot.

Because she was eager to imagine how she might change her fantasy, Renee used another therapy exercise to continue the character analysis started with the stick figures. This time, instead of diagramming the fantasy on paper, she laid out colored crayons to represent the different characters. Using three-dimensional objects gave her a chance to move the characters around and experiment with different fantasy plots. In a dramatic moment in therapy, Renee talked about how angry she was with the Rapist and the Stupid Things. She reached out, grabbed the crayons that represented the men, and broke them in half. By releasing her anger, she was beginning to change this fantasy plot that had always felt stuck.

As another step toward healing, Renee decided to try to reduce her need for the fantasy by experimenting with when she would allow it to occur. She decided to work at staying more present during sex with David. She would stop the fantasy if it came up during lovemaking and use it only during masturbation.

Within a couple weeks of doing the character-exploration exercises, Renee noticed the fantasy plot change dramatically. She explained, "One day, when I was touching myself, the fantasy was playing out as it usually does. But all of a sudden, I imagined the Coach saying, 'Come on, you guys, let's get out of here.' *And they did.* The woman and all the men just stood up, walked out, and left the Victim alone. At that instant, the sexual excitement drained right out of the fantasy." By changing the plot to make it end before the girl climaxed, Renee had defused the fantasy of its erotic potential. In transforming the content, she had also made her old fantasy less upsetting. "I finally saw that the girl really needed to be left alone. That felt important for me, too, in healing," she said.

Renee had another breakthrough in healing when she considered, "What might the girl need, in order to feel safe?" That question led Renee to imagine her real, adult self showing up as a new character in the fantasy and offering comfort and compassion to the Victim. "I pictured myself wrapping the girl in a blue blanket, holding her, and nurturing her. I gave her what she needed." In real life, Renee had gone without protection and comfort when she had needed it most. As an adult, she could develop compassion for the little girl she once was and who had been betrayed and abused. Transforming her fantasy gave her a powerful way to soothe these old hurts and reclaim her sexuality for herself.

The next time she had sex with David, Renee focused on what was happening in the present. She employed the stop-thought technique whenever any fantasy would start to creep in. To her delight, she found this more conscious approach to sex gave her much more enjoyment than she had experienced before.

While Renee was pleased with her progress, she was disappointed in how her relationship was going. The more skills Renee practiced to help her stay present, the more critical and unhappy David became. When she tried to initiate sex, or to be more assertive during lovemaking to get what she wanted, he reacted with displeasure. He was losing control of the sexual scene—control he had enjoyed while she had been silent and off in her fantasy world. Renee explained, "Just as I was trying to connect with him more, he backed off. I felt like he was running away from me."

In fact, she was right. David was literally running from her and had already started a new relationship with another woman. As she had feared when she first started working on her fantasies, David was leaving her.

During the years when she managed to function sexually by relying on her fantasy, Renee wasn't facing the problems in her real-life relationship with David. Over the years, he had tried repeatedly to improve their sex life and had often encouraged her to talk to him more openly in bed. Back then, however, Renee was too afraid to tell him about her unwanted fantasies. She wasn't ready for the level of trust that he wanted to experience. He had misread her pained silence and felt rejected by her. He grew tired of trying to improve their intimate relationship on his own. Now that she was finally getting back her own voice about sex, David was too emotionally exhausted to listen. He didn't have the energy or commitment anymore to work with her as she learned new habits that she considered healthy and necessary for sexual enjoyment. Instead, he decided to make a fresh start with a different partner. As a result, they both decided to go their separate ways.

Although saddened, Renee was left with a sense of healing in her fantasy life and a commitment to find a new partner who would be nurturing and honest with her. If her old Victim fantasy crept into her thoughts during sexual arousal, she spontaneously revised it, with a more satisfying conclusion. "Before, I used to feel like I had to surrender to my fantasies. I felt paralyzed, like I couldn't move and I couldn't talk," Renee explained. "But now, it's the opposite. I can go to fantasy, if I want. I realize that when I fantasize now, it's about me, and I'm involved in creating the fantasy."

Once during masturbation, when she imagined hearing the familiar voice of the Coach saying, "She likes it," Renee was able to speak up for herself and answer loudly, "Yes, I do." That affirmation helped end the old fantasy dynamics and reminded her that she was fully deserving of pleasure in her sex life and capable of transforming her fantasy life to meet her present needs.

At forty, Kris had worked hard to overcome and heal from an unhappy childhood. She had grown up with parents who always seemed at war with one another emotionally. In addition, her mother had sexually molested her when she was a girl. Kris could remember once asking her mom to stop touching her genitals, and her mother responded by laughing in her face. Each time, the abuse never ended until Kris came to a climax.

In therapy, Kris had made good progress in repairing her damaged self-esteem and recovering from past abuse. She was in a committed, long-term relationship with a woman named April who was supportive and caring.

Yet, despite all the recovery work she had done, Kris could not get rid of a disturbing sexual fantasy. She attended a fantasy workshop, hoping to find out why a certain recurring fantasy left her feeling so ashamed and upset. After the workshop, Kris decided to continue using the new exercises to analyze her fantasy in more depth.

At the workshop, Kris started by writing down a synopsis of her fantasy plot. She called it "The Takedown."

A male stranger comes to my house to do some repair work. Even though he's dressed in his work clothes, it's obvious that he has an erection. I start to make lewd comments about his body. I say things like "I see you're ready to do more work than you came for." Or "You look like you want to take a reading with that rod." I walk up and undress him, undress myself, then lie down naked on the floor. I point to his penis and say, "Bring that tool over here." He walks over to me and starts to get into a position to fuck me. I say, "I'm not ready for you yet, but get ready to enter when I tell you." I'm

*masturbating, and he has the head of his penis touching
my outer vaginal lips, waiting for me to give the signal.
As I'm about to climax, I tell him, "Almost, almost,
Now!" Then he can enter me. I like having that power
over him, making him wait. Once I come, the fantasy
disappears, and I'm left feeling ashamed.*

As she had listened to other women explore their fantasies in-
depth at the workshop, Kris became even more determined to get
to the bottom of this fantasy that had been tormenting her for so
many years. As a woman in love with another woman, she was
upset to be fantasizing about rough sex with a man. But she had a
hunch that her dislike for the fantasy went well beyond sexual
orientation issues. As she explored the theme of the fantasy, she
could see that the dynamics were completely at odds with everything she loved about her real-life relationship. Her fantasy was
about cold, angry sex between power-hungry strangers, while in
her real life, sex was an expression of love between equals. Yet, the
fantasy felt essential to achieving orgasm.

After the workshop, Kris used an exercise designed to help
her step into the minds of her two fantasy characters. When she
had experienced the fantasy in the past, she had always felt like a
Voyeur, watching herself interact with the repairman. Now,
though, she imagined reading the minds of both characters and
putting their unspoken motivations into words. When she did, she
was in for a surprise.

Although Kris had always thought the fantasy was about the
woman having power over the man, she was shocked to discover
that the repairman thought *he* was the one in charge. She described the repairman's thoughts this way: "Oh, boy, I'm ready
for this." "I'm getting what I want here." "You dumb fuck, you
can't tell me when I get to come. I'm in control of my penis. I'll get
off when I want."

When she wrote down the woman's thoughts, she imagined

her thinking: "I want to get fucked." "You're the dumb fuck, and I'm in control." "I have the power to make you wait. I get to climax first."

Once she had recorded these thoughts, Kris could see that both characters used each other in this fantasy. Each one imagined having all the power. Each one treated the other as a sex object. Each one thought of the other as a "dumb fuck." They both imagined they had won, but their victory was hollow.

Looking back at her written fantasy plot, Kris underlined what she considered to be key phrases that were always included in her fantasy. Then, underneath these phrases, she identified the underlying emotions and relationship dynamics. She wrote down such comments as "lack of intimacy," "alienation," "exploitation," "rage," "loneliness," "a lack of respect for self and others." Next, she considered, "Do these qualities remind me of any other relationship?" Again, Kris was in for a surprise.

In many ways, her fantasy recapitulated the abusive relationship between her mother and her father. "They always seemed to be locked into this sick way of treating each other. Each one wanted to have power over the other one, but it was a false power. They each wanted to be in control, but they were both massively out of control. What they had was a mutually unsatisfying relationship."

Although Kris's parents had both died long ago, she saw that, on an unconscious level, she had been keeping them alive in her fantasy life. She realized she had always hoped they would find a different way to relate, and that their life story would have a happier ending. Like other children of dysfunctional families, Kris had grown up hoping she could somehow fix what was wrong between her parents and end their fighting and mutual torment. In an important breakthrough that helped strengthen her self-esteem, she realized, "I was the one who survived living in this abusive home. I came out intact. It was their problem, not mine. I'm tired of feeling responsible for them."

With this new understanding, Kris was finally able to get past her shame and bring herself to talk with her partner about the details of her upsetting fantasy. April was supportive and eager to help Kris learn how to enjoy sex without relying on fantasy. Together, they planned how to use new techniques to disrupt the function of her old fantasy. At orgasm, for instance, the point in her sexual response cycle when Kris was most likely to shift into fantasy, April would say "I love you" and help her stay present. They also experimented with using dildos (coincidentally, one of April's fantasies) to add more vaginal stimulation during sex.

After the first time Kris had sex without the fantasy, she said, "I never realized sex could be so powerful, not power filled." Gradually, she found herself feeling less numb during sex and more aware of her body's sensations. She became more willing to initiate sex and more eager to experiment with different styles of lovemaking. "My sense of dread around sexuality finally went away," she said.

Eventually, Kris was able to bring her fantasy work to a sense of closure by using a guided visualization exercise. She imagined her parents standing before her. They told her, "You don't need to worry about us anymore. We did love each other, but we didn't know how to express our emotions differently. We never got to have the kind of relationship we really wanted, or that you wanted us to have." As the image began to fade, Kris imagined her parents turning their backs and walking away from her, hand in hand.

With the understanding she had gained about her old fantasy, Kris said she couldn't imagine replaying it during sex. In getting to the core message of the fantasy, she had peeled away its erotic power. Yet, she didn't turn her back on the value of fantasizing in general. For years, she had used fantasy as a reliable route to orgasm. Now, she realized, she was free to imagine new erotic fantasies that contained the kind of sexual energy she wanted to bring to her own mind and celebrate in her real-life relationship.

❦

When we set out to change an unwanted fantasy, we are taking a bold step. This process won't always go smoothly, or bring the results we want when we want them. Some women do this healing work and find that their troublesome fantasies go away and never return. Others find that their unwanted fantasies return during times of stress or anxiety. Some women find their unwanted fantasies remain powerfully erotic, even when they are no longer dependent on using them, while other women feel the old fantasies have lost all erotic charge.

Once we heal an unwanted sexual fantasy, the benefits often carry over into improvements in other areas of our lives. A woman named Allison said she used to think of sexual fantasy as a bird in a cage. "It was a big, ugly bird that made horrible screeching noises. My fantasies were something I wanted to cover up. I'd imagine throwing a cover over this birdcage to shut up the screeching. In reality, that meant avoiding any sexual urges or feelings. That was the only way I knew how to keep the bird quiet."

Since she has healed her unwanted fantasies, though, Allison has acquired a new view of fantasies and a new attitude about her own sexuality. "Now, I can take the blanket off this cage whenever I want. And the bird has turned into a wonderful creature that has beautiful, colorful feathers and marvelous songs. I've discovered that fantasies can actually be fun. I feel no guilt about them now, and no shame about sex. If I hadn't healed my fantasies, I never would have attained feeling like a normal, sexual person."

CHAPTER 9

Sharing Fantasies with Lovers

In the film, *When Harry Met Sally,* Harry (Billy Crystal) and Sally (Meg Ryan) walk through a park and chat about their sexual dreams and fantasies. He goes first, describing a comical scene in which he imagines himself making love before a panel of Olympic judges. The first two judges rate his sexual performance highly, but his mother, disguised as an East German judge, gives him a miserable score.

Sally then shares her recurring sexual fantasy, which she's been having since adolescence. It's always about a faceless man who rips off her clothes. When Harry asks whether it ever goes any further, Sally replies No, but sometimes she imagines herself wearing different clothes.

In the film, Harry and Sally share their sexual fantasies as a way to get to know one another better. It's a cute scene, with a clever punch line and no significant consequences.

In real life, however, it's often a different story. People vary in how comfortable or how awkward they feel discussing sexual matters, and in how guarded or how open they are about their most personal thoughts. Some partners choose to keep sexual fantasies off-limits to protect their relationship, while others are anxious to explore and actively tap into this resource to enhance how they relate as a couple.

Research underscores what many women have told us in interviews: sharing sexual fantasies can be a tricky business. After surveying dozens of studies on sexual fantasy for an article in a 1995 edition of *Psychological Bulletin,* one research team concluded, "Although there is very little information about this issue [of whether partners share fantasies], the data available suggest that only a minority do." Among the highlights of scholarly findings: Women are more inclined than men to share a sexual fantasy with a partner, but men are more likely to react to a partner's fantasy with jealousy. Men and women who express the most guilt about having sexual fantasies also believe that their fantasies hurt their relationships and their partners, even though the partners may not be aware of these sexual thoughts.[1] No wonder, then, that sexual fantasies remain a big secret many of us never tell a lover.

When women have decided to share their intimate sexual thoughts with a partner, they report a wide range of reactions, concerns, and repercussions. Many women say that sharing fantasies brought them closer to their partners, enhancing intimacy and improving their sex lives. Other women report, however, that sharing fantasies generated emotional distrust and highlighted sexual incompatibilities in their relationships. For better or worse, sharing fantasies can profoundly influence how a woman and her partner relate as a couple.

Some women share fantasies in words alone, by talking about them with a partner or by listening to a partner describe his or her fantasies. This type of interchange can take place in a non-sexual setting, or when sexual passions have been stirred up. Talking about fantasies can be an enjoyable part of foreplay, adding to sexual arousal and excitement.

Some couples stage a more active dance, playing out fantasies together with a partner during sex, perhaps even with elaborate costumes or props. Again, women report a wide range of experiences. Some couples enact one partner's favorite fantasy, while others invent new fantasies that draw on both partners' imaginations and erotic desires. When two people develop an ability to talk comfortably about how their unique fantasies have influenced them personally and as a couple, they can create a special type of rapport that deepens emotional intimacy.

While many women describe valuable personal growth, sexual healing, and improved relationships as a result of sharing fantasies, others are left with regrets. Outcomes can range from pleasantly surprising to unpredictably disappointing. Only in the movies, it seems, can a couple reveal their most private sexual thoughts and expect no consequences.

WHY WOMEN KEEP THEIR SEXUAL FANTASIES SECRET

Many of the women we interviewed told us they had never revealed the details of their sexual fantasies to anyone before, including their partners. Among the women who have shared fantasies, most of them reported that they were extremely cautious about when, and with whom, they revealed the contents of their erotic imagination.

The difficulty with revealing any fantasy is that once it's been shared, *it can't be unshared*. And, because there are no guarantees about the outcome of disclosure, women sometimes agonize over whether opening up this type of discussion would be good or bad for themselves, their partners, or their relationships. The reasons so many women keep quiet about their fantasy lives vary widely, but often reflect personal privacy issues or fear of a partner's reaction.

PERSONAL PRIVACY ISSUES

Because fantasies are both personal and sexual, it's common for women to feel embarrassed about them, protective of them, or shy about revealing them. In some cases, this reticence comes as a result of not understanding enough about fantasies. A lack of information has left many of us too puzzled about the meaning of our own fantasies to discuss them with a partner. As one woman pointed out, "How can I share these weird thoughts with someone else, when even *I* don't know why I have them or what they mean?"

Some women report feeling embarrassed by the overt sex and the intensity of sexual passion conveyed in their fantasies, the sexual activities portrayed, or the unconventional settings, images, and characters their fantasies contain. Concerns about sexual orientation can also keep women quiet about their fantasies. Heterosexual women sometimes hesitate to describe same-sex fantasies to male partners, while lesbians can be reluctant to share fantasies about men or penises with women lovers. Yet, as we've already seen, fantasies don't necessarily reflect our true sexual preferences.

For women who adhere to strict religious teachings that condemn sexual thoughts, or who grew up in a sexually repressive environment, sharing sexual fantasies may be akin to confessing their sins. In these instances, women said they have avoided talking about their fantasies because they feared they would be judged as unworthy, sick, perverted, insatiable, or sexually loose.

Without a common vocabulary to describe our fantasies, or a mutual understanding of how fantasies function for us and where they can come from, many of us have felt as if we haven't known enough about this subject to talk comfortably. Some of us may have felt at a loss to describe unscripted fantasies, for example, which are seldom portrayed in commercial erotica or pornography. Similarly, we may never have heard anyone else describe a scripted fantasy that compares to our own.

Maintaining a well-protected erotic imagination can reinforce a strong sense of individuality and freedom. Leah, a hetero-sexual woman who often has sensory fantasies about women's breasts, said she has deliberately avoided telling her husband about her fantasies. "We've been together for seventeen years, and by now I know that there are some needs a spouse can never meet," she said. "When we make love, he's very tuned into my body. We have a great sex life. But I don't think he wants or needs to hear every thought and emotion I'm experiencing. This is my private space, and I prefer to keep it that way. I like to maintain my individuality in our relationship by having my own thoughts."

Another woman described the special enjoyment of going off in her mind, into her very private fantasy world, then returning to her real-life partner. "After climax, when I return from the fantasy to the present, I feel like my husband's arms are waiting there to catch me," she said. "It's very welcoming, like coming home."

When women are particularly attached to certain sexual fantasies, or enjoy them precisely because they function so reliably, they may be reluctant to talk about them out of a fear that, once revealed, these fantasies could lose their erotic power. Indeed, as we've heard in previous chapters, the very act of putting a sexual fantasy into words can change how we feel about it and how well it continues to work for us.

Some women are cautious about revealing their fantasies because they are waiting for the right partner, or the right moment. They may covet and guard their favorite fantasies as if they were precious jewels, only wanting to reveal them to a partner who could appreciate and understand their beauty and value. One woman with a Beloved-type fantasy (involving prolonged foreplay in a warm wading pool) explained, "I've avoided talking about or acting out this fantasy of mine, because I don't want to waste it on just any partner. And I haven't yet found a partner who I've felt would really appreciate it, like I do. I don't want be disappointed by how it might turn out. If you save a fantasy, treasure it just for yourself, then it's always there for you to enjoy. Whenever you need it, you can dust it off and know that it will look, taste, smell exactly the same. It's wonderful to have something so reliably pleasurable, all for yourself."

When women keep their fantasies private, they don't have to worry about their fantasies becoming contaminated by a partner's potentially negative judgment or misguided interpretation. Without distraction, a fantasy can continue to serve as a highly personal creative outlet. Not discussing a fantasy may help preserve its erotic charge and potential. One woman summed up how many others feel when she said, "If I share it, it won't be my *private* fantasy any longer."

Fear of a Partner's Reaction

Many women hesitate to share fantasies because they worry about a partner's reaction. We may worry about how our partners would feel, knowing that we fantasize at all. Or, we may wonder how our partners would react if told the details of a particular fantasy. We may choose not to share these private thoughts out of fear that a partner would become jealous of a fantasy, judge us harshly for its contents, or encourage us to act it out.

Judging by the stories women have shared, these fears are reasonable. Partners who subscribe to widespread cultural views about sexual fantasies may misinterpret the real meaning of a woman's fantasy, or assume it's a true mirror for her deepest desires.

One women, for instance, decided not to tell her husband about her most common fantasy, involving a romantic, Pretty Maiden scenario. He reacted by guessing that it was about being raped. "He had heard on a talk show that women fantasize about being overpowered, and he just assumed this was true for me. I got so angry," she said.

A woman who enjoyed Wild Woman fantasies, in which she imagined a parade of male sex partners, avoided talking with her husband about these thoughts. "He would find it too wild. Either he would think I'm a pervert who wants group sex, or he would feel disappointed, like he was not meeting my expectations in bed. Really, though, this fantasy is not something I would ever want to be a part of. It just adds variety to our monogamous sex life."

Similarly, a woman who often fantasized about a well-endowed former lover kept these sexual thoughts to herself to avoid stirring up jealousy in her relationship. She explained, "My husband doesn't talk to me about his old lovers, and I know he doesn't want to hear about mine." Indeed, a woman may decide to keep her own fantasies under wraps if she feels insecure about hearing her partner's fantasies—especially if she assumes that they feature more attractive, younger, or more buxom females than herself.

Women who had unpleasant or awkward experiences with sharing fantasies were reluctant to bring up the subject again. Kelly, a woman in her late twenties, stopped telling her husband about her Pretty Maiden fantasies after one bad experience. She had wanted the sharing to bring them closer as a couple, but her good intentions backfired. As Kelly recalled: "I started by describing a fantasy to my husband about a mystery man who would see me dressed up in an elegant restaurant, then sweep me off my feet. But after I told him just this one story, he asked me not to share anymore. He said he feels insecure now and expects me to be unfaithful if I'm having a fantasy about someone else. Ultimately, I regretted sharing this fantasy, even though it was an open moment between us. Ever since I told him about it, he's been harassing me about being unfaithful—which I never have been. I can't imagine sharing anything else about my fantasies with him again."

Women who suffer from unwanted sexual fantasies are often wary of sharing because they fear their partners would not respond with compassion. The contents of unwanted sexual fantasies can feel so disturbing and shameful that the risks involved in sharing them may seem to outweigh the benefits.

Indeed, in our research, some women survivors of sexual abuse did report negative experiences with sharing fantasies. Survivors frequently said they kept quiet about the specifics of their unwanted fantasies until they had some assurance of emotional safety. One survivor explained what can happen when a partner does not respond appropriately. She said, "I finally pulled together the courage to tell my boyfriend about my horrible recurring fantasy about abusive sex with my grandfather. Just when I wanted comforting, my boyfriend accused me of enjoying the incest more than sex with him. I was so upset with his reaction, I broke up with him. Before I ever share anything about my fantasy life again, I'll check out a future partner more carefully."

WHY WOMEN REVEAL THEIR FANTASIES

Although there are many good reasons for wanting to keep our fantasies private, there are also times when it's desirable, appropriate, and even necessary to share sexual fantasies with a partner. Some women, for example, decide to share fantasies for sexual enrichment. They may talk about or enact fantasies to spice up a flagging sex life, expand on their sexual repertoire, or explain the intimate details of what they want to do in bed. Sharing can be a step toward enacting a fantasy. Or, as some women report, just talking about fantasies can add to arousal and intimacy.

Women may also be motivated to reveal their fantasies for healing purposes. As we've seen in previous chapters, fantasy concerns can sometimes threaten intimacy and may need to be addressed to avoid or overcome a crisis in a relationship.

A DESIRE FOR SEXUAL ENRICHMENT

Because they grow out of our personal and sexual experiences over a lifetime, fantasies contain a wealth of information about our sexual interests, styles, desires, fears, and enjoyments. Thus, revealing them can sometimes be a good way for us to open a dialogue that can improve sexual relating and increase satisfaction.

A young graduate student named Tiffany, who has been struggling to overcome a sexually repressive upbringing, said she asked her new husband about his fantasies as a way to help inspire her own sexual imagination. "I told him I can never think of any fantasies. My sex life has always felt constricted, tied up in my intellectual head. When he told me about his fantasies, I was excited and honored to know that he trusted me enough to share. I also felt more comfortable with the idea of inventing some of my own. We are slowly learning more about each other."

A woman named Juliet decided to share fantasies with her lover in hopes that she could improve their stale sex life. She said: "I wasn't happy with the way our sex life was going, and so I asked him to describe a fantasy to me. Then, I told him a fantasy of mine about sexually adventuresome gargoyles who take me captive in a cave. I emphasized the graphic details about how the gargoyles were skilled at performing oral sex. It was a definite hint that this is what I want more of during lovemaking. I also explained that I see myself, in my fantasies, as someone who protests at first, but eventually screams for joy and delight because she gets so swept up in desire and pleasure. In real life, I have a hard time letting go so completely."

At first, Juliet said, her boyfriend was embarrassed to be talking about the subject of fantasies. But she could tell by his physical response that he was also excited by the conversation. "He definitely listened to me, and I listened to him. We both learned more about what the other one wanted to experience during sex by describing our fantasies, and our relations have improved since then."

Nikki, a forty-four-year-old woman, decided to share a special fantasy idea with her new boyfriend early in their relationship, as a way to get to know more about each other's sexual styles and interests. She was also curious whether Alex, a dead ringer for the actor Wesley Snipes, might be interested in eventually acting out the fantasy. Although it began as her fantasy, it shifted into something more mutual as a result of their intimate conversations. They haven't yet played it out, but the very process of creating it together has increased their sexual hunger for each other. Nikki describes their fantasy as a "work in progress":

> I told Alex that I respond to loud colors like red and jade and purple. He told me his favorite color is red, so we've decided there's going to be a lot of red in this scene.
>
> We both like to move, too. I know there's going to be slow dancing in this scene. So we've got music and movement, for who knows how long. Maybe all night.
>
> And I absolutely love to be undressed. I want to watch Alex's face as he discovers what it is I have on underneath. I have a serious lingerie habit. I love the stuff. It makes me feel more sensual. I like the touch of lacy fabric on my skin. I'm looking forward to having him unhook my fanciest bra, because I know he's into breasts. He told me. I'm pretty chesty. He likes my breasts almost as much as I do.
>
> Most of the time I wear flat, sensible shoes, but Alex says he'd like me to wear high heels. When I asked why, he explained how nice they make a woman's legs look. After he told me that, I happened to see some shoes on sale, in my size, with three-inch heels. I bought them and left them out where he could see them. His eyes lit up when he spotted them. We are definitely doing the shoes in this fantasy.
>
> Now, this may sound corny, but I also imagine us sitting for a while so we can feed each other. I'm sorry, but I like to eat. Especially chocolate. Godiva milk chocolate. He likes this idea, too.
>
> Then, we plan to get into foreplay. Slowly. I don't

like to be groped. It would have to move slowly. I recently saw in a florist's window a bottle of Chocolate Body Paint. That sounded fun, so I bought that, too, along with a little brush. Then I told him about it. That's going to get used, too, during this slow foreplay.

I'm very affected by music, particularly saxophone music. Ideally, I would climax at the height of one of my favorite jazz soloist's pieces. When we finally do act out this scene, I know I'm going to keep the lights on, and my eyes open. I like to watch. And I like to talk. Sex without talking is not nearly as exciting to me, and I don't mean that "ooooh, baby" stuff. I'll want to know what he's feeling, so we can connect on that deep level.

Alex is getting anxious to do this fantasy, but I'm in no rush. You can't do what I have in mind in an hour. We'll need all night, at least, and we're still finding new things out about each other that we'll need to add to the scene. I'm still discovering things, by just talking with him, that I didn't know about me. And it's the same for him.

The thing with this fantasy is, when we finally act it out, we won't be acting. It's going to be the real thing because we've both been involved in creating it to fit who we really are and what we really like. I know that there's nothing harmful in this fantasy, except for the calories.

A NEED FOR HELP WITH HEALING

When fantasy concerns stifle or threaten intimacy, women may feel compelled to talk about this subject directly. In particular, talking about disturbing fantasies can be a helpful step for women who are attempting to heal or change their unwanted thoughts. Several women described how their partners offered help and support in healing, once they understood the dynamics and cause of unwanted fantasies. When partners respond in such positive ways, the experience of sharing can be healing for the woman and beneficial for the relationship.

Betty, for instance, had an intrusive Victim fantasy that replayed an assault she had experienced years earlier. After sixteen years of marriage, she finally decided to tell her husband about the fantasy. "He knew that I was planning to attend a fantasy workshop," she explained, "and he asked me if a fantasy was bothering me. I finally told him a little about it, not in any great detail, but only that it was a rape scenario. He listened quietly, and held me afterward." She hadn't shared the fantasy earlier in their marriage, she said, "because I was afraid he wouldn't understand, as even I don't. I was afraid he wouldn't want to make love to me again if he knew that I was thinking such a bizarre thing." By sharing the general nature of the fantasy, however, and receiving his comfort, she felt strengthened and supported as she set about healing.

A woman named Claire found that her healing progressed almost as soon as she dared to talk to her partner, Eric, about her fantasies. She had been avoiding sex to avoid her Pretty Maiden fantasies, which reminded her of some negative sexual experiences she had as a child. Because she could see that their relationship was heading for a crisis, she decided to overcome her fear and tell him what was bothering her. She said: "Once I told him, I knew there would be no more hiding in fantasy. From then on, whenever we made love, he might look at me and know that I'm not there. But it was a risk I had to take if we were to have a chance as a couple. To my delight, Eric opened his arms to me in a way I couldn't have predicted. He didn't show any signs of being disgusted, which was my worst fear. I had hoped he would be sympathetic, but he went way beyond that. He told me he was grateful that I had talked to him, and that he wanted to help me work through this. He felt honored that I would risk telling him something I'd never told anybody else before. He held me for a long time as we talked. Afterward, he said we had come a million miles that night in connecting with each other."

Similarly, a woman named Lisa, whose unwanted Dominatrix fantasies focused on erotic power and control, had to overcome feelings of vulnerability and fear to share her fantasies with her partner, Kay. She chose to reveal her fantasy because she knew this step could be an important part of her healing work. "I was afraid Kay would fear me, or not feel safe around me, or think of me as some kind of sick monster," she said. Often, her fantasies involved threesomes, in which Lisa saw herself tying up sexual partners. "In these fantasies, I told the other women when they could climax, and that power excited me," she explained. When her partner reacted to her stories only with support, though, Lisa felt relief and acceptance. "She was sweet and helped me feel safe talking about these fantasies. Working together, we were able to begin changing some of my destructive fantasies. This felt really new and exciting to me, and brought us closer."

GUIDELINES FOR DISCUSSING SEXUAL FANTASIES

Whatever motivates us to talk about fantasies with a partner, we are more likely to have positive experiences when we respect our own limits and comfort levels and pay attention to some general guidelines. When we are clear about why we are sharing our own fantasies, or listening to a partner speak about fantasies, we can proceed more confidently, increasing the likelihood of a positive, valuable discussion.

SHARING IN SAFETY AND IN STEPS

Sexual fantasies are such private and personal thoughts that no one should ever feel forced or compelled to disclose them. Talking about fantasies works best when both people in a relationship know they have options as to if, when, where, how, and how much they reveal about their fantasy lives. Before we begin to share fantasies, it's important to agree to stop the conversation at any time if either person feels uncomfortable.

When women decide to share a fantasy, they want their partners to be nonjudgmental listeners. Women said they appreciated partners who could listen to them share fantasies, appreciate their creativity, and perhaps pick up new ideas for future lovemaking. One woman said, "I remember a wonderful lover who made a point of inviting me to allow my fantasies to be present while we were making love. I never felt like I had to tell him the details of my fantasy life, but I knew he was open. It made me feel so comfortable about my sexuality, just having that permission to be real and honest with what I was experiencing during sex."

Although partners sometimes intuitively understand what women want them to learn from their fantasies, other times they need to have this information spelled out more directly. "I guess lovers aren't necessarily mind readers," said one woman. "I thought I could tell him my fantasy, and he'd automatically know what I wanted more of during sex. He didn't get it, though."

Conversations about sexual fantasies tend to be more productive when the two people know each other well and are open to talking about sex. If both partners view fantasy in much the same way, then they don't have to be worried about the other's reaction.

When a woman is unsure how her partner will react, however, she may want to begin by testing the waters to find out if the partner is interested in talking about fantasies at all. If even general questions—such as "Do you ever have fantasies?"—lead to cues indicating that a partner is feeling uncomfortable or threatened, that's usually a good signal to stop talking about fantasies. This kind of conversation can go slowly, with sharing happening in stages if both partners feel comfortable about proceeding.

A woman named Ellen, for example, took time to talk with her husband about sexual fantasy in a general way to establish some mutual understandings. "We talked about the different kinds of fantasies we enjoy and why we like them," she said, "I feel like we came to a deeper understanding of each other. It created a new level of intimacy, where we felt safe describing our most personal thoughts. I felt like it opened a new realm for us, as a couple. We both revealed something personal, and we both felt better afterward."

SELECTING WHAT TO SHARE

Women need to exercise good judgment in deciding how much detail they want to share about their fantasy lives. A partner may be intrigued with some aspects of a fantasy, yet feel put off, threatened, or hurt by other details. Even though fantasies don't necessarily reflect a woman's genuine desires, talking about fantasies in a sensitive, often carefully edited manner, can be a subtle way to educate a partner about sexual styles, interests, and preferences.

Bobbi, for example, was very selective about which parts of her Beloved-type fantasy she chose to share with her husband. When he asked her if she ever had sexual fantasies, the following favorite fantasy came easily to her mind:

I'm with a man I've never met in real life. He's a cowboy and an animal lover, self-confident and strong, yet also tender. We spend the whole day together and discover that we have many common interests. He showers me with attention, hanging on my every word, and looks at me with burning desire. At his home, we eat, drink, listen to music, dance close. Then he begins to whisper his feelings for me. He says that I'm the only one who has ever made him feel this way. This excites me and makes me want him, too. His first kisses are gentle, and I return them that way. Then he kisses me more aggressively, and I return that energy. When we undress each other, I notice his lean, taut stomach, his

*contoured legs, his dark chest hair. As he caresses me,
he makes me feel worshiped, adored, safe, and very
sexy. He takes me to the edge with breast stimulation
and oral sex, then thrusts inside me. We begin slowly,
then go at it with wild abandon. We climax together,
then cuddle in bed for the rest of the day, talking and
touching.*

However, when Bobbi described this fantasy to her husband,
she told him only the part that she thought he could relate to: the
actual sex scene. She shared that she imagines a man giving her
lots of breast stimulation and oral sex. Bobbi didn't think her
husband would understand why all the talking, kissing, eye contact, slow dancing, and other evidence of emotional connection
were so important in her fantasy, and so arousing to her. "It did
excite him to hear that I had fantasies, and we had great sex
afterward," she said, "but he's still much more interested in the
physical details of sex, and I'm into the emotionality of the experience."

Although there's no guarantee that talking about fantasies
will be a positive experience, many women have found this a step
toward greater self-knowledge and enhanced intimacy. In general,
women have been most positive about their decision to share a
fantasy when they have had a good reason to do so, such as
wanting to feel closer or wanting to experience some new things
sexually. Talking about fantasies also seems to get easier with
experience, as a couple's comfort level increases and their mutual
understanding grows.

GUIDELINES FOR ENACTING FANTASIES

Sometimes, sexual fantasies do reflect our real desires. We may be
curious and even excited about experiencing for real something

we, or our partners, have enjoyed only in the erotic imagination. Women sometimes see acting out a fantasy as a way to satisfy healthy curiosities, stimulate sexual passions, and expand the range of activities they can enjoy in sex. Acting out a fantasy, however, is not without risks, no matter how optimistic our expectations.

The essence of fantasies is that they are *unreal*. They can improve on reality. As the person who invents a particular fantasy, we get to control every detail as it unfolds. If we don't like one setting for a fantasy, we can change it in an instant to be more pleasing. We can easily make the characters in our fantasy do whatever, and say whatever, we most desire. And in our fantasies, great sex never gets interrupted by doorbells, phone calls, or wakeful children. In real life, however, we lose this total control. That's why, when women enact their fantasies for real, anything's bound to happen during lovemaking.

The aftermath of enacting a fantasy is similarly unpredictable. When women described situations of enacting fantasies, some said they were delighted with the experience, while others found their favorite fantasies backfired and they lost a pleasurable route to sexual satisfaction. This unpredictability has caused some sex therapists to go so far as to caution couples against enacting fantasies. Drs. William Masters and Virginia Johnson, for example, concluded, "Sexual fantasies that are tried in real life often turn out to be disappointing, unexciting, or even unpleasant, resulting at times in a complete loss of the erotic value of the fantasy."[2]

Just as we can evaluate our personal fantasies to determine whether they function well for us, or whether they cause us problems, we can also consider whether acting out fantasies will hurt or harm our relationships. Fantasy enactments should be avoided if they might lead to risky or criminal behavior, feel out of control, hinder recovery, lower self-esteem, cause sexual problems, or undermine intimacy. Attention to safe sex should extend to making sure that neither person is physically or emotionally harmed as a result of playing out a fantasy.

Generally, women described the most positive sexual experiences when they approached a fantasy playfully, with mutual consent and clear guidelines agreed upon ahead of time with their partners. They also kept sexual fantasy in perspective as something that might be fun to try out, but that never became more significant than one's own self-respect, safety, or the sanctity of a real-life relationship. They honored their own limits and intuition and were similarly sensitive to their partners' needs, desires, and comfort level. These women also felt they had learned something important that they wanted to share with other women.

INITIATING PLAYFULLY

Instead of telling their partners directly that they want to enact particular sexual fantasies, many women prefer a playful approach that is more subtle and less risky. This sort of initiation tends to work well when partners are in a receptive mind-set, and when women approach fantasies with a low key, casual attitude. The primary agenda of this approach is to have fun and explore where curiosity might lead.

Women sometimes tiptoe toward acting out a favorite fantasy, carefully dropping hints to gauge a partner's willingness to play along. A woman might start by suggesting only a small part of a fantasy at first, then weaving in more elements of her fantasy gradually, if she gets a positive reaction. As one woman explained, "When I initiate fantasy play, I tell myself to accept possible rejection and be open to making changes. I know that, if my partner turns down a suggestion, he's not rejecting *me*."

Some couples bring their fantasies to life in a subtle way, simply by adding special dialogue or behaviors to their usual lovemaking rituals. One woman turned up sexual heat by whispering "you beast" to her husband during sex, without telling him that she was mentally playing out a scene from a favorite romance novel. Another woman was delighted when her lover took time to acknowledge her sensory fantasies by lighting her perfumed bedroom candles before they had sex.

Jojo, a single woman in her twenties, wanted to coax her lover into playing out a Pretty Maiden fantasy in which she's blindfolded, gently tied to a bed, and then pleasured all over. In the fantasy, she enjoys the sensual surprise of not knowing which part of her body will be stimulated next. Hoping to experience this kind of sexual seduction in real life, she hinted to her partner that she would like to try bondage or blindfolds as part of sex play. "I brought it up jokingly, so he wouldn't think I was asking for too much, or that I was unhappy with our sex life as it was," she said. "He did it lightly, holding down my hands during sex. I liked that, and so did he. It didn't feel awkward or uncomfortable."

A playful approach to enacting fantasies can help couples create spontaneous sexual adventures. One woman recalled a memorable sexual experience when she and her college boyfriend acted out some fantasies on the spur of the moment. She said:

> My roommate went away for the weekend. My boyfriend and I borrowed a video camera and were just fooling around with it when we decided to make porno movies of ourselves. We didn't talk about it much beforehand. We just turned the camera on, and things started happening. Before I knew it, I was tied up on the bed and Kurt was dancing above me in my roommate's underwear. We had never done anything like that before. I'd repeat it, without a doubt. I found it very liberating.

Ashley, a woman in her thirties, said she and her lover discovered playful new ways to give each other sexual pleasure as a result of talking about their fantasies. Her lover was delighted to learn that he was the subject of her Beloved-type fantasies. After she described to him a typical script, which involved extended foreplay and lots of eye contact between passionate lovers, they spent the night together. "He did as many things to me as he could, based on the fantasies I had told him about," Ashley said. "I went nuts. Having him act out my fantasy in this way was like a dream come true."

After they played out her fantasy, Ashley's lover asked her if she would like to try out one of his. "I agreed, not out of obligation, but because I felt excited to try something new," she recalled. "He asked me to tie him to the bed and stimulate him with different objects—ice, a makeup brush, my fingers soaked with body lotion. I did so, gladly. My self-confidence increased, because I knew I could give him pleasure and that he wanted to receive it from me. Our relationship became more mature because we both felt we could tell each other a lot more after that night."

A problem women sometimes encounter with a playful approach to enacting fantasies is that, because it's so indirect and subtle, there's no guarantee that the partner is really open and receptive to the experience. The importance of mutual understanding and communication became clear to Anita, a young mother, when she attempted to set up a romantic Wild Woman fantasy with her husband. She sent her children off to a friend's house for an evening. Before her unsuspecting husband was due to arrive home, she dimmed the lights, decorated the house with flowers and candles, chilled some wine, and laid out a trail of lingerie from the front door to their bed, just like in her favorite fantasy. He walked in the door, turned on the lights, and blurted out, "What's this laundry doing all over the floor?" As her fantasy fizzled, Anita realized that she had skipped an important step of making sure her husband was ready for and wanted to participate in her fantasy.

CLARIFYING GROUND RULES

Because sexual arousal can sometimes impair judgment, negotiating with a partner about the details of acting out a fantasy can be an important step to take before the sexual heat is turned up. Clarifying ground rules in advance can help tilt the odds toward a positive experience with acting out fantasies, especially when the type of fantasy being considered involves new, unusual, challenging, or "kinky" behavior.

Agreeing on ground rules doesn't have to involve heavy negotiations. This step also can be undertaken with a playful attitude, such as one woman's suggestion to her lover, "Let's get crazy tonight." She made it clear, as part of her invitation, that she wanted to act out fantasies as a onetime sexual fling. She wasn't interested in creating a new norm for their relationship. "It was kind of an adventure," she said. "We tried out a bunch of things we were both comfortable doing—a little light bondage, some fun things with vegetables. I was recently divorced and enjoyed this chance to get a little wild. My new lover and I felt free enough to experiment together, and we made sure not to do anything that hurt either of us." As a result, she said, "We satisfied our curiosity. Although it was fun for one night, there was nothing that we wanted to do again. Once was enough for both of us."

Many women who enjoy acting out fantasies which involve bondage and assumed control by a partner say that good communication and advance planning are essential to ensuring a positive outcome. Couples may agree on a "safe word" or gesture ahead of time to signal that they want to stop acting out the fantasy.

Sandra, who enjoys sex play involving dominance and submission, explains, "I only do these things with partners I know well, feel safe with, and trust completely. Part of a safe S/M scene is making sure that you negotiate the rules ahead of time, before you begin to play. You need to be able to talk about sex and explain what you want to do, and what you don't want. We decide ahead of time who will play which roles, and what our safe words will be if anyone wants to stop. If anyone says 'no,' at any time, it has to stop right then," she said. "Otherwise, it's the same thing as rape. If you're playing with power and sex, and you're agreeing to give up some of your power to someone else for the night, you'd better know what you're getting into."

ACTIVELY HONORING LIMITS

Once partners begin to act out a sexual fantasy, they need to feel comfortable about stopping or changing the experience any time it begins to feel awkward, uncomfortable, or threatening. This element of mutual consent needs to be ongoing throughout the sexual experience, so that either partner can pull out of the fantasy play at any time, without shame or blame. By actively honoring one another's limits during sex, a couple can steer clear of fantasy hazards, traps, and future regrets.

When Gigi and her lesbian partner talked about sexual fantasies, for instance, her partner described a bondage scenario. Gigi offered to act it out, because she thought it would make sex more exciting. After talking more, however, and taking into account Gigi's abuse history and her struggle to change unwanted, abusive fantasies, they decided not to enact it. Instead, as a way of increasing sexual excitement without bringing potentially damaging energy into their lovemaking, they decided to act out a sensory fantasy that was purely verbal and didn't require them to take on roles related to power. Gigi said, "Our new fantasy involved imagery of an ocean wave, a cave, or a field of flowers, with my voice communicating what I am discovering or where we are going next. I would try to create the sensual aspects of each place by talking about its sounds, smells, or view. My hand would become the wind, wave, or lightning, as it touched her body."

Valerie, a young, single woman with an adventurous attitude about sex, had a few unpleasant experiences when she tried to interest partners in acting out her Wild Woman fantasies about having sex in semipublic places. They either balked or reacted to her suggestions with ridicule. To avoid further disappointment, she decided to keep her own fantasies to herself and instead encouraged partners to suggest fantasies they might want to act out. That way, she was in a position to choose whether or not to proceed with a particular scenario. One partner eagerly proposed a number of things they might do. She said, "He asked me to strip, to masturbate, to be tied up, to be fed, to crawl, to be silent, to dance erotically, to undress in public. I DID THEM ALL, because they felt like fun games and adventures. I enjoyed being the recipient of all that passion and lust gained from me and my action."

If either partner fails to respect the other's limits, however, a fantasy experience can backfire, potentially damaging a relationship. Carly, for example, had long entertained a Wild Woman fantasy of having sex in an airplane bathroom. When she tried manipulating an unwilling boyfriend into acting it out with her, both of them wound up feeling annoyed and disappointed. She described the experience: "The first time I was going on a plane trip with my new boyfriend, I joked about my fantasy beforehand, letting him know I was up for it. Then, once we were airborne, I asked him in a flirtatious manner, but with no misconception in my meaning, if he would like to join me in the ladies' room. He declined, seeming tired from the trip and a little embarrassed. It disappointed me that he didn't want to take that risk. Instead of letting go of the fantasy and respecting his limits, I pouted for a while and stopped talking to him. Later in the flight, I suggested it again. Then he seemed annoyed and turned me down more forcefully. By the time the plane landed, I was upset with him, and he was irritated with me."

PREPARING FOR SURPRISES

No matter how good the intentions or how careful the planning, fantasy enactments are likely to produce unforeseen outcomes and unexpected results. Some surprises are delightful, and others are distressing. From the stories that women have shared, successful outcomes seem dependent on individual personalities, circumstances, expectations, and good timing.

Some women discovered they enjoyed acting out a fantasy precisely because it involved taking on a made-up role. One woman, for instance, pretended to be a "rich bitch," and her boyfriend pretended to be her houseboy, whom she seduced. She said, "The fact that we were *acting* enabled us to do things we weren't quite comfortable doing *for real.*"

Other women, however, were disappointed after indulging a fantasy because they realized the sentiments and sexual intensity being enacted were not genuine or long-lasting. Maria, for example, finally got an opportunity to act on her recurring fantasy of reconnecting with an old boyfriend. One afternoon, when she spotted him in a restaurant lobby, "it was like a scene in a movie. We dropped the packages and briefcases we were carrying and ran into each other's arms." They wound up in bed together that night, and the sex was passionate and loving, just as she had imagined. But the next morning, when she went to the airport to see him off, he kept her at arm's length. "That's when my beautiful fantasy went boom!" she said. "He was so mean to me at the airport, so cold, so distant. I felt hurt, used, and disappointed, like I had made a fool of myself."

Acting out fantasies is seldom a positive experience if either party is being dishonest or manipulative with the other. Women have reported feeling tricked or disappointed after engaging in fantasies over the Internet, for example, where the potential for a partner to be hiding behind a disguise is high.

Helen, a divorced woman in her late thirties, was using a computer bulletin board one day for professional research. Her research took a new turn, though, when a man she was corresponding with electronically asked her what she was wearing. "Our conversation got more and more personal, until we were actually having cybersex. I have to admit that it was exciting. The conversation got so graphic that I climaxed, sitting in my home office, right in front of the computer screen." The man gave her his home phone number, and she later decided to give him a call. When she did, though, she was surprised to hear a woman answer the phone. Her computer "date" had never mentioned that he was married. "I realized that, even though I'd had this exciting cyber-sex experience, I was still a divorced woman in my thirties, all alone in my apartment with my computer," she said.

By bringing fantasies into real life, and losing the control over them that we maintain when they stay within the imagination, women sometimes encounter unexpected annoyances and inconveniences. This was the case for Leslie, who invited her husband, Mike, to act out one of her treasured fantasies one summer night. Hand in hand, they walked to the stable behind their farmhouse. As Mike prepared two of their horses for a midnight ride, Leslie, an avid horsewoman, stripped off all her clothes. Mike gave her a boost onto her favorite mare's back, then got onto his own horse, keeping on his jeans and boots. She said:

> We took off on a thrilling ride, just as I had been fantasizing about. I could feel the heat coming up from my horse and smell the fresh-cut hay in the fields. When we began to canter, I could feel my hair blowing and my breasts bouncing. All of those sensations felt wonderful, and I loved how Mike watched me. The experience also offered me a way to share with him the joy I feel on horseback. When I'm riding my horse, I feel free and uninhibited. My fantasy was about bringing him into this world that I'm so passionate about. The experience was almost perfect, except for one significant detail. I hadn't expected how much it would hurt to ride naked and bareback. To Mike's disappointment, and mine, I was much too sore to have sex that night.

Another woman was surprised by reality when she tried acting out a coveted fantasy that combined two of her passions: food
and sex. Having her husband coat her body with rich chocolate,
then lick it off of her, was just one aspect of a detailed, sensory
fantasy. She explained:

> We wanted to have a second baby, and I began thinking
> of lots of ideas about how I wanted things to be when
> we conceived. I wanted to go away somewhere special,
> just the two of us. We would have dinner in a fancy
> restaurant, with flowers, wine, and candles. Then we
> would go to a hotel room where no one would hear us
> or interrupt us. We would undress each other. We both
> really like chocolate, so I wanted us to coat each other
> with chocolate fudge topping. That would be just the
> first layer. Then we'd spread on ice cream, Cool Whip,
> then more chocolate. Licking all that off each other
> would be sort of an appetizer for sex.

When they tried acting out her fantasy in real life, though,
she was disappointed to discover that it was an intensely ticklish
experience. "We had to stop what we were doing and take a
shower in the middle of it," she said, "and it nearly killed me to
waste all that chocolate." Nonetheless, they didn't let the failed
experiment ruin their evening. "We showered, then went right
back to making love. We're pretty sure that was the night our
daughter was conceived."

Some women act out their fantasies only to find that they are
more turned off by them than turned on. Gwen, for example, was
anxious to test out one of her favorite fantasies of sex with her
husband in his office. "In the fantasy, I pictured my husband
sitting at his desk, thinking about me. He gets so horny he can't
stand it, and starts masturbating. I show up then, and he switches
from masturbation to intercourse with me," she said. When Gwen
suggested playing out this fantasy one night at her husband's

empty office, he was eager to comply. But she was surprised by how differently she felt during this experience. "In real life, watching him masturbate didn't arouse me. It made me feel sad, for some reason. It wasn't gratifying."

Another woman was surprised and subsequently upset when her male partner became very attached to her fantasy. "The fantasy was more of a verbal game, in which I would pretend to be his nubile young student, and he would be the brilliant professor. It was fun at first, but it got old for me. I began to feel like a sex tool," she said. "He wanted to use it every time we had sex. It seemed that I didn't matter anymore, and that he wasn't really attracted to me. He was more turned on by the fantasy of a young, less successful woman, than by me. Finally, I told him I didn't want to play that game anymore, and he said okay."

Shannon, a single woman in her early twenties, never expected the outcome that resulted from enacting one of her fantasies with a boyfriend. "As sort of an experiment, I proposed that for one evening he would be the woman and I would be the man. At first, he was skeptical. Eventually, as I refused to abandon the idea, he began to get into the role. By the end of this particular night, we were both completely convinced that we had swapped sexes. He was in my clothes and I was in his. Later, after we broke up, I found out that my old boyfriend had become a habitual cross-dresser." Such surprising results can't be predicted in advance.

The unexpected consequences of acting out a fantasy may not be apparent until long after the sexual experience ends. Megan, for instance, had long entertained a fantasy of having sex with one of the South American musicians who traveled through her town a couple times a year. One day, during one of their performances, she and her dream lover began flirting. Afterward, the musician found her in the crowd and introduced himself. They wound up spending the day getting acquainted, listening to music, and enjoying each other's company. That night, she decided to carry out her fantasy and have sex with him. The sexual contact was even better than she had imagined. But in the months that followed, he kept calling her from all around the country, wanting to marry her so he could move to the United States permanently. She said, "I had only been focused on fulfilling my sexual fantasy and hadn't realized he had his own agenda going, too."

CHALLENGING SITUATIONS

A number of the women we spoke with had experimented with acting out fantasies that involved more than one partner. In threesomes, and other combinations of multiple partners, the likelihood of being able to establish and maintain consent, trust, safety, and control in the situation is greatly diminished. As we discovered in previous chapters, the desire for multiple partners in fantasy can reflect a desire for increased stimulation and attention. In reality, though, these situations involve more people who bring their own, often unexpected, agendas to play.

Krista, a thirty-five-year-old artist's model, had long entertained a fantasy of being naked with another woman. "I've had this fantasy ever since I was about seven and saw an episode of the television show *Gilligan's Island* in which Mary Ann and Ginger were taking a mud bath together." As a heterosexual adult, her fantasy became more graphic, with Krista imagining herself touching and being touched by the other woman. She had tried telling a few male lovers about the fantasy, "but their response had been either disgust or patronizing amusement."

Finally, Krista told her fantasy to a new lover named Rudy, who happened to be a photographer. She said:

> He accepted it as a real part of me and offered to help make it a reality by arranging a nude photo shoot of me and another female model who was into this sort of thing. Initially, the experience was a great success. The other model had a lithe, boyish figure like mine. She

responded well to all of Rudy's camera directions. He would say, "Rotate slowly, touching each other. Look into each other's eyes. Slide your hand down into Krista's pubic hair. Kiss. Lie on your back and let Krista lie in your lap." After a while, though, we didn't need so much direction from him. We started exploring each other's skin of our own accord. It was the first time I had ever touched a woman's breast and, though it never went much further than that, it was more than worth the wait. Enacting the fantasy changed me. I felt like it erased my fear of really looking at another woman's body and appreciating female flesh.

What Krista hadn't expected, though, was the jealousy that welled up in her once she recognized how intensely pleased Rudy had been to watch her with another woman. Later, when they looked at his photographs together, he singled out one picture to admire. "It showed a back view of the other model's butt rearing up to the camera. Not only did I resent that he was taking pleasure in looking at another woman's genitals, but I hated her for displaying them to anyone else but me. Much as I liked accepting my own urge to look at women, I wish I didn't know how much Rudy wants to look at them, too. I wanted to rewind and erase the experience, and turn the fantasy back into make-believe."

Another woman, Carmen, initially refused her husband's requests to act out threesomes. "Then, one New Year's Eve, one of my best girlfriends wound up staying at our house for the night. My husband convinced us to have a threesome with him. The weird part was, the other woman and I enjoyed being intimate with each other. That was pleasing. But neither of us had much fun with my husband. Afterward, she and I stopped being friends. It was just too uncomfortable. We couldn't go back to where we were as friends, before we had this sexual experience. Not long after that, my husband and I broke up."

Vanessa, a forty-two-year-old lesbian, found herself drawn

into a threesome scene almost by accident, when she was younger and more of a risk taker. "In my twenties, I thought I was into anything and everything until I had this one encounter that taught me I had my own limits with enacting fantasies." Here's what happened:

I went into a lesbian bar one Saturday night, by myself, and sat on the last open barstool. A tall woman with a Texas accent was on the next stool. She introduced herself as Candy, called me "Sugar," and bought me a drink. She told me she used to be a Playboy *bunny. She introduced me to her husband, Rod, who was sitting on the other side of her. He and I got into a pool game, and the three of us wound up shutting down the bar. We got along well. Then, Candy invited me to come home with them for a private party. I said, "Listen, your husband's good-looking, but I only sleep with women. I'm not into guys." She gave me her business card and said to call if I ever changed my mind. The next day, I told a couple friends where I was heading, and they promised to check on me if I hadn't come home by evening.*

When I got to Candy's house, she was delighted to see me. She brought out her old Playboys, *to prove that she really had been a bunny. I was impressed. They had a nice pool table, too, so I stayed a while. By late afternoon, I was ready to leave. I started to go home, but Candy got me up against the pool table and gave me a big kiss. I fell for it. The next thing I knew, I was in their bedroom with her. She promised me that, if we kept going, Rod wouldn't join in. He'd go walk the dog or something. Sure enough, I heard Rod and the dog go out, and Candy and I began to really enjoy ourselves. All of a sudden, there was a third body in the bed with us. It was Rod, back from his walk a little early. I said, "That's it. I'm out of here." I showered, got dressed,*

*and left. They were still in bed together. Once I was
outside, I reached into my pants pocket for my keys. I
pulled out a piece of paper I hadn't remembered putting
there. It was fifty dollars. I had prostituted myself and
didn't even know it! I felt so guilty about being a hooker
for a day that I didn't spend the money for a week.
Finally, I gave in and bought a toaster oven.*

USING FANTASY TO INCREASE INTIMACY

Although women's experiences with acting out fantasies vary
widely and don't follow a predictable pattern, the most satisfying
enactments we heard about tended to be described by women in
ongoing intimate relationships. This is understandable, since it is
in these situations where couples are most likely to establish and
build the honesty, trust, and emotional openness necessary for
guiding any successful experiment with fantasy.

For some couples, certainly, this kind of foundation may be
in place at the start of the relationship. But generally, it takes time
for two people to become comfortable, open, and sensitive enough
to step into the other's private fantasy world. Even if they invent
new fantasies together, as a mutually enjoyable aspect of sex, each
of them brings to the relationship a separate sexual history and
previous individual experiences with fantasy. The challenge to a
couple is to blend these unique histories, sexual styles, and maturity levels in a way that increases intimacy and enhances sexual
enjoyment for both of them.

Deliberately using fantasy within a relationship also requires
flexibility from both partners, so that a couple can avoid turning
fantasy play into a relationship rut. In the most satisfying situations we heard women describe, fantasy is seen by both partners as
a creative outlet, but never an obligation. In addition, fantasy
enactments tend to work best when they reinforce the dynamics a
couple wants to enhance in their relationship, such as caring, respect, and playfulness.

Just as relationships evolve over time, so do couples change and experiment with the ways that they put fantasies to use. Many couples begin to experiment with fantasy play after the newness of a relationship wears off, and they settle into a long-term partnership. Fantasy can become a way to keep a sexual relationship fresh and exciting. Some couples, for example, use fantasy to pretend that they have just met, reliving the thrill of falling in love.

Beyond adding sexual excitement, exploring fantasy within the context of a relationship can also offer a couple a new route to growth and a deepening of intimacy. Often, it's only with the wisdom of hindsight that a couple can appreciate how sexual fantasy has shaped, and been shaped by, their relationship over time.

❧

One couple in their forties, Paula and Jason, never set out deliberately to use fantasy as a personal growth tool or marital aid. Looking back over the twenty years of their marriage, however, they can see how sexual fantasy has played an important role in the life they have shared. At different stages in their relationship, sexual fantasy has been a source of excitement, fear, anxiety, emotional pain, sexual tension, and intense pleasure. At times, it's also been a catalyst for changing how they relate sexually. Over the years, they have discovered that the comfort to discuss sexual fantasies is deeply and profoundly shaped by the personal and emotional growth each partner accomplishes separately.

When they met in their twenties, their sex life was exciting and spontaneous. "As a young man in love with a new partner," Jason recalled, "I remember wanting to try it all. My fantasies had been about all the different ways I had dreamed of having sex, and now I wanted to experience all those things in real life."

Paula loved that sexual experimentation and spontaneity. She said, "On the spur of the moment, if it felt safe and sounded good to both of us, we'd have sex outdoors, on a train, or even after hours at work." One night, on a whim, they went to an X-rated movie and made love afterward. "I remember getting really turned on, but not feeling satisfied," she said. "I felt distracted by all the porn images that kept replaying in my mind, even after orgasm." For Jason, too, that night "didn't feel quite right." At the time, though, neither of them shared their reaction with the other. They just didn't return to the adult theater.

In fact, talking about their feelings was a skill that took both of them time and maturity to develop. In those early years together, sexual fantasy was an unspoken concern for both of them. Jason can remember feeling anxious, even though he enjoyed the novelty of their sex life. "With each new thing we tried, I wondered, would this improve our sexual relationship? Or would Paula dislike me if we act this fantasy out?" Paula, meanwhile, was wondering, "Is this going to be the new standard for how we have sex? What if we go too far?"

After a few years, their relationship shifted into a different stage. Once their children were born, their sex life became more rushed and less adventuresome. By then, Jason had satisfied much of his sexual curiosity. He felt ready for more warmth and less thrill. Paula, as a new mother, often felt tired and less responsive sexually. She worried that their sex life would never be the same.

To stir up her sexual interest, Paula got in the habit of reading pornography before they had sex. She found the bold images and juicy stories arousing, but worried about what she might be doing to herself. "I wondered if this was going to become the only way I could get aroused."

One night, based on a porn story that had turned her on, Paula told Jason she'd like it if he would act as if he were a cocky older man seducing a young woman. "I liked the tension between the man's self-assurance and directness and the female's innocence and curiosity."

Jason felt uncomfortable with her request and refused to play along. "I was in a double bind. If I went along and acted out her fantasy, I felt like I wouldn't be myself. But if I said no, she would get angry and feel rejected. We'd get into these snits. I didn't see a solution." It didn't help that he misunderstood her fantasy. He assumed Paula was trying to re-create how she had felt about an old lover. He thought, *"I don't stand a chance against this guy in her fantasy."* In fact, Paula wasn't even thinking about a specific person. She just wanted to create the excitement that had become a conditioned part of her sexual response.

Even though they both felt a lot of tension, they still didn't address their concerns together. Instead, Paula retreated into her fantasy life by herself. She said, "My fantasies didn't seem like something we could share comfortably, yet I needed them to function. We just sidestepped talking about them for a while. I kept using fantasies to help me get aroused and climax. We were able to keep having sex regularly and we loved each other, but we weren't making any progress as a couple."

Over the next ten years, as they both matured and gained more confidence as individuals, their relationship shifted again. They got better at expressing their feelings. Jason said, "Our emotional connection seemed to suddenly jump ahead as the most important thing for both of us." Around that time, they both realized that they felt strong and secure enough as a couple that a disagreement about sexual fantasies wasn't going to ruin their relationship.

While making love one night, Paula started mentally replaying her old fantasy of an older man seducing a younger woman. Only this time, she pictured a really young female—so young, in fact, that Paula was suddenly reminded of her own sexually innocent eight-year-old daughter. Instead of getting turned on, she felt repulsed. When she tried to push the fantasy out of her mind, her body shut down. She felt sexually flat and started to cry.

Jason interrupted lovemaking, took Paula into his arms, and asked, "What's wrong?"

Paula explained that she'd been turning to fantasies for years because she was worried that she couldn't get aroused without them. Hearing that, Jason felt as if a missing puzzle piece had dropped into place. He said, "I had always thought these fantasies were things you wanted to happen, something you really desired and *preferred*. Now, things fit into place more."

He later remembered that night as "a milestone in our relationship." In retrospect, Paula felt relieved that Jason had never agreed to play out her seduction fantasies. She said, "I could see that he had been wanting our whole relationship, including our sex life, to be built on equality."

After that night, they continued talking more openly about sex. Gradually, they made deliberate changes in their sexual relationship. They set aside uninterrupted time for lovemaking. They experimented with new kinds of foreplay. Intentionally, they made love a few times without going all the way to climax. And they even started talking more *during* sex.

With these changes, Paula found her old seduction fantasies about strangers shifting to new, more playful fantasies about Jason. She said, "I started weaving in the present with whatever erotic scene I was imagining. If I pictured us having sex on a beach, for instance, our top sheet became a beach blanket. These new fantasies felt more fun. They also felt more like real life than acting or make-believe." Instead of feeling like a necessity to get her aroused, fantasy started feeling like her choice.

Jason noticed changes, too. "I've become more conscious of the subtle, enjoyable images of sex that play through my mind. Sex is so much more satisfying to both of us now. It feels so close and authentic with who we really are." They both have learned to feel more free when they talk about sex, and more accepting of each other's desires and fantasies. Paula said, "We no longer have to feel secretive or ashamed of what's going on in our thoughts during sex." Unlike their early years together, when sex was exciting but never really discussed, now it's more exciting precisely because they *do* talk about it.

And instead of treating sexual fantasy as a delicate subject they both tiptoe around, they have learned to joke and even laugh about fantasies. One recent evening in bed, Paula turned to Jason and asked, "What's it called when you whisper your favorite fantasy in your lover's ear?" He was stumped, but they both broke out laughing when she answered, *"oral sex."*

Looking at their long, shared history of dealing with fantasy issues, Jason made one last observation. "The whole subject of fantasy has gone from a hidden, threatening issue to something we both feel can be creative and fun."

CHAPTER 10

Creating Favorite Fantasies

In her own way, every woman who shared her story for this book is memorable. We remember some, in particular, because the fantasies they described were so original, passionate, unusual, funny, or poignant. We remember others because of their courage to weed out unwanted sexual fantasies that had stubbornly taken root in their minds, often due to influences that were beyond their control. And, we remember a few in particular because something in their stories thrilled our senses and inspired our own fantasies to take flight.

Collectively, these women remind us of the wonderfully creative, erotic power of the female imagination. Although our fantasies are often strongly influenced by the culture around us and past sexual experiences, we also have the power to deliberately shape, control, and filter our fantasy life to better suit our individual interests, sexual styles, relationship needs, and as-yet-unsatisfied desires.

The fantasies women have shared with us, in all their rich variety, also demonstrate the infinite possibilities for creating new sexual thoughts for our own pleasure. The personal histories we've heard remind us that we've all known how to fantasize ever since we were children. Over the years, some of us may have forgotten how to spin stories and images from the air. Perhaps we underestimated the value of fantasizing, dismissed it as child's play, or unknowingly allowed our sexual imagination to be limited, repressed, or influenced by outside sources.

Given all that we have learned about women's sexual fantasies, we have new opportunities to put this wisdom to use. As our own best fantasy makers, we can change fantasies we don't like, expand on fantasies we enjoy, and seek out new sources for the specific kinds of fantasies we want to experience more. We can exercise more choice in our fantasy lives, and use it to lead us wherever we decide to go.

GIVING OURSELVES PERMISSION

Caroline is a quiet, serious twenty-three-year-old teacher who was inspired to deliberately get in touch with her fantasy life for the first time after attending a fantasy workshop with some friends. Throughout most of a two-hour group discussion on sexual fantasy, she sat quietly as the other women in the room described their experiences. She occasionally looked surprised as the women she thought she knew well shared their favorite Dominatrix and Wild Woman fantasies and reminisced about their adolescent crushes, first kisses, and earliest sexual thoughts. Near the end of the session, as the participants were reflecting on all they had learned from one another, Caroline finally spoke up.

"I just don't know how to *do* this fantasy stuff," she said, sounding exasperated. "It's a place my mind will not seem to go, no matter how much I'd like it to. And from what I'm hearing from all of you, I'm missing out on something that sounds like fun."

Caroline went on to explain that she had grown up in a family where "suppressing the appetites" was considered praiseworthy. "My parents were moral, honest, working folks who taught me to be strong-willed and self-reliant, and I thank them for that. But they also raised me to be suspicious of anything that had to do with sex. I wound up feeling afraid that I might lose myself in sexuality, if I ever really got into it. When I finally started having sex, it was so difficult for me to draw any pleasure from the act. Now, I find that I have to really concentrate on my body's reactions to feel much of anything. Orgasms, when they happen, feel like finely tuned, mechanical events. Meanwhile, my husband is this sensual guy who wants our sex life to be playful and fun. It seems so easy for him to just relax and enjoy his body, and mine. Frankly, I'm pissed off that this whole sexuality thing has to be so damn hard for me. From what I'm hearing, fantasies might help me let go and enjoy sex more, if only I could learn how to create them."

A few weeks later, we received an exciting letter from Caroline. The discussion group had stirred up her dormant erotic imagination. By learning more about sexual fantasy, and all the benefits that it offers us, she felt a new permission to explore this part of her mind. In fact, she had just created her first sexual fantasy. She enjoyed it not only because it turned her on, but also because the Beloved-type fantasy fit with how she wanted to define sexual pleasure for herself, on her own personal terms.

"I know myself well enough to understand that I don't want to be silly about sex, in order to enjoy it. If I'm going to invent fantasies, I want them to be a continuation of what I like most in my real life," she explained. "This new fantasy is all about me, just as I really am, and all about my husband, just as he is—except that, in the fantasy, his fingernails are neatly manicured and very smooth." Intuitively, Caroline had figured out how to use fantasy to improve on reality. She was thrilled and proud to be able to share her first sexual fantasy with us:

I am sleeping, clean and warm in a deep, soft bed in a quiet, private place. My husband, a gentle, sensual, beautiful man, comes in silently and smiling as he watches me breathe. He touches my face lovingly. I'm wearing loose-fitting pajamas. As I lie still, half asleep, he climbs into bed beside me and caresses my body as he undresses me. I keep my eyes closed, and let my usual self-consciousness continue sleeping. Meanwhile, though, I allow my body to awaken. I feel and respond and become aroused. We do not need to speak. He strokes my sides and thighs (with those well-manicured hands). I feel my nipples become erect. My body's full, uninhibited sexual response excites us both. Our separate skins enjoy touching and playing together. Finally, we both climax, long and richly, then sleep soundly.

For Caroline, and for all women who wish to create new fantasies, giving ourselves permission to play with our fantasy lives is the best place to begin.

RECOGNIZING MOMENTS OF OPPORTUNITY

From women who have shared their stories, we've learned that inspirations for sexual fantasies are all around us. They await in the books we read, the movies we watch, the music we hear, the dreams that arouse us, the foods and smells that titillate our senses, the partners who share our sexual pleasure, and the strangers we know only from a distance. Sexual fantasies can be inspired by almost any experience, image, or sensation that an individual woman recognizes as erotic.

We can greatly expand on inspirations for new fantasies by paying attention to these moments of erotic opportunity. The most fleeting encounters or episodes can fuel our fantasies, if we are aware enough to appreciate them and recognize our own response. A new fantasy might start with something as mundane as peeling an orange and sucking the juice from our fingers. Or stepping from a bath and noticing how the droplets of water roll down the skin. Or making eye contact with a stranger who shares a brief elevator ride. One woman said she and her husband had been going to the gym together for months before she took the time, one morning, to appreciate how sensuous his arm muscles looked as he worked out on a weight machine. Similarly, writer Sallie Tisdale described a chance moment of erotic opportunity in her book *Talk Dirty to Me:*

> I walked out, not long ago, at eight-thirty on a clear, fragrant spring morning. Gnats were stirring in the still sunshine and no one else was about. I was still sleepy, thinking only of the morning paper and a cup of tea as I walked down a path between apartments. Suddenly in the hush of the day I could hear the repeated moans of a woman through a curtained, half-open window. Her voice was breathy, catching in her throat, climbing higher in tone and louder in volume. I stood rooted to the path for a few seconds, saw the open window next to me with the white curtain fluttering in the slight breeze, and then walked on. . . . Her guttural, meaningless sounds infected me with desire like a virus caught from the air. I could barely walk a straight line to the sidewalk.[1]

To inspire our own fantasies, we can pay attention to whatever it is that tweaks our own desire, whether it's music or poetry or scenes from nature or nude photography. Later, we can call these thoughts and experiences to mind again, during times of private genital pleasuring. Connecting new erotic thoughts with sensations such as clitoral stimulation helps reinforce their erotic power and effectiveness as new sexual fantasies. To deliberately link what's happening in our minds and our bodies, we can think our favorite sexual thoughts *and* touch ourselves.

As we've already heard, women sometimes draw erotic pleasure from sources and images that don't seem to be sexual at all. A woman who is a watercolor artist enjoys sensory fantasies about velvety flowers opening their petals and releasing their perfume. A woman who teaches yoga pictures swirling images of red and violet as she makes love. She shares these kinesthetic fantasies with her lover, imagining that their bodies are exchanging auras of colorful energy during sex.

Although we can certainly learn from hearing about how other women make use of these inspired moments, the fantasies that we enjoy the most are those that strike a particular chord in us. Our most satisfying fantasies feel right because they reflect our own erotic style. One woman, hearing a suggestion at a workshop that fantasies can be inspired by scenes from nature, said pointedly, "Yeah, but what's *nature* got to do with it?" Fantasies are valuable to us only if they connect with our individual sense of the erotic. Each of us holds a unique palette that we can use to paint our own fantasies.

READY-MADE SOURCES

We don't have to be artists, poets, or pornographers to create our own sexual fantasies. If our sexual creativity needs a boost, we can try on ready-made fantasies by reading erotica or romance fiction, or watching films that celebrate and expand on our definition of the erotic. Then, if we like, we can imagine ourselves in the scenes we like best.[2]

Geraldine Kudaka belongs to the new wave of women writers producing a wide variety of erotica for other women to enjoy. (She edited *On a Bed of Rice,* an anthology of erotica by Asian-American writers.) When a woman sits down to read a book of erotica, Kudaka says, she's giving herself permission to express and play with her own sexuality. "It can be reassuring for a woman to hear that it's okay to want to have sex, and it's okay to think about sex. These books tell a woman, 'I'm not a freak for sitting here, being horny. Horny is okay.' " Kudaka adds, "Erotica can really please the mind and open up the senses. The best stories can push the edge of sexuality, and spark desire for us in new ways."

And once we understand exactly what it is that sparks desire, and why, we have a new source of inspiration for our own fantasies. *Desire can build on desire.* Some women, for instance, may find themselves inspired to think about sex in new ways, with new images, after reading a passage such as this one by Tanith Tyrr. Her erotic story "Sacrament" describes the first sexual encounter between a Japanese-American couple this way:

> This is sacred, this most ancient of rituals. My body is a holy sacrament which he worships with growing delight, his tongue flicking as rapidly as a serpent's on the altar of my breasts, my belly, my thighs. Hesitant, then hot and demanding, he buries his face in my holy cunt, my sacred womanhood, and worships me to orgasm after orgasm. I am Goddess, I shout, as waves of pleasure come crashing over me like the moon-called sea.
>
> I clasp him to me and we press together, moving inexorably with the rhythm of tides. We surge forward violently and then draw back, readying for the final embrace. Thou art God, I cry out softly.
>
> Stallion, goatfoot god, golden phallus of the sun, his cock fills me as if I have never been empty, as if I will never again be empty. I clutch his lean, tautly muscled body to me.
>
> We plunge together, bucking and twisting, sacred bull and rider locked in the ancient dance. He rises like the sun, limned in glory. My body is the full moon, moving to cover him in the sky, and our joining eclipses the Earth. Again and again, until our backs arch and our mouths open wide in a rictus of uncontrolled pleasure.

As I ride the cresting waves of orgasm, I hear him
cry out, high and wild. In my mind I see two birds flying
freely, beyond the prison walls and for home.[3]

Romance writers tell stories about sex in a different way. In
romance novels, typically written by women and for women, contemporary writers such as Stella Cameron include explicit love
scenes that deliberately touch on all of the senses. Cameron wants
her readers to vicariously feel everything that the heroine and hero
experience in these scenes. "My readers tell me that, on some level,
it's sexually stimulating for them to read these books. Reading
romances may make them more receptive to sex in their own
relationships," she said. In a recent novel called *Sheer Pleasures,*
Cameron also describes a first-time sexual experience between two
lovers. Cameron's sexually inexperienced heroine, Phoenix, and
her worldly hero, Roman Wilde, play out a passionate encounter
that reads like this:

> Her body wept for him, wept for what he promised.
> Several times he sent a finger reaching inside her and she
> whimpered. She also felt him reach away from her and
> heard him find something that crackled. A condom. She
> should have known he would always be ready for mo-
> ments like this. His teeth, fastening lightly on a nipple,
> blocked her train of thought. Her back arched and Ro-
> man's response was to suck.
>
> While his finger reached, his thumb played over the
> nub that has passed beyond aching. Holding her about
> the waist with one arm, he worked that bud of flesh
> until she clawed at him with her fingernails and cried
> out in meaningless pleas.
>
> The inferno erupted. Phoenix clung to him, con-
> sumed, only to cry his name over and over as he raised
> her hips and drove her down on him, drove himself into
> her waiting, wanting body.

There was a burning, a breaking, a sweet torture. She accepted and contracted about him, welcomed him deep within her.

For an instant he paused, breathing raggedly, his skin wet beneath her hands. "You said this wasn't the first time."

"Don't stop."

"Oh, my God." He muttered against her lips. "You're unbelievable."

He was unbelievable.

It was unbelievable.

His great hands bracketed her hips and moved her. His pelvis jerked to meet each descent.

"Now?" Phoenix shouted the word and knew what it meant. It meant the beautiful, searing, consuming flame that shot to her womb, to her breasts, to her knees.[4]

In the same way that reading can set our erotic imaginations in motion, watching films can also give us ready-made ideas for new fantasies. Women who want to minimize violent or otherwise abusive sex scenes in their own fantasies can deliberately seek out films that portray loving, mutual, or playful qualities of sex. Deborah, a woman who was healing from sexual abuse, said she was thrilled to fantasize that she was Sarita Choudhury, the Indian actress who played opposite Denzel Washington in the cross-cultural love story *Mississippi Masala*. Deborah said: "In the film, the two characters take time to know each other well before they ever have sex. That struck me as unusual. When they finally did make love for the first time, it had meaning. It was touching to see them looking into each other's eyes and smiling. When I saw them lick, stroke, and suck each other's dark skin, I could tell they were happy to have found each other. Even their feet became part of their joyful lovemaking and sexual exploring.

"When I took this love scene into my own fantasy life, I had a whole new vision for what sex could be. In my own life, I never experienced sex with a man who didn't rush or force me. This fantasy let me imagine how it would be to receive respect, and let passion build up slowly."

BECOMING OUR OWN FANTASY MAKERS

Georgine was twenty-eight years old when she was involved in a car accident that left her paralyzed from the waist down and put her in a wheelchair. A beautiful woman by anyone's standards, with long, wavy hair, smooth skin, and high cheekbones, she stopped thinking of herself as sexual after the accident. "Once the injury happened, I just shut down my sexuality for a while. I didn't give myself permission to even fantasize about sex."

One morning, about two years after the injury, she was surprised when a jet of hot shower water hit her in the crotch and triggered a tingling response in her genitals. That was the first sign that she had gradually recovered some sensation below the waist, and she recognized the erotic potential of that moment. She thought to herself, "Maybe there's still hope for me to be a sexual person."

Georgine began to get back in touch with her sexuality by encouraging herself to fantasize. "I started using tanning beds as a place to let my imagination take off. Under the lights, I'd feel warm all over. I'd kind of drift off into these explicit fantasies. At first, they involved sensations that helped me relax. I remembered how it used to feel to lie in the warm sun and feel cool blades of grass against my bare skin. Gradually, I began to respond sexually. I would lubricate. Then, I started creating the same feelings by imagining myself with a partner."

Eventually, Georgine turned her bedroom into a place where she could deliberately encourage her sexual fantasies to unfold. "My bedroom set has a huge vanity, and I keep my bed perpendicular to that, so that when I look up, I see this huge mirror. I light candles and incense to stir up my senses. I fill my room with lovely colors. Oh, and I have a collection of hats. Depending on my mood, I might put on a tiara with rhinestones or my great-grand-mother's fur."

With that, Georgine broke into laughter. "Imagine," she went on, "if I told people that I put on my fur coat, my rhine-stones, and sit on my bed with a glass of champagne, waiting for the spirits to guide me to sexual pleasure. They would probably think I was bonkers, right? But I've had some very satisfying, very erotic experiences since I've become my own fantasy maker. I've imagined myself as Muffy, an aging cheerleader with big breasts who is afraid of getting older. She's into younger men. I've been a rather slutty character in a red wig and heavy makeup who likes to hang out in bars. I've imagined myself wearing a hippie outfit from the sixties. In that fantasy, I imagine a certain gentleman I really like coming into my room, wearing a long, black jacket. He stands at the foot of my bed so that I can see his reflection in the mirror. The light is really soft. He takes off his clothes and does whatever I ask." When she has a particularly vivid fantasy, Georgine said, "I literally feel the heat from my imaginary lover's body."

When Georgine sees herself in a mirror now, she recognizes a sexual woman who happens to get around in a wheelchair. Since she embraced her fantasy life, she has been reminded of how much she enjoys sensual, sexual energy, and how much pleasure awaits within her own erotic imagination.

⁂

The final five stories we'll hear were shared by other women who have learned to appreciate the value of sexual fantasies. They have been inspired by a variety of sources to create their own original fantasies that they clearly love. Their stories demonstrate how we all can craft new fantasies that feel more like our own authentic creations, not something imposed on us. Finally, their stories remind us that sexual fantasies are our most personal creations, changing with our unique life experiences.

NADINE:
COURTROOM DRAMA

Nadine is a single, high-powered trial lawyer in her thirties who keeps her sexuality well concealed during the day behind conservative suits and a businesslike demeanor. One day at work, however, an opposing lawyer named Malcolm jokingly told her he was working so hard on an upcoming case that he dreamed he had appeared in court—naked.

Nadine remembered how Malcolm had looked the previous week when she happened to see him working out at the gym. He was wearing shorts that showed off his tanned, muscular legs. Nadine appreciated a buffed male body, and especially liked dark-haired men. In a flash, she imagined how the rest of Malcolm must have looked in his dream.

Later, when she had more time, she decided to invent a new Wild Woman fantasy set in the familiar territory of the courtroom. She wrote it down so that she could have fun playing with the language, adding legalistic puns and sexual innuendo, along with the specific kind of sexual stimulation she most enjoyed. Each time she saw Malcolm after that, she enjoyed recalling the fantasy and knowing that he didn't have a clue in terms of what direction her imagination had traveled. She also adopted a new habit of wearing her sexiest lingerie under her business suits whenever she had to appear in court. She shared her fantasy:

Somehow I entered Malcolm's dream, too, and saw him naked in the courtroom, using his cell phone to tell an office clerk to bring him some clothes. When he looked up and saw me, with his intense blue eyes, he acted as if we were conducting business as usual, and handed me a demurrer to read. As I looked down to digest the legal document, I realized that I, too, was improperly dressed for the courtroom. Instead of my usual business suit, I was wearing a purple merry widow from the Victoria's Secret catalogue, thong panties, pull-up stockings, and spiked heels. I asked to borrow Malcolm's cell phone so that I could call my office, too, but he was not obliging. In fact, he said that I could only use the phone if I let him practice undoing the clips on my garter belt. I really needed to use that phone, so I stipulated to his request.

Even though he claimed to be an old hand at garter belts, my outfit gave him trouble. Somehow, he thought he could undo the clips by kissing and fondling my breasts. Then he insisted that I bend over and grab hold of the jury box railing, so that he could get a better grip from the rear. Even though I doubted his competence by this time, I went along, continuing to read the demurrer.

Malcolm softly ran his fingers over my bottom and strayed a bit, touching lightly on my vaginal lips, which were moist and warm by this time. I dropped the demurrer. He managed to unclip the two rear garter clips, but when I turned around and asked respectfully for the phone, he said that he wasn't finished. Two more clips remained to be undone. By this time, I couldn't help noticing how excited he was. I kneeled in a prayer for relief and began to suck his hard cock. He lifted me up, faced me, and perched me atop the railing. I wrapped my legs and heels around him as he pushed inside me. We nearly tumbled off the rail and into juror number three's seat, but Malcolm held me tightly with his muscular arms. Licking, pushing, and kissing, we came together in a series of sighs and sweetness.

WANDA:
MEDITATIONS ON PLEASURE

When Wanda and her husband, Luke, first met during the 1970s, they often spent time together at a meditation center. They've drifted away from Zen practices since then, although Wanda still brings to lovemaking the lessons about mindfulness that she first learned in a spiritual context. She especially enjoys feeling calm, aware, and in the moment during sex, hearing her own breath, appreciating the buildup of sensations in her body, and enjoying the exciting rhythms she and Luke create together. In her favorite fantasies, she often finds new ways to enhance these experiences.

Because her master bedroom is located right next to her teenage daughter's room, however, Wanda also feels compelled to keep the sounds of lovemaking somewhat hushed. One night, she and Luke went to see the movie *Ace Ventura: When Nature Calls*. In one scene, comedian Jim Carrey pretends to be meditating, while in reality he's having sex. That scene inspired Wanda to create a new sexual fantasy that felt playful and spiritual. Because it highlights a sense of privacy, the fantasy also helped her to more fully enjoy sex. In her new fantasy:

> *I imagine that I'm a college-age meditation student who has received special permission to use a secluded ashram in the woods for a weekend retreat. Although I'm expecting to be alone, I discover that another Zen student has arrived before me, planning to have the ashram all to himself for his own spiritual retreat. (He looks just like Luke did, back when we were both in our twenties.)*
>
> *Since neither of us is eager to change our plans, we agree to share the space. We quietly go about our separate tasks, beginning our silent meditation early in the morning when the air is cool. Sitting cross-legged on the ashram floor, several feet apart, we are positioned at an*

angle so that we each can steal glances at one another. As the sun streams through the big picture window, the day grows hotter. We both begin to unbutton and remove items of clothing. This becomes a subtle striptease, with our hands moving slowly and sensuously across our own increasingly bare skin.

Although we are trying hard to concentrate, we cannot help but be aware of each other. As our clothes litter the floor around us, we find it harder and harder to keep our minds on meditation. Although we're still not talking or touching, every now and then one of us releases a groan, knowing it will attract the other's attention. Toward dusk, when we're both completely undressed and clearly aroused, we finally turn and embrace each other. As we move together, our sexual energy combines with the sense of comfort and safety that I enjoy in real life with Luke. Our breathing, which we have practiced keeping calm and steady during meditation, continues to feel peaceful even as we are becoming more excited.

Once we're actually having sex, fantasy merges with reality. For a moment in both fantasy and in reality, his cheek rests against my cheek. Our heads turn toward the picture window in our bedroom, which frames a view of a graceful tree, its branches swaying in the breeze. Then I turn my head so that I can see my lover's face. His eyes are also open, and I can see him swooning and writhing in ecstasy. To see Luke enjoying such pleasure is a real turn-on for me, and hastens my own orgasm. My climax feels like it is honoring life, our love, the safety and comfort we bring to one another, and a spiritual connection to nature. The Zen energy of this fantasy lets our natural, erotic chemistry build calmly, quietly, but powerfully.

ROCHELLE:
POETIC PLEASURES

When the poet Rochelle Lynn Holt was a little girl growing up in Chicago, she would announce to her parents, "I'm going to bed now to turn on my dreams." Her earliest sexual fantasies cast her as a Pretty Maiden in distress rescued by such Hollywood heroes as John Wayne, Clark Gable, and Humphrey Bogart.

In her twenties, after a woman friend introduced her to the poetry of Anaïs Nin, Rochelle began to fantasize about women. When she read romance novels, she would imagine the love scenes playing out with a woman in the role of the daring cowboy, soldier, or other hero. Meanwhile, in real life, she had lovers of both sexes.

Once she reached her forties, and AIDS became a risk, Rochelle turned her erotic attention to what she considers "safer paths." For example, she says, "Water has become a primary lover, whether in a private pool where jets beneath the surface can engender literally multiple orgasms in a swimmer who fantasizes about whomever, or in the ocean when I am pleasantly or wildly pummeled by the waves."

One such fantasy, a prose poem called "Pleasures," demonstrates how sensation, nature, and language can combine to inspire new kinds of erotic images. It begins:

The pleasures of waves lapping the shore which is your body at night when you lay the ocean of your self down for a long session of dreams letting another time sweep over your subconscious floating effortlessly the body at once both the waves and the sandy shore over which the water washes feeling cleansed and massaged by tongue by fingers that are gentle and loving this pleasure of the sea and its song the message between tides under the whitecaps gone all memory of past or fears of future only now swimming in the moment of nature at the period when there is nothing else on water but waves beneath full moon and diamonds below shimmering like jewels . . .

BRENDA:
ELECTRONIC FOREPLAY

For Brenda, a married woman in her forties, a sense of humor and flair for drama have come together in unexpected ways to inspire new sexual fantasies. One night, she and her husband, Tony, were acting out charades at a party. When she made a sexually suggestive gesture to enact the movie title *Guess Who's Coming to Dinner?*, she could tell from the look in his eyes that he got turned on. And that turned her on. Once they got home, she asked Tony if he wanted to keep playing charades. He was more than happy to continue. As they acted out movie and book titles that got more and more erotic, they both wound up undressed and well on their way to a night of memorable lovemaking. Since then, they have discovered that inventing fantasies together keeps their sex life exciting and fresh in middle age.

They regularly use all sorts of telecommunications devices to expand their fantasy repertoire and to share new ideas they want to explore in lovemaking. On a typical day at their separate offices, they might use private e-mail and voice mail to set new fantasies in motion. "This way, we can have hours of extended foreplay before we ever get home from work," Brenda said. "It's like we've been making love all day long." She describes a recent example, in which she pretended to be a demanding Dominatrix:

I was sitting at work, and the thought of Tony's erect penis just popped into my mind. I knew that he'd enjoy hearing how I was thinking about him, so I picked up the phone and connected with his private voice mail.

Faking a Russian accent and a stern voice, I said, "This is Natasha, the horse trainer. (We live on a farm, and he takes care of the stable.) I will be home soon, and I want you to be ready for me. When you curry the mare today, take your time. Pay a lot of attention to her flanks and back. Whisper in her ears. She loves that. And be sure to have a big, hard carrot ready for her. The stallion has been acting frisky lately. Let's be sure to exercise him—vigorously."

Within an hour, she had gotten a response from Tony via her private e-mail. He wrote:

"This is Boris, your dutiful stable boy. I wanted to assure you that I got your message. I'll try to do every-thing you asked, in a way that will really please you. I have some new ideas, too, about what that frisky stal-lion wants. I think he's ready for a good workout."

By the time they arrived home, Brenda said, they were both excited about climbing into an imaginary hayloft. As they have woven these new fantasies together, they also have discovered that they both enjoy thinking back on their shared sexual adventures. Each time they have invented and acted out a fantasy, they have expanded on the erotic material available to replay in their minds. "We love to talk about other times we've been sexual together, other fantasies we've invented," Brenda said. "I can describe to Tony how I felt the first time we ever made love, for example, and that alone might bring us to climax. He makes me feel as if I'm his greatest lover, and that really appeals to me."

Whatever roles they choose to play in their fantasies, Brenda and Tony never lose sight of who they really are, and how they feel in the moment. "Fantasy offers us a way to bring our wit, our humor, and our wisdom into lovemaking," she said, "but it's always about who we truly are. In our fantasies, no matter what characters we're playing, nothing else matters except for the two of us and the love we share."

ELENA:
PURE GOLD

Elena, a hardworking stockbroker in her late twenties, was surprised when a sexual fantasy spontaneously emerged one night because of a chance, nonsexual encounter. She had been seeing her current boyfriend, Rick, for nearly six months. Before the holidays, the two of them had been talking about going away together, but couldn't seem to find a time when they both could take a break.

Several days before she had the fantasy, Elena had been feeling more stressed than usual. Later, she recalled how this new sexual fantasy first came to mind:

> *It had been a really hectic week, leading up to a three-day holiday weekend. During my lunch hour, I decided to do some last-minute Christmas shopping. My office is near a street lined with small boutiques, so I decided to try my luck there. The window display in a tiny little shop caught my eye. It was filled with bottles of aromatherapy oils, massage lotions, and bath salts, in all different shapes and colors. My attention was drawn to a certain bottle with sensuous curves that reminded me of Aladdin's lamp. It contained bath oil that shimmered, even in the pale winter light. As I picked it up to look closer, a saleswoman appeared at my side. She was lovely, with soft, chestnut brown hair that framed her creamy complexion. When she spoke, her voice had a soothing, almost musical quality.*
>
> *She told me that the bath oil was pure and smelled like spring rain. The large, shiny flakes suspended in the liquid were real gold. She wrapped her long, delicate fingers around my hand and showed me that shaking the bottle ever so gently would cause the golden particles to float through the oil like snowflakes in a paper-*

weight. She held her hand over mine until the contents of the bottle became still again, then walked off to help another customer. I left without buying a thing but felt refreshed, as if I had just awakened from a wonderful dream.

I returned to work and forgot all about the experience until that night. I'd been working late at home, trying to finish some year-end reports. My boyfriend, Rick, stopped by my apartment unexpectedly. He said he'd been thinking about me all day. He began to massage my tight shoulders, and convinced me I needed a break. Before long, we were stretched out on my living room floor, watching the lights twinkle on my Christmas tree. We began to make love. As his kisses and touch made me feel more and more aroused, I imagined that I was climbing a long, winding staircase that led to a doorway. I reached the top of the stairs just as I began to climax, and the doors flew open to reveal a room that shimmered with gold. For a fleeting moment, right at orgasm, it was as if I became the gold. After my orgasm faded, my mind was still filled with an image of swirling, golden droplets, and I felt incredibly calm and relaxed, for the first time in days.

I loved the fantasy so much that I decided to share it with my boyfriend. Not until I was describing it did I make the connection between the sensory images of gold and the bottle of bath oil. Rick listened closely, caressing my face and smiling tenderly at me as I described my unusual encounter in the perfume shop, and this golden moment in our lovemaking. Then he said, "When we have sex, you make me feel like I'm gold, too."

On Christmas Eve, Rick handed me a beautifully wrapped package. Inside, I was thrilled to find a bottle

of the golden bath oil and a reservation for a weekend at
a romantic inn.

᪥

Sexual fantasies occupy a special place in our minds and can create wonderful pleasure in our bodies. Until we dare to mindfully enter this realm, without fear of what we might discover, our wisdom and creativity can remain hidden, even from ourselves. If left unexplored or allowed to be misunderstood, women's sexual fantasies might seem mysterious, strange, frightful, or even silly. When we take time to appreciate and understand our fantasies, however, we discover a marvelous personal resource that we carry with us throughout life. Embracing our fantasies is a way of honoring ourselves. As we know ourselves better, we become more free to celebrate our natural erotic rhythms with whatever thoughts quicken our pulses and please our hearts.

End Notes

PREFACE

1. Nancy Friday's *My Secret Garden,* an anthology of women's sexual fantasies, was considered groundbreaking when published in 1973 (New York: Trident Press; in paperback from Pocket Star Books, New York, 1991). She later published two more volumes of women's sexual fantasies: *Forbidden Flowers* (Pocket Star Books, 1991) and *Women on Top* (Pocket Star Books, 1993).

CHAPTER 1

1. More than twenty years ago, Helen Singer Kaplan wrote that "sex is composed of friction and fantasy" (*Psychology Today,* October 1974). Since then, many studies have documented the universality of sexual fantasies.

   In an article by Harold Leitenberg and Kris Henning ("Sexual Fantasy," *Psychological Bulletin,* 1995, Vol. 117, No. 3, 469–96), the authors reviewed the research literature on sexual fantasy and concluded that approximately 95 percent of both men and women have sexual fantasies. They wrote, "Contrary to Freud's assertion, sexual fantasy is not a sign of sexual dissatisfaction or pathology. Instead, sexual fantasies occur most often in those people who exhibit the least number of sexual problems and the least sexual dissatisfaction."

2. We have explored individual women's sexual fantasies within the context of their life experiences. Similarly, Gina Ogden, Ph.D., in *Women Who Love Sex* (New York: Pocket Books, 1994), stressed the significance of life experiences in shaping all aspects of women's sexuality. "For women," she wrote, "sexual function is more than a set of actions, more than the physiological events scientists know how to measure in the laboratory. It is a function of women's *whole lives*."

CHAPTER 2

1. Studies that have focused on gender differences with regard to sexual fantasy were summarized in the Leitenberg and Henning article, cited above. B. J. Ellis and D. Symons, Ph.D., concluded in a 1990 article (*Journal of Sex Research*, 27, 527–55), that women and men display "substantial sex differences in sexual fantasy." Steven R. Gold and Ruth G. Gold, in a study on gender differences in first sexual fantasies, concluded, "Females would more often describe [their first sexual fantasy] as being related to a specific person or relationship, whereas males would more often describe the event leading up to the first sexual fantasy as being due to a visual stimulation or to nonrelationship sex play." (*Journal of Sex Education & Therapy*, Vol. 17, No. 3, 1991, 207–16) J. K. Davidson's findings about the five most popular sex fantasies of men and women were published in 1985 (*Journal of American College Health 34*, 24–32).

2. *Dangerous Men and Adventurous Women*, edited by Jayne Ann Krentz (Philadelphia: University of Pennsylvania Press, 1992), is an anthology of essays by writers of romance fiction. In a 1984 study by C. D. Coles and M. J. Shamp (*Archives of Sexual Behavior 13*, 187–209), the writers concluded that female readers of romance fiction engaged in more frequent sex than

nonreaders and were more likely to use fantasy to enhance sexual experiences.

3. In a study entitled "Sexual Fantasies, Gender, and Molestation History" (by John Briere, Kathy Smiljanich, and Diane Henschel, *Child Abuse and Neglect*, Vol. 18, No. 2, 1994, pp. 131–37), the authors explored the sexual fantasies of adults who had been sexually molested as children. They concluded: "Subjects with histories of childhood sexual victimization reported more sexual fantasies than did their nonabused peers. . . . Sexually abused women reported more sexual fantasies of being physically forced than did women without sexual abuse histories or men regardless of molestation history."

4. In *Making Violence Sexy: Feminist Views on Pornography* (New York: Teachers College Press, 1993), a collection of essays edited by sociologist Diana Russell, Russell wrote, "Although rape, torture, and murder of women has not quite been institutionalized in the United States, these forms of violence have been institutionalized in the media. . . . Sexually violent images sell. . . . Watching movies of females being raped, tortured, and killed is now a favorite leisure activity for many Americans, particularly for teenagers" (260–61).

5. Rose Solomon, "Just Desserts," in *Ladies Own Erotica*, by the Kensington Ladies' Erotica Society (Berkeley, CA: Ten Speed Press, 1984), 151–52.

6. Marge Piercy, "Wet," in *Mars and Her Children* (New York: Alfred A. Knopf, 1992), 128–29.

CHAPTER 3

1. In *The Erotic Mind* (New York: HarperCollins, 1995), author Jack Morin, Ph.D., explores the meaning of eroticisim and describes the importance of peak erotic experiences. He wrote, "By the time we reach adulthood we've all discovered that, by itself, sex can be little more than a collection of urges and acts. But the erotic is intricately connected with our hopes, expecta-

tions, struggles, and anxieties—everything that makes us human" (3).

CHAPTER 4

1. *By Force of Fantasy* by Ethel S. Person, M.D. (New York: BasicBooks, 1995), explores the many functions and purposes of fantasies of all types, including sexual fantasies. She wrote, "Fantasy . . . is a major mode of adaptation in which hope and investment and the future remain alive. Fantasy postulates a better tomorrow" (37).
2. The quote by Lonnie Barbach is from *For Yourself: The Fulfillment of Female Sexuality* (New York: Anchor Books, 1976), 77.
3. Rochelle Lynn Holt, "The Pleasure of Feeling Inside Your Body," in *Erotic by Nature: A Celebration of Life, of Love, and of Our Wonderful Bodies,* David Steinberg, ed. (Santa Cruz, CA: Red Alder Books, 1988).

CHAPTER 5

1. In *How to Make Love While Conscious: Sex and Sobriety* (New York: A Hazelden Book, Harper San Francisco, 1993), author Guy Kettelhack discusses fantasy issues of significance to those who are in recovery.

CHAPTER 6

1. The sex therapy exercises referred to in Gale's story, designed to help couples relearn touch in a more caring way, were developed by Wendy Maltz. She explains them in detail in her book *The Sexual Healing Journey: A Guide for Survivors of Sexual Abuse* (New York: HarperPerennial, 1992), and in an educational video, "Relearning Touch: Healing Techniques for Couples" (Eugene, OR: Independent Video Services, 1995).

CHAPTER 7

1. In *Sexual Dreams* (New York: Fawcett Columbine, 1994), Dr. Gayle Delaney compares sexual dreams and sexual fantasies. She wrote, "Our sexual dreams are generally quite different from our sexual fantasies in several ways. Our sexual fantasies are usually erotically exciting, they unfold in a predictable manner, and they follow a fairly uncomplicated story line. Our sexual dreams, on the other hand, are sometimes not at all erotically exciting; there are usually all sorts of surprises, interruptions, and twists in the plots; and the story lines can be very complex indeed. Most of us call up sexual fantasies to turn us on, whereas our dreams come unbidden and sometimes shock the daylights out of us" (7).

CHAPTER 8

1. A more in-depth discussion of the conditions for healthy sexual intimacy was included in "The Maltz Hierarchy of Sexual Interaction," by Wendy Maltz, first published in the *Journal of Sexual Addiction and Compulsivity* (Vol 2, No. 1, 1995, Brunner/Mazel, Inc., 5–18).

CHAPTER 9

1. Research on guilt about sexual fantasies was summarized in the Leitenberg and Henning article, cited above. Specific studies dealing with partner issues include the previously cited study by Davidson and a 1986 study by Davidson and L. E. Hoffman ("Sexual Fantasies and Sexual Satisfaction," *Journal of Sex Research, 22,* 184–205). Researchers B. Buunk and R. B. Hupka, in a 1987 study ("Cross-Cultural Differences in the Elicitation of Sexual Jealousy," *Journal of Sex Research, 23,* 12–22), concluded that among subjects from seven different countries, women were less likely than men to feel jealous about their partners' sexual fantasies.

2. The Masters and Johnson quote is from *Masters and Johnson on Sexual Loving* by William H. Masters, Virginia E. Johnson,

and Robert C. Kolodny (Boston: Little, Brown and Company, 1986), 274.

CHAPTER 10

1. Sallie Tisdale, *Talk Dirty to Me* (New York: Doubleday, 1994), 87–88.
2. Among the many volumes of erotica catering to women readers and to specific racial and ethnic populations are: *On a Bed of Rice: An Asian American Erotic Feast,* edited by Geraldine Kudaka (New York: Anchor Books, 1995), *Erotique Noire,* edited by Miriam Decosta-Willis (New York: Doubleday, 1992), and *Pleasure in the Word: Erotic Writing by Latin American Women,* edited by Margarite Fernandez Olmos and Lizabeth Paravisini-Gebert (New York: Plume, 1994). Down There Press (San Francisco) regularly publishes new volumes of erotic writing for women. *The Wise Woman's Guide to Erotic Videos,* by Angela Cohen and Sarah Gardner Fox (New York: Broadway Books, 1997), includes reviews of 300 adult films and sexual enrichment videos available from video rental stores or by mail-order. *Passionate Hearts: The Poetry of Sexual Love,* compiled and edited by Wendy Maltz, is an anthology of erotic poetry celebrating the joys of healthy sexual intimacy (Novato, CA: New World Library, 1996).
3. Tanith Tyrr, "Sacrament," in *On a Bed of Rice*, edited by Geraldine Kudaka (New York: Doubleday, 1995), 95–96.
4. Stella Cameron, *Sheer Pleasures* (New York: Zebra Books, 1995), 223–324.

Index

Wendy Maltz, M.S.W., is an internationally recognized psycho-therapist and expert on sexuality with more than twenty years of clinical experience addressing sexual and relationship concerns. A frequent lecturer, she is the author of *The Sexual Healing Journey* (hailed by Harriet Lerner as "remarkable . . . rare, useful, and encouraging") and the editor of *Passionate Hearts: The Poetry of Sexual Love*. Her work has been featured in *New Woman, Cosmopolitan,* and many other publications. She lives in Eugene, Oregon.

Suzie Boss, a journalist and editor, has written for the *New York Times, Newsweek,* and *Travel & Leisure*. She lives in Portland, Oregon.